THE
EVERYTHING®
Dog Book

Dear Reader,

Whether you are a first-time or long-time dog owner, with a canine addition to the family you are in for some of the most special moments of your life. In our opinion, a family is not a family without a dog (or several!). To help you maximize your relationship with your dog, which includes all aspects of his care, we have written *The Everything® Dog Book*, now updated and revised in a Second Edition. In it you'll find answers to some of the most confounding issues you'll face—training challenges, nutrition, basic health care, even behavior problems—all explained in ways to put you and your canine companion at ease and on track to enjoy many satisfying years together.

We get excited just thinking about our dogs waiting for us at home—their happy welcomes when we walk through the door, the "gifts" they bring us to let us know we're loved, the softness of their heads when we pet them, the delight they take in their walks and playtime—so many special moments in each and every day. We hope this book helps you find the same joys in your life with your dog(s) and that your years together are the best ever.

Time for a treat!

Carlo De Vito & Amy Ammen

Welcome to the EVERYTHING® Series!

These handy, accessible books give you all you need to tackle a difficult project, gain a new hobby, comprehend a fascinating topic, prepare for an exam, or even brush up on something you learned back in school but have since forgotten.

You can choose to read an *Everything®* book from cover to cover or just pick out the information you want from our four useful boxes: e-questions, e-facts, e-alerts, e-ssentials. We give you everything you need to know on the subject, but throw in a lot of fun stuff along the way, too.

We now have more than 400 *Everything®* books in print, spanning such wide-ranging categories as weddings, pregnancy, cooking, music instruction, foreign language, crafts, pets, New Age, and so much more. When you're done reading them all, you can finally say you know *Everything®*!

QUESTIONS?
Answers to
common questions

FACTS
Important snippets
of information

ALERTS!
Urgent
warnings

ESSENTIALS
Quick
handy tips

DIRECTOR OF INNOVATION Paula Munier

EXECUTIVE EDITOR, SERIES BOOKS Brielle K. Matson

MANAGING EDITOR, EVERYTHING SERIES Lisa Laing

ASSOCIATE COPY CHIEF Sheila Zwiebel

ACQUISITIONS EDITOR Kerry Smith

DEVELOPMENT EDITOR Elizabeth Kassab

PRODUCTION EDITOR Casey Ebert

Visit the entire Everything® series at *www.everything.com*

THE
EVERYTHING®
DOG BOOK
2nd Edition

Choose, raise, and train
your perfect canine companion

Carlo De Vito
with Amy Ammen

avon, massachusetts

To my wife, Dominique, and my sons, Dylan and Dawson. And to Chief, Cinderella, Sadie, Lulu, Exley, Chelsea, Bentley, Storm, Cheri, Pepi, Red, Benji, Max, Burton, Timothy, and Jo. They have all taught me a great deal about dogs, and even more about being a better human being.

An Everything® Series Book.
Everything® and everything.com® are registered trademarks of F+W Publications, Inc.

Published by Adams Media, an F+W Publications Company
57 Littlefield Street, Avon, MA 02322 U.S.A.
www.adamsmedia.com

ISBN 10: 1-59869-591-6
ISBN 13: 978-1-59869-591-5

Printed in the United States of America.

J   I   H   G   F   E   D   C   B   A

Library of Congress Cataloging-in-Publication Data
is available from the publisher.

This publication is designed to provide accurate and authoritative information with regard to the subject matter covered. It is sold with the understanding that the publisher is not engaged in rendering legal, accounting, or other professional advice. If legal advice or other expert assistance is required, the services of a competent professional person should be sought.

—From a *Declaration of Principles* jointly adopted by a Committee of the American Bar Association and a Committee of Publishers and Associations

Many of the designations used by manufacturers and sellers to distinguish their products are claimed as trademarks. Where those designations appear in this book and Adams Media was aware of a trademark claim, the designations have been printed with initial capital letters.

Photographs copyright © 2008, by Mary Bloom.

This book is available at quantity discounts for bulk purchases.
For information, please call 1-800-289-0963.

Contents

Acknowledgments

I want to thank Amy Ammen for writing the training sections of this book in its first and second editions. Amy is one of the most accomplished dog trainers I have ever met, and I admire her commitment to helping dogs and their owners learn to live together with respect, manners, and joy. Learn more about her at *www.dogclass.com*.

Top Ten Components of a
Happy, Healthy Dog

1. Love and Companionship
2. Just Leadership
3. Safety and Security
4. Sound Nutrition (food, water, and treats)
5. Veterinary Care
6. Exercise
7. Grooming
8. Toys and Games
9. Comfortable Beds
10. Family

Introduction

▶ BENTLEY WAS THE answer to a sixth-grader's dreams. He was a confidant, a play pal, someone to talk to late at night. He was never judgmental, always loyal: someone who would definitely sneak downstairs with you for a late-night snack, and one who would fight for space on the bed with you—covers and all. In short, he was my best friend. Bentley was a godsend who arrived at my door at what just happened to be three days before my twelfth birthday. Bentley was a Dalmatian.

He had an extremely square head for a Dalmatian and a deep, broad chest. And of course he had a tremendous number of spots. He had one large circle around his eye. My grandmother used to say to him, "Bentley, you smudged your mascara again." With his red collar and wonderful, bouncy gait, he was what every child envisioned a Dalmatian to be. He loved attention, food, sleeping, and running.

My family and I have many great memories of Bentley. There was the Saturday when the entire family went food shopping and left him alone in one room. I can proudly say that he did not go to the bathroom while were gone at all. Instead, he rewarded us by tearing up the entire kitchen floor. Then there was the time we came home and the kitchen table looked like the *Titanic* going down to its watery grave—he had gnawed one of the legs entirely off. There was also the time my parents were entertaining out-of-town clients: During the dinner, Bentley clawed his way into the pantry and ate a whole cake, as well as assorted pastries. I remember the shriek my mother gave when she found out. I flew down the stairs only to find her chasing the dog around the table, his face covered in chocolate. He thought it was a game.

Bentley didn't only do naughty things, of course. There was the time he protected my little brother from a German Shepherd who had roamed into our yard. He loved to sleep near the fire and insisted on lying on the living room floor in the middle of every holiday. I even took Bentley to college with me one semester, where he kept me warm in my poorly heated room in the winter, attended many tennis matches and baseball games, and became a well-known personality on campus.

Every family who has had a dog has these same types of stories and memories. While dogs come in a variety of physical packages, they are all big where it counts—personality. In the character department, they are all colossal. People who are lucky enough to open up their lives and let in a friend as true and loving as a dog find a bond that transcends the verbal. It does not have the intimacy of a human relationship, but it doesn't have its deceits and disappointments, either. Dogs do not know how to lie. There is something in the magically expressive eyes of a dog that is difficult to explain to someone who does not understand. If you have a dog, you already know what I mean. If you're thinking of getting one, you're in for the experience of a lifetime.

It would be nice if dogs didn't require instruction booklets, but they do. There are lots of things that you need to know, not only for your dog's sake, but to strengthen the bond between you. Training is key, and that's why Amy Ammen wrote the training chapters. She's an amazing trainer who has trained countless pets privately and in groups. She has trained dogs in each of the AKC Groups to high-level obedience trial titles.

Dog owners need to know about their breed's histories and traits, grooming requirements, nutritional needs, basic healthcare, how to pre-pare their home and family for a dog, and much more. I am lucky to have met many dog professionals in my life since I lost Bentley. Thanks to them I understand that dog ownership is more than just feeding an animal and taking him to the vet when he's sick. It's more than just enjoy-ing the unconditional love dogs give. It's about being partners as well as friends.

May your life with your dog give you as much joy on a daily basis as mine have for me, and may this book help you give your dog everything he needs.

CHAPTER 1

Dogs and Where They Came From

You find them in ancient cave paintings. You find them in masterpieces by Renaissance artists. You find them on greeting cards, stationery, bookmarks, linens, and decorative home accessories. You find them in different lands, as part of vastly different cultures, in all sizes, shapes, and forms. What are they? Dogs. For millennia, dogs have been an integral part of our lives, protecting us, helping us, and loving us. In turn, we have shared our homes, our food, even the raising of our children with these animals who are so dear to us.

Joining Forces with Humans

The history of dogs is so closely woven in with the history of people that historians and archaeologists cannot agree on when or how they were introduced. Prehistoric people may have found many good uses for dogs. Once domesticated, dogs were used as early warning detection devices against human or animal intruders. They would defend people's caves and camps as their own, and so they must have been excellent protection as well as an alarm system.

FACT

Numerous cave paintings depict dogs hunting alongside humans as far back as 5000–4000 B.C. Five primary types have been identified: greyhounds, pointing dogs, mastiffs, wolf-type dogs, and sheepherding dogs.

Obviously, the greatest use early people had for their canine companions was hunting. Once the dog was part of the human family, and once humans were part of the pack, hunting together became a valuable common interest. There is also conjecture concerning how far back humans used dogs to guard livestock. Of course, as a dog fancier, one must wonder in the end, what attracted dogs to people? According to dog experts there were mainly three things—food, fire (for heat in winter), and community.

Lloyd M. Wendt, a noted historian of the human/dog connection who wrote the very detailed book *Dogs*, believes that the relationship between early humans and domesticated dogs can first be traced back 100,000 years to northern Africa and the Middle East. Wendt also noted that 10,000 years ago, Algerians were drawing hunting scenes on cave walls, depicting the hunt, with dogs on leashes.

The Roles of Ancient Dogs

Historians place the working aspect of the human/dog relationship at approximately 80,000 years ago, with the advent of the spear. Spears gave humans a weapon to fend off aggressive animals, as well as something to kill them with. It was probably about this time that humans and dogs began hunting together in earnest.

As humans became more adept at navigation on the sea, they also began to seek dogs that were optimal for specific tasks. Great wolflike animals were bred for hunting wolves, bears, and lions in Abyssinia and Persia. The largest and best of the herding dogs came from Tibet. And the fastest hunting greyhounds came from Egypt.

The Lhasa Apso is one of the oldest known dog breeds. It originated in Tibet and was introduced to the United States in the 1930s as a gift from the thirteenth Dalai Lama.

The Egyptians

Of course, the dog achieved its first great fame among modern people in Egypt. Dogs played an important part in everyday life—so much so that they were incorporated into the religion. The god Anubis was portrayed as a dog or as a mixture of a human's body with a dog's head. It was not uncommon to have the form of a dog sculpted to rest on the sarcophagus of a deceased king. The dog served to deter grave robbers and as a symbol of a guide who would lead the entombed through the afterlife. The Egyptians so loved their dogs that theirs was the first civilization that had a law to punish humans who were cruel to dogs.

A richly decorated wooden casket dating to circa 1300 B.C. shows Tutankhamen in his chariot pursuing Nubian soldiers who are being harassed by his Assyrian dogs.

The Greeks and Romans

Alexander the Great and later Roman emperors were also fond of dogs. Because the Greeks and Romans traded with the Egyptians, dogs became popular with the Hellenic aristocracy. However, the Greeks used dogs for a variety of purposes. Unlike the Egyptians, who prospered in semi-isolation, the Greeks and the Romans were products of the very heavily populated and mercantile-minded Mediterranean and Middle Eastern cultures. Life was competitive and land came at great cost.

Learning from the Persians and their other warlike neighbors, the Greeks began to use two dogs. One was large and massive in build, with a large, broad face, known as the Molossian. The other was also large, with a rather pointed snout, and was somewhat fast and sleeker. This one was known as the Laconian Hound. Aristotle was a fan of both dogs, saying that the Laconian female was gentler and smarter, but by no means fit for war, and that the Molossian was the dog of choice.

The Molossian was named for the tribe that had made it well-known, which came out of northern Greece. The Molossian of Alexander the Great's time is the ancestor of today's Mastiff. For centuries it was recognized as the ultimate dog of war—large, strong, fearless, and smart. The Greeks and then the Romans used these beasts in war for something like a cavalry charge. The Laconian Hound was developed, it is believed, in Sparta. It was fast and brutal, but of a sleeker build than the traditional Mastiff.

The first literary classic pairing of a man and his dog comes from the Greeks. One of the first classic pieces of literature known and studied for centuries, *The Odyssey*, features the story of Odysseus, warrior of the Trojan War, attempting the long, treacherous, and adventurous journey home. After many years away from his farm and kingdom, the hero of the story is not recognized by those people who knew him long ago. Despite his claims, he is only believed when his faithful hound—by then old and impaired—crawls to his master, for whom he has been faithfully waiting. Upon greeting him, Odysseus's dog dies, wagging his tail, happy at his master's feet.

FACT

There are tales of multiple dogs who served as kings in Scandinavia. In the sixth century, a Swedish king sent a dog to rule Denmark, declaring that whoever told of his death would himself die. The dog was eventually overcome by larger dogs. In a dispute among rulers in Norway, when King Eysteinn conquered a particular territory, he put his son in charge. The people killed him, and the king asked them then to choose to be ruled by a slave or a dog. They chose the dog, which lived an extremely opulent life for three years until being killed by wolves.

If dog was man's best friend in Greece, another dog was the mother of Rome. According to myth, a she-wolf found and fostered two abandoned brothers, Romulus and Remus. The two would go on to found Rome, which Romulus named for himself after he overpowered and killed his twin.

It was the Romans who first outfitted their war dogs with thick leather collars, studded with sharp metal blades to keep other attacking dogs off of them. Dogs were instrumental in Rome's rise. As its famous roads were built and expanded, guard posts all along the way were manned by small militia and hosts of guard dogs. The roads were kept safe for Roman use. The Romans also used their large dogs as beasts of burden. It was not unusual to see dogs, along with cattle, oxen, horses, and ponies, pulling carts of all sizes from all different parts of the empire.

Dogs in the Middle Ages and Renaissance

In the period after the fall of the Roman Empire, the bubonic plague, or Black Death, was one of the galvanizing events. It was during this time that the dog acquired much of its more negative lore. During the plague, in which fleas transported the deadly disease, historian Mary Elizabeth Thurston points out in her book, *The Lost History of the Canine Race*, that the dog was now on its own. Most livestock was killed by the disease, and people killed each other over food. Few people during this period kept pets. Ownerless, dogs ran wild, usually in packs, eating corpses and killing in groups.

During feudal times, the aristocracy assumed ownership of many fertile lands, especially the great forests in which many animals and other natural resources were still abundant. During this time, the hunt became very ritualized, and many different dogs were used to pursue many different kinds of game. Lords and barons had different dogs to take down deer, bears, bulls, wolves, large fowl, and foxes, and they had other dogs for small game, mostly vermin. Others were bred for specific duties, such as tracking, coursing, and retrieving on land and in water.

Thurston points out that Henry I of England had a kennel of 200 dogs for huntsmen to train, care for, and deploy. As the aristocracy grew, so did their land claims. And unless you were someone of rank, you could not rightfully take game from a claimed preserve.

It was not until after the fall of the French king in the late 1700s, during the French Revolution, that ordinary people were allowed to hunt in the largest and most heavily stocked game forests. In the early 1800s many lands across Europe were opened up in an attempt to dissuade the masses from overthrowing various monarchies. These policies were part of larger political agendas, which all worked to varying degrees. However, one thing was an absolute success—sport hunting became popular to the extreme.

The Victorian Era

Queen Victoria was a devoted dog fancier, and when her husband, Prince Albert, suddenly sickened and died in 1861 at the age of forty-two, the saddened queen grew even fonder of her gentle pets. In her lifetime she raised more than fifteen different breeds of dogs. According to noted historian Paul Johnson, "She formed passionate attachments to animals when a child, and the vehemence with which she fought for their rights persisted to the end. At her various jubilees, prisoners were released all over the Empire provided that she personally signed their remission. There was only one category she refused: those convicted of cruelty to animals, which she called 'one of the worst traits in human nature.'" The queen was especially fond of a favorite Spitz, who was actually allowed to jump on her breakfast table.

Due to Victoria's love of canines, the dog reached an all-time high status. Your choice of dog conveyed whether you were a sportsman or a true lady. Dogs helped people fulfill their aspirations toward a higher station in life. Indeed, it was in this period that many dog classifications began. It was also a time in which many new dog breeds were bred by varying groups, especially hunters.

In the 1700s and 1800s, many of the sporting breeds, such as the German Shorthaired Pointer, Weimaraner, Vizsla, and other hunting dogs, were bred because middle-class Europeans had more time for hunting as recreation, and they wanted one dog to perform a series of functions for which the European aristocracy could previously afford to keep several breeds. Likewise, smaller, toy breeds also became more popular, and many breeds which were hitherto unknown came to the fore.

FACT

Bulldogs were originally bred to bait bulls during bullfights, and the breed was in danger of disappearing after the sport was outlawed in Britain in 1835. However, dedicated breeders patiently cultivated the breed and crossed it with other breeds to create new ones, including the Bullmastiff and the Bull Terrier.

The different species we are so familiar with today are the result of the continuing quest to find the perfect dog. In many cases throughout history, people have bred dogs for different characteristics, such as size, speed, and hunting abilities to produce dogs for a variety of uses. This period was the golden age of the dog.

Dogs and Their Distinguished American Owners

The United States may not be known as the country where dogs are especially cherished—for example, in France almost all dogs are welcome in restaurants, whereas in the United States only registered service and therapy dogs are—but that doesn't mean it doesn't have its share of people who adore their canine companions. In fact, dogs have been alongside the settlers of the United States of America since the country's infancy. There are whole books devoted to dogs who've shared the White House with the presidents and other famous people and their dogs. Here are just a few.

FACT

The Chesapeake Bay Retriever is one of the dogs that can claim a North American heritage. It is an active, versatile dog that was originally bred to hunt waterfowl. Its body and temperament can withstand demanding weather conditions.

George Washington

George Washington was known as an avid lover of canines. He was very fond of hunting and often had packs of dogs at Mt. Vernon, his home outside of Washington, D.C. Washington was known as one of the main people who helped establish the Treeing Walker Hound, a prized Coonhound in this country today. Washington was known to let his favorite dogs have the run of the house, much to Martha Washington's dismay. His favorite hounds were Sweet Lips and Vulcan. Vulcan once stole the main course of a holiday dinner off the kitchen table. Mrs. Washington was upset, but Washington himself found the episode humorous.

FACT

After the American defeat at the 1777 Battle of Germantown, a Fox Terrier appeared in General Washington's camp and wound up in Washington's tent. Its collar told that it belonged to British General William Howe. Washington, ever the gallant soldier and lover of dogs, sent the dog back under flag of truce to Howe, and the two exchanged polite notes.

Fala and FDR

President Franklin Delano Roosevelt's favorite pet was his black Scottish Terrier known as Fala. Fala was ubiqitous in Roosevelt's world, and the only person who was allowed to feed Fala—no matter who had prepared the meal—was the president himself. Roosevelt happily brought the dog with him everywhere he could.

During World War II, FDR took Fala with him. Republicans—eager to find any weapon against the seemingly invincible Democrat—commenced a whispering campaign against Roosevelt, saying he spent taxpayers' money sending a USS destroyer to go back and pick up the dog that the president had erringly left in the Aleutian Islands. This was a blatant falsehood. In response, FDR addressed these rumors in September 1944: "The Republican Leaders have not been content with attacks on me, or my wife, or my sons. No, not content with that, they now include my little dog, Fala. Well, of course, I don't resent attacks, and my family doesn't resent attacks, but Fala does resent them. You know, Fala is Scotch, and being a Scottie as soon as he learned that Republican fiction writers in Congress had concocted a story that I had left him behind on the Aleutian Islands, and had sent a destroyer back to find him—at a cost to the taxpayers of two or three or eight or twenty million dollars—his Scotch soul was furious. He has not been the same dog since. I am accustomed to hearing malicious falsehoods about myself—such as that old chestnut that I have represented myself as indispensable. I think I have a right to resent, to object to, libelous statements about my dog."

FACT

At the Franklin Delano Roosevelt Memorial in Washington, D.C., a statue of Fala sits beside his master. He is the only presidential dog to be so honored.

Fortunately for Roosevelt, he did not have to experience the death of his beloved pet. Roosevelt died in April 1945, and it was a grieving Fala who went to live with Eleanor Roosevelt at Val-Kill, their country residence. Fala died on April 5, 1952, two days short of his twelfth birthday, and was buried beside his master in the rose garden at the Roosevelt home.

General Patton and His Bull Terriers

The famed U.S. General George Patton was an avid animal lover. Shortly after World War I, he purchased the first of many Bull Terriers he would come to own for his daughters, Beatrice and Ruth Ellen. They named the dog Tank. The loveable Tank was stone deaf, but the girls loved him. The family took to stomping on the floor to call the dog, and he responded. Tank had a great love for Patton himself, as well as his family, and he was always present for his master's return, greeting him at his front door.

On March 4, 1944, Patton bought his most famous Bull Terrier, which he named William the Conqueror. Patton himself called the dog Willie. According to the Patton Society, Patton wrote the following journal entry when he first bought Willie: "My bull pup . . . took to me like a duck to water. He is 15 months old, pure white except for a little lemin [sic] on his tail which to a cursory glance would seem to indicate that he had not used toilet paper . . ." Jingle bells and U.S.-issue dog tags were affixed to Willie's collar so everyone could hear him wherever he went. The two were devoted to one another. Like Fala, Willie outlived his beloved master, who died in December 1945.

Dogs in Our Lives Today

In today's world, for every kind of lifestyle people lead, there is a different kind of dog. There are tiny dogs and giant dogs, hairless and shaggy, pedigreed and mixed breed. Dogs also perform a variety of different jobs—they sniff out narcotics or explosives, search for missing people, excel at certain sports, hunt, and assist those with handicaps. Then there are the dogs who are simply dogs.

The popularity of dogs is booming in just about every part of the world. The clubs and organizations dedicated to certain breeds help newcomers not only learn more but do more with their dogs. Small dogs that are easier to transport and care for are becoming increasingly prevalent in urban areas. Dog owners have more options than ever, not only in selecting their breed of dog, but also in choosing everything their dog needs, from food to accessories to health care. For many beloved canines, it is a great time to be a dog.

FACT

Upon her death in 2007, the late hotelier Leona Helmsley left $12 million to her Maltese, Trouble, and also requested that the dog be interred with her in her mausoleum upon its death.

On the other hand, it's a fact that caring for a dog is not for everyone. In the end, a dog is still a dog—a living being whose genetic makeup dictates that it behave in certain ways that are not always compatible with ours. It is each person's responsibility to be a conscientious and compassionate caregiver to the animals they bring into their lives. Like our ancestors who worked alongside our dogs' ancestors, we owe them the respect they deserve. Perhaps you, too, will contribute to the wealth of art and literature that helps celebrate our enduring relationship with dogs.

CHAPTER 2

Choosing a Dog

Amazingly, when you ask people how and why they chose a particular dog or breed of dog, most confess it was a random choice. Maybe their kids had been pestering them for a dog for a while, and one day they just decided to go get one; maybe someone down the street had a dog who had puppies and they took one; maybe they were passing a pet shop and fell in love with a fuzzy face in the window. Although these can all be ways to bring a wonderful dog into one's life, they can also be recipes for disaster—for the people and for the dogs.

Not Just Unconditional Love

There is nothing better than coming home from a hard day's work to a tail-wagging, sloppy-tongued mop of a dog who can't wait to greet you. Dogs are bouncy and loving and wonderful—there's no getting around it, they're exceptional companions. They are fun and friendly, and they love attention. They love to play, go for long walks, and be mischievous.

But before selling yourself on only the nice things about them, remember that no matter their size, coat type, or activity level, dogs are a tremendous amount of responsibility. It's fun to cuddle up with a dog while watching television or take him hiking and running; it's fun to play with a dog at the beach, in a park, or in the snow. But dogs are also completely dependent upon the care of their keepers for everything from food to exercise to training—and they don't take a day off.

FACT

Every year, thousands of dogs are left homeless and are sheltered in dog pounds and rescue homes all across the country. Often this is no fault of the dog's. When the cute puppy turns eight months old and starts showing an ornery streak, some families don't have the time or patience to handle it, and that can be the last straw.

When an over-obliging owner suddenly finds himself with a dog who growls when she's told to get off the bed, well, the dog may become a casualty. Often, people give up their dogs because they don't fully understand all the care requirements necessary to keep a dog healthy and well-behaved. They find out that Dalmatians require too much exercise; they didn't know St. Bernards grew that big; they learn that their tiny Maltese is a mischievous ball of fire. Then, for reasons completely unknown to her, a once-beloved dog may find herself at the shelter, cowering at the back of a cold pen as countless strangers peer in on her and countless other distressed dogs bark and howl around her. At the same time, the removal of a dog from the home can be a traumatic experience for the children and adults who came to love her—despite the behavior that eventually led to her being given up.

This handsome adult Vizsla looks great while standing still in this posed position. Such a photo could cause you to want to own this kind of dog. What you can't see, though, is the dog's nature, and for the Vizsla, this is mega-energy. Owners who don't understand that Vizslas need *lots* of exercise could become frustrated easily (and often).

In a day when razors, pens, diapers, and even spouses are disposable, dogs are no exception. Unfortunately, they pay for being disposable with their lives.

Top Reasons Why Dogs Are Given Up

It's sad, but true. According to the National Council of Pet Population Study and Policy, these are the top ten reasons cited by people who give up their dogs:

1. Moving
2. Landlord issues
3. Cost of pet maintenance
4. No time for pet
5. Inadequate facilities
6. Too many pets in home

7. Pet illness
8. Personal problems
9. Biting
10. No homes for littermates

Think hard about whether any of these circumstances could lead to your thinking about giving up your puppy or dog. If so, you should wait before getting one.

The Right Dog for You

Don't let the above scenarios become the reality for you or your family. With the help of this book, you can avoid being someone who gets the wrong dog for what might seem like the right reason. What you want—and what will bring the most joy for your family and your canine companion—is to make a choice that can practically ensure that you will end up with a dog who is right for you in all the important ways.

Before you get a dog, ask yourself some important questions:

- What kind of life do you lead? Do you travel frequently? Are you constantly running around taking kids to after-school activities? Are you a single man or woman? Are you getting ready to retire? How old are your children?
- Do you want an active dog, a laid-back dog, a big dog, a small dog, a hairy dog, a hairless dog, a slobbery dog, a neat dog? With more than 150 different breeds recognized by the American Kennel Club alone, you can really pinpoint the kind of dog that will suit your lifestyle.
- How much room do you have, and what kind of house do you live in? Are you obsessively neat? Are you excessively sloppy?
- How much time do you have for the dog? When you come home are you eager to get outside and exercise or do you want to relax and watch TV?
- Do you like to entertain?
- Should you get a puppy or an older dog? If you get a puppy, will someone be home during the day to housetrain and socialize him?

- Do you have a fenced-in yard?
- Does everyone in the family want a dog or are you caving in to a demanding child?

As you consider these questions—especially if you're making a decision for a family—you'll find that more questions come up and that there is actually a lot to consider. The more you think now, the less you'll be surprised or disappointed by later.

Looking at Lifestyle

Lifestyle decisions aren't all about interior decorating or fashion, though those things are certainly part of it. When it comes to choosing a dog, it shouldn't be based on whether you think he'll look good with your sofa, or whether he'll go well with your English garden. How reflective a dog is of whether your clothing choices run to Ralph Lauren or Levis shouldn't matter, either. A dog is not an accessory; he is an animal with a mind and personality all his own, and having one is like having another person in the house.

QUESTION?

How much time do I need to have for a dog?
If you've owned a dog before you may have a sense of how much time it takes to care for one properly. If you haven't, you need to give the matter some serious thought. Besides the time you need to spend taking care of a dog's most basic needs for food, water, going to the bathroom, exercise, grooming, and overall health (and that's a lot right there), you need to factor in the time you must spend interacting with your dog. Dogs are social animals who thrive on companionship.

Analyze what you do every day. What is your idea of fun? Is it roller-blading? Riding your bike? Watching a movie or sports on television? Going hiking? Going on little day trips in the car? Going to the park or beach and lying out in the sun? Do you work? If so, is it part-time or full-time, and what are your hours? Do you like to come home, shower, and go back out to dinner and the movies or your favorite bar? Are you allergic to pets? You have to ask yourself these kinds of questions when you are choosing a dog so that you can pick the dog that's best for you.

If you're an in-line skater, you want to know that when you come home, you can suit up, put a leash on Rover, and bring him along. You want a dog who shares in that fun. You need an athletic dog who has the stamina and explosive energy to keep up with you. You don't want some sedentary hound who's panting after the first half-mile. Likewise, if you like going for an evening stroll, you don't want some drooling half-lunatic pulling you around the block like a crazed demon. You want a good dog who is happy plodding along at a leisurely pace while you enjoy the evening air together.

Maybe you need a dog who can keep up with your children and whom you can trust with them. You need your dog to be a companion and playmate for your kids to share in their well-behaved fun.

Puppy or Adult

This is a question most people don't stop to think about, but they should. Typically, when people think of getting a dog, they think about getting a puppy. They think of the cute ball of fluff running around the house making the family laugh. They want to nurture and raise the dog from a pup.

Do You Really Want a Puppy?

Think about it: Do you really want a puppy? Is a puppy the best fit with your family's lifestyle? Having a puppy is like having a two-year-old in the house. Puppies want to get into everything, and they use their mouths to explore. They need to chew, and if you don't supply a variety of toys, they'll chew what's available.

It's a fact: Puppies are adorable. Who wouldn't fall in love instantly with this Irish Setter puppy? One look into those soulful eyes is all it takes.

Puppies need to be kept on very strict schedules in order to be house-trained. That means taking the puppy out first thing in the morning, several times during the day, and last thing at night. It means monitoring the puppy during the day to try to prevent accidents from happening. It means making a real commitment to training and socializing, because when your puppy gets big and she doesn't know what's expected of her, she'll make the rules. It may be cute to have your puppy curl up on the couch with you or sleep in your bed or jump up on you to greet you, but then don't be surprised if you meet with resistance when your pup's grown up and you don't want her doing those things anymore.

What Older Dogs Have to Offer

When you get an older dog, you obviously miss the adorable stages of puppyhood. You miss the complete experience of growing together from the time he's ten to twelve weeks to twelve to fourteen years old. But you do get other things in return. Older dogs are generally calmer; they're usually housetrained; they're more set in their ways; and people report that they seem grateful to be in a new home in which they're loved and appreciated.

There's also the feel-good part of getting an older dog, because whether you adopt one from a shelter or a purebred rescue group, or just take one in from a neighbor, you are essentially saving that dog's life. Yes, you are inheriting behaviors that the dog has learned from his previous owners or circumstances, but contrary to the old saying, you *can* teach an old dog new tricks. And if you approach getting an older dog as conscientiously as you would approach getting a puppy, you're sure to find one whose temperament suits you ideally.

QUESTION?

Am I doing the right thing?
You may be more confused now than when you first started thinking about getting a dog! Remember, there is no right or wrong answer. The final decision is what's best for you and your family. It's understanding the pros and cons that go into that decision that will truly make it the right one in the end.

Adopting an older dog doesn't limit your choices much, either. It doesn't mean going to the dog pound and rescuing a mangy mutt on death row. There are many older dogs available—both purebred and mixed-breed—that are physically and mentally sound. The obvious thing about taking in an older dog is that you're making a difference in a dog's life. But the thing you need to consider is: Is an adult dog going to make a difference in your life?

Purebred or Mixed Breed

There are arguments for welcoming both a purebred or a mixed breed into your home. Purebred dogs are those that have been bred "pure" over several generations. In so doing, they have certain traits that are fixed, such as the Basset Hound's long ears, the Golden Retriever's silky coat, or the Pug's corkscrew tail. Of course there are variations between individuals, but when you see a Great Dane, you should know it's a Great Dane and not an Irish Wolfhound.

After investigating breeds, you may find that no one particular purebred especially does it for you. Or maybe it simply doesn't matter to you how much you know about your dog's genetic makeup; you may just want a mixed-breed dog. Yes, a mutt! Some of them may not be the most beautiful dogs you've ever seen, and you may never be sure whether their instincts are coming from retriever blood or terrier blood or perhaps a bit of everything, but like their purebred cousins, mixed breeds can make superlative pets.

FACT

Mixed-breed dogs often marry the best traits of the dogs they're descended from. It is fun to try to guess what breeds went into making your dog. In some cases you'll know—if your Lab bred the Australian Cattle Dog next door by mistake, for example—but in many cases you won't know at all. When you don't, it's fun to guess and speculate.

In the end, neither a purebred nor a mixed breed is going to be a better dog than the other. Both are just dogs. The important considerations are, again, how well your lifestyle accommodates your dog's basic needs. If he's a big, hairy purebred or a big, hairy mix and you're a neat freak who lives in a fifth-floor walkup, things might not work out. Whether you choose purebred or mixed, you have to realistically assess the amount of time and energy you have to take care of your dog the way she deserves (and needs) to be taken care of.

For many, a mixed-breed dog has everything they want and need. Besides getting a dog whose appearance is utterly unique—like this scruffy fellow—there's the fun of trying to guess which breeds contributed to the look. Are they any less lovable? No way!

Finding Your Dog

So, you've thought about the kind of dog you want based on the way you and your family live. Now, how do you go about finding that dog? As you begin your search you'll find you have plenty of options. As when you shop for anything, though, some are sounder than others. Read on before making a too-hasty decision.

From a Breeder

If you've decided on a purebred puppy, consider buying your dog from a breeder. These folks are passionate about their breed!

You may think this is like asking a Chevrolet salesman if he himself would buy a Chevrolet. What do you think he's going to tell you? "Oh, no, I think you're much more a Honda type. Honda's down the road." Not likely. But if you get a good breeder, she may indeed tell you just that.

Breeders will interview you, too, which will help you decide if the breed is truly right for you. A breeder may ask you how often you like to go hiking, say, or how often you travel. You may realize you're not the sportsperson you thought you were, or that your schedule is tighter than you thought. Then again, you may be relieved to hear that a breed you thought was too active actually doesn't need as much exercise as you thought, and the breeder has helped you figure out how to fit in a good workout for the dog without compromising your daily habits.

Another great thing about talking to breeders is that you will get a good sense of who you want to get your puppy (or older dog) from. The person who's especially helpful, or with whom you "click," or whose dogs seem the most well-behaved and mellow of the lot you've spoken with—this is the person from whom you want to acquire your new family member. You should feel comfortable calling your breeder at any time during your dog's life to ask him about any kind of problems you're having. If your pup's chewing is getting out of control, if housetraining isn't working, or if your adult dog suddenly goes lame, it's nice to know there's someone you can call who not only knows the breed, but knows your dog personally.

A responsible breeder will tell you all about your potential puppy's or older dog's past—what the parents and siblings are like, whether there's working stock in the bloodlines, what kind of traits she's been breeding away from (or for), particular health problems to look out for, and much more. In fact, a breeder who doesn't want to inform you of all these things, particularly health records for breeds prone to hip dysplasia or other genetic conditions, is one to stay away from—she's probably got something to hide.

Responsible breeders want their puppies or older dogs to find homes in which they'll be loved and cared for as real family members for the duration of their lives. Many of them will put in writing that if for any reason you can't keep the dog any longer, you should contact them first before surrendering the dog to a shelter.

Be advised, though: there are plenty of breeders who don't ask the tough questions. There are many who don't have any scruples at all. That's why it's important to find a reputable breeder whom you can trust. Many breeders are willing to take the time to ask you the right questions. If they don't, you should wonder how much care they take in breeding their dogs.

From Purebred Rescue

Technically, a rescue dog is a purebred who has been rescued from a former home or from a pound or shelter and is currently homeless. Most AKC breed clubs sponsor purebred rescue groups. When a dog is dropped off at the shelter or taken into the dog pound, if that dog is believed to be purebred, the shelter calls the contact person for the local rescue group. If the rescue coordinator believes the dog is a purebred of the breed with which he is involved, that dog is taken from the pound and housed in a foster home until the rescue organization can find the dog a new, permanent home.

Rescue groups are typically run by breeders who are very concerned about dogs in general. They are networks of people who have extremely big hearts and only want to see the dogs find a good home. Much of the cost of fostering is picked up by the family that is sheltering the dog in their house, and the adoption fee you pay for the dog helps offset that cost.

ALERT!

To have a positive experience with a positive outcome, before you begin searching for a dog through a purebred rescue organization, think about the qualities you're looking for: male or female; younger or older; good with kids; good with cats; etc. The more specific you can be with what you're looking for, the easier your search and the more helpful the organization can be.

It is natural to wonder if rescue dogs or others that have been abandoned have something wrong with them. After all, if they didn't, wouldn't they still be with their first family? The great thing about the fact that these dogs are fostered with "real" people is that they can be evaluated. The rescuers learn about the dogs' behaviors so they can explain to people what they might have to deal with. Many rescue dogs need some stability to help regain their confidence, and foster owners spend a lot of time working with such animals to ensure that they'll adjust to a new home.

The network of purebred rescue volunteers is extensive, and with the Internet it's easier than ever to investigate your options. Simply do a Web-based search for the breed you're interested in, plus "rescue," and let the search begin.

From a Pet Shop

Once upon a time, buying a puppy from a pet shop was a common experience. Today it is becoming less common. The decline in pet shop sales has to do with the way they operate.

A responsible breeder ensures that his dogs are bred for a purpose, that they're properly raised and socialized, and that any health problems have been addressed. He takes care to breed two dogs who complement each other in order to produce the best possible dog, most emblematic of the breed standard or ideal. Responsible breeders ask you a lot of questions before they agree to sell you a puppy, and they try to match your personality with one of their puppies.

Pet shops claim to get their dogs from breeders, but pet shops need variety and volume. The breeders who sell to them tend to produce dogs with little or no concern about breed standards, temperament, or health problems. Pet shops know that puppies are most appealing when they're six to eight weeks old. That means that to get them to the store by that age they are usually separated from their mother and littermates at four to six weeks of age—far too early. These pups miss the critical developmental benefits of staying in their first family for as long as they should, and their new families pay the price in health and behavior problems later in life.

Does this mean good dogs don't come from pet shops? No. Some people who bought their dogs at pet stores have perfectly fine pets; others bought their dog at the mall, only to find out that the dog has a major health or behavioral problem.

Ask the people in the store a lot of questions. Where are the puppies from? How old were they when they came to the store? What kind of health guarantees does the store have? How long do you have to obtain a thorough veterinary health exam? How are the puppies kept—are the cages clean, do they have water, what are they fed, etc.? Use common sense. It may break your heart to leave the pleading puppies behind, but it may be best for you and your family.

ALERT!

There are many reasons to be wary of purchasing any animal in a pet shop, and health is at the top of the list. This doesn't mean that all pet shops sell dogs they know may have problems. But you want to be sure you don't bring home a pup or dog who will steal your heart and then break your bank with health and behavior problems.

If you do buy a puppy from a pet store, ask the staff a lot of questions about its background and whether the store provides any guarantees of the puppy's health. Take the puppy to a veterinarian right away for a first physical, and if the vet suspects any problems, speak with the store staff immediately.

From a Shelter

Almost every county in every state operates a local animal shelter where unwanted pets can be taken. Shelters typically house dogs and cats, though they may also take in rarer pets like iguanas, rabbits, ferrets, and birds. Dogs who end up there are often brought in by their current owners, though sometimes the dogs are found on the side of the road and are brought in by a concerned citizen who can't shelter the animal. Others are brought in by the local animal control department.

Sometimes the shelter is able to provide lots of information on a particular dog, and sometimes it has none. People who work in shelters are often the best judges of the dogs in their care and can tell you how they respond to certain situations and to other dogs.

In short, if you don't care about purebred vs. mixed breed, there are plenty of dogs that need good homes in these shelters. When you bring them home, they need a little extra loving and space before they can become confident, but they'll make it up to you with love and admiration. In many cases, they're a little older and are already housetrained, but you should still expect to go through an obedience course with your new dog at the very least.

FACT

Approach a visit to the shelter as you would a search for a rescue dog or even a visit to a pet shop that sells puppies: Think through what it is you want in a dog before you get there, talk to the shelter personnel to find out as much about the dog(s) you're interested in as possible, look for signs of poor health or behavior, ask about the shelter's policies for adoption and possible return, and use common sense. The saddest, most desperate dog in the shelter may not be the best match for your family, no matter how sorry you feel for him.

From Other Sources

Relieving neighbors or friends of a puppy or dog is probably one of the least desirable ways to get a dog. Why? Maybe your neighbor has great fashion sense, knows all the newest, hottest bands, hangs out with cool people, has a great job—but what does she really know about dogs?

Often people have puppies to give away because their dog got pregnant. Sometimes they've bred her to another dog, and sometimes she's found a beau of her own. Sometimes they know who the other dog is, sometimes they don't.

In many cases, you really don't know what you're getting. And that's when you have to ask yourself a lot of questions. Is my friend really good to his dog? Did he read up on what to do with a pregnant dog? Did he go to their veterinarian for advice and regular care? Do I like my friend's dog? Have I spent enough time with that dog to know whether or not I like her?

Sometimes "friends" come up with dogs when they find a stray and try to find it a good home. This is more common than you think. Make sure to ask as many questions as you can. Try not to be moved by the sad story. You need to find yourself a pet that you can live with for a long time. Although many fine pets have been found this way, make sure to think about it before you bring one home. In short, a real friend won't try to sell you a dog you don't need. Think about the person who's trying to give you the dog, as well as about the dog itself.

CHAPTER 3

Exploring Different Breeds of Dogs

With hundreds of dog breeds from around the world to choose from, how do you go about deciding which dog is right for you and your family? The truth is, you probably have some ideas about what kind of dog you like already—but you should still think carefully about your choice. Even if you grew up with a particular breed, it doesn't mean it's right for you now. Read on for discussions about the characteristics of certain groups of breeds.

Going to Dog Shows

The best way to find out about the idiosyncrasies of various breeds and to really get a good look at them is to go to dog shows. You'll find representatives of just about all the AKC breeds at a dog show, and best of all you'll find their breeders, the people who understand them best.

You may think a Beagle will suit everyone in your family fine. He'll be small enough for the kids, solid enough to be played with, active enough to go on family outings, and not so big he'll take over your small house. When you go to the dog show intent on meeting some local breeders and finding out if they have puppies available, you may see the Beagles in the ring and decide that something about them doesn't appeal to you at all. They always have their noses to the ground; they bark at other dogs too often; they seem aloof. And just as you feel your heart sink, your daughter tugs your sleeve and says, "Look, what's that?" and you fall in love with a West Highland White Terrier.

Seeing is believing, and being able to talk to breeders is invaluable. Breeders are used to dealing with people in the same situation as you. Also, they want to ensure that the dogs they breed go to the right homes for them. A Husky breeder would not recommend that one of his pups go to a home in which the primary caretaker was wheelchair-bound. That wouldn't be fair to the person, and it wouldn't be fair to the dog.

How do you find local dog shows to attend? You can call the American Kennel Club and ask for show information. The AKC's customer service number is (919) 233-9767. You can also find show information on the AKC's Web site, *www.akc.org.*

Categorizing Breeds

Whether you own or are interested in a purebred or mixed-breed dog, your friend will behave in ways that have been bred into him over the centuries by people who wanted a breed to perform a certain function. If you wonder why your retriever is always bringing you something in his mouth when you come home, it's because every cell in his body is programmed to bring in downed birds to earn his keep. When he brings you a favorite toy, he's doing the next best thing.

This section is intended to help you better understand your dog or to help you shop for the kind of dog you think would best suit your lifestyle—one that's a diehard loyalist, one that will run and play all day, one that wants to curl up on your lap for hours. Reading about the traits and the histories of some of the most popular breeds in each of the seven AKC groups will do this for you. But remember, every dog is an individual. That's why it's important to talk to other owners of the kind of dog you have or are interested in.

Purebreds and the AKC

The American Kennel Club recognizes more than 150 individual breeds of dogs that are classified into seven groups. The groups are defined by key features in personality and breeding. They are:

1. Sporting
2. Hound
3. Working
4. Terrier
5. Toy
6. Non-Sporting
7. Herding

Sporting Dogs

The Sporting Group is made up of some of the oldest breeds registered by the AKC. Many of the dogs in this category were bred for hunting. Specifically, they were bred for one or two of the following purposes: to point, retrieve, or flush game birds. That is why the Sporting Group is broken down into pointers, retrievers, and setters.

The Sporting Group is home to many of the AKC's most popular breeds, including the Labrador Retriever, the Golden Retriever, the Cocker Spaniel, and the German Shorthaired Pointer. These were dogs bred for specific purposes, and most are still doing the jobs for which they were bred. While many people who have these dogs will never need them to do anything but be the family pet, when given the opportunity, these breeds will begin to automatically use their hunting instincts, pointing and retrieving with abandon. These traits can be some of the most enjoyable aspects of owning a sporting dog. It's wonderful to see your Weimaraner go on point while running a hedgerow; it's fun to have your retriever tirelessly fetch a tennis ball from a lake or the ocean; it's reassuring to have your spaniel go back and forth in front of you on a walk (this is called quartering in the hunt field). But be forewarned: your dog is a dog, and one day she may come back with not just a ball or toy, but with fresh kill.

The Labrador Retriever is just one of the retrievers in the Sporting Group—but he is by far the most popular. The Lab has been the #1 breed in America since the early 1990s, and that's in large part because of his wonderful disposition.

Aside from that, the Sporting breeds are renowned for their outgoing personalities. Many of them, suited to the right families, make wonderful family pets. They also make good watch dogs (as opposed to guard dogs). They are known to be sociable but are not known to be overly aggressive and will always let you know when someone is approaching.

FACT

The Irish Water Spaniel, the largest of the spaniels, is now relatively rare. It is the only surviving breed of water spaniel developed in the British Isles. All Irish Water Spaniels alive today can trace their lineage to one dog: Boatswain, who was born in 1834.

It is important to keep in mind that the early breeders of these dogs wanted them to be able to hunt all day and bred them for strength and stamina. The better and longer the dog worked the more highly prized it was. While that's great news if you're a hunter, it's particularly important to remember when you buy one of these breeds. They tend to be very active. You should ask the breeder about the parents of your soon-to-be pet so you know about their temperaments and exercise needs, as well as about any health problems that might run in the family. In alphabetical order, here are the breeds in the Sporting Group:

- American Water Spaniel
- Brittany Spaniel
- Chesapeake Bay Retriever
- Clumber Spaniel
- Curly Coated Retriever
- English Cocker Spaniel
- English Setter
- English Springer Spaniel
- Field Spaniel
- Flat-Coated Retriever
- German Shorthaired Pointer
- German Wirehaired Pointer

- Golden Retriever
- Gordon Setter
- Irish Setter
- Irish Water Spaniel
- Labrador Retriever
- Nova Scotia Duck Tolling Retriever
- Pointer
- Spinone Italiano
- Sussex Spaniel
- Vizsla
- Weimaraner
- Welsh Springer Spaniel
- Wirehaired Pointing Griffon

Hounds

The Hound Group includes some of the dogs whose ancestors were the earliest companions and assistants of humankind. Sleek sighthounds like the Saluki are believed to be thousands of years old. Alexander the Great hunted with hounds in the third century B.C. This group also offers the widest range in size of any group. The smallest hound is the Dachshund, which actually comes in two sizes: Standard and Miniature. The Mini Dachshund weighs up to 11 pounds, the Standard, up to 32 pounds. He is also the only dog in this group who is neither a sight- nor a scenthound exclusively, but rather was bred to hunt smaller game "to ground," going gamely into burrows and dens for small animals, like a terrier. The largest dog in the group is the giant Irish Wolfhound, who weighs a minimum of 120 pounds. There is the fleet and agile Whippet, and the lumbering Basset Hound.

FACT

The more the merrier! Two popular hounds, Beagles and Dachshunds, come in multiple sizes. Beagles can be under 13" in height, or 13-15" in height; Dachshunds can be Standard (16-32 pounds), and Miniature (11 pounds and under). Dachshunds also have three coat types: smooth, longhaired, and wirehaired.

Hounds generally are grouped together because they will actually hunt down prey and either corner or kill it. They will not wait for the hunter but will let the hunter know where they are by various types of barking. Hound people make a distinction between "barking" (the sound most dogs use to communicate) and "baying" or "tonguing," which refer to the different types of sounds made when hounds are on the scent trail. As a hound tracks a scent, she lets out what is often referred to as a "song."

The Beagle is a scenthound, which means she uses her nose to hunt. She is the breed upon which Charles Schultz based his internationally beloved cartoon character, Snoopy, and it is no wonder. Beagles have personality to spare!

Hounds are generally categorized into two distinct types: scenthounds and sighthounds. The scenthounds are the trackers who hunt with their noses. These include Bloodhounds, Beagles, Foxhounds, and Bassets.

Sighthounds hunt by vision. The Afghan Hound, the Pharaoh Hound, and the Irish Wolfhound fall into this category. All had very specific uses, and many date back either to the feudal hunts or to ancient Egypt. The Irish Wolfhound hunted wolves; the Harrier and the Petit Basset Griffon Vendéen hunted rabbit and other small game; the Otterhound hunted otter; the Scottish Deerhound hunted deer; the Rhodesian Ridgeback hunted lions.

FACT

The Norwegian Elkhound is Norway's national dog. It was bred to hunt moose and can trace its lineage back to the Vikings. It has the characteristic thick coat, prick ears, and curled tail of a spitz breed and in this sense is unique among the other hounds.

Hounds tend to be social and easy-going—a necessity when working in a pack. Bred for stamina so they could go all day, hounds need sufficient exercise. They were bred to use their voices, their noses, and their acute perception, so owners are forewarned that they will—and do—become easily distracted by smells and movements too refined for our limited senses. Their preoccupation with their sensory worlds has led misguided owners to label them as hard to train, stubborn, or willful. The truth is, you have to be pretty interesting to get the full attention of your hound. Your unconditional love and understanding count for a lot with your hound, and he is mighty happy in a live-and-let-live relationship. These are the members of the Hound Group:

- Afghan Hound
- American Foxhound
- Basenji
- Basset Hound
- Beagle
- Black and Tan Coonhound
- Bloodhound
- Borzoi
- Dachshund

- English Foxhound
- Greyhound
- Harrier
- Ibizan Hound
- Irish Wolfhound
- Norwegian Elkhound
- Otterhound
- Petit Basset Griffon Vendéen
- Pharaoh Hound
- Plott
- Rhodesian Ridgeback
- Saluki
- Scottish Deerhound
- Whippet

Working Breeds

Most of the dogs in the Working Group were bred for labor-intensive jobs such as hauling, guarding, and even soldiering. Many of these date back to the Romans, where guarding property and family was paramount. However, there were other jobs to be done. The Greater Swiss Mountain Dog was used to drive cattle, and was the most popular dog in the Alps until about fifty years ago. The Portuguese Water Dog was the fisherman's dog, used to retrieve items—or people—that had fallen overboard or to carry messages from one boat to another. The Newfoundland was bred for hauling in huge fishing nets laden with fresh fish. Saint Bernards were rescue dogs, saving lives throughout the Alps. And of course, the Alaskan Malamute and the Siberian Husky were sled dogs that pulled people back and forth across frozen tundras in very dangerous conditions.

There are many popular dogs in the Working Group, most notably the Rottweiler, Doberman Pinscher, Akita, and Mastiff, which were bred primarily as guard dogs. They are powerful dogs, and when properly trained and socialized, they make invaluable friends. These dogs will risk life and limb to protect their families and are a great source of pride and love. However, there are many people who have given these dogs a bad name.

Because they are large, powerful dogs, if they are not properly trained and socialized with other dogs, they can become a menace. It is not in their nature—it is in the nature of the people who own these dogs and then train them to be that way.

The noble and handsome Siberian Husky is as hardworking as he is handsome. A rugged individualist who gives his all to those who care for and keep him, it is said that once a Siberian wins your heart, you are gone for good.

The Rottweiler is the best example of this kind of misuse of natural instincts. Rottweilers, by nature, are very sociable dogs. They are even cuddly and fun-loving, like big teddy bears. But they need to be socialized at a young age and given proper obedience training. Take that same dog and encourage his aggressive behavior, and you have a dog that is a danger to his family, other people, and other animals. These dogs are not inherently malicious, they're trained by irresponsible, immature thugs into ticking time bombs, giving those people a false sense of power.

FACT

The Great Dane is a member of the Working Group, and an impressive dog she is! Standing at about thirty-two inches at the shoulder (nearly three feet tall!), her large head and ears give her an even larger appearance. This giant is gentle, though—you would never know she was once used to bring down the fierce wild boar. Her coat can be many colors, from a creamy fawn to a patchwork Harlequin.

That said, the breeds in the Working Group make exceptional family pets. It's a matter of socializing your dog with other dogs, animals, and people from an early age, and treating your friend with respect and dignity. Do this, and you will have a loving, devoted family member who is, in fact, wonderful with children. The breeds in the AKC Working Group are:

- Akita
- Alaskan Malamute
- Anatolian Shepherd Dog
- Bernese Mountain Dog
- Black Russian Terrier
- Boxer
- Bullmastiff
- Doberman Pinscher
- German Pinscher
- Giant Schnauzer
- Great Dane
- Great Pyrenees
- Greater Swiss Mountain Dog
- Komondor
- Kuvasz
- Mastiff

- Neapolitan Mastiff
- Newfoundland
- Portuguese Water Dog
- Rottweiler
- Saint Bernard
- Samoyed
- Siberian Husky
- Standard Schnauzer
- Tibetan Mastiff

Terriers

What would the one word be that could describe the majority of breeds in the Terrier Group? Spunky! The dogs in this group are by turns tenacious, lovable, energetic, and downright funny. The Terrier Group is mostly made up of a number of wire-haired, smaller dogs that were originally bred to help land owners and gamekeepers keep undesirables off their properties—namely raccoons, foxes, rats, weasels, and badgers.

The word "terrier" finds its root in the Latin word *terra*, which means earth. And that's what many of these dogs were used for. They were bred from way back to dig out animals that went to ground for cover or safety, then kill them or chase them out. They would bark and dig simultaneously, driving away vermin, or fighting their adversaries right there in the den's entrance. Indeed, many dogs in the Terrier Group have short, strong tails that many a gamekeeper or huntsman used to pull the little fighters out when it seemed the dogs might be getting the worse end of the scrap—or when it seemed that the contest had been decided.

In the 1800s, dog fighting, though a cruel and inhumane sport, was popular. While Mastiffs and Bulldogs were the most prized in the area, breeders decided they needed a new dog, and so several new breeds were created in this period. Many were achieved by crossing certain breeds with terriers, which added fleet movement and tenacity to their part of the match. Usually married to them were brawn and size. The resulting breeds are no less lovable than any other breed of dog. Many of these dogs get lumped under the rubric "pit bull"—a term referring to the time when two dogs were thrown into a pit and fought to the death (an abhorrent practice that is outlawed today).

The Cairn Terrier hails from Scotland, where he got his name because of his ability to find prey in the "cairns," or natural mounds of stones found throughout that country. He is a wonderful all-purpose companion, large enough to keep pace with any member of the family, yet small enough to be portable and easy to care for.

Don't be fooled by the terriers' packages—just because many of them are small and oh-so-cute doesn't mean they are good apartment dogs or "accessory pets." Many of them are very high-energy animals who require extensive exercise. Learn as much as you can about any that interest you before deciding on one as your dog.

For the most part, terriers are well suited to urban, suburban, or rural life. However, they are determined little dogs and will require training in many cases to keep them on the straight and narrow. Like some of their larger brethren, these dogs need firm rules along with love and a real leader in the house to keep them from acting out in ways that could be destructive to the home and yard. The AKC-recognized terriers are:

- Airedale Terrier
- American Staffordshire Terrier
- Australian Terrier
- Bedlington Terrier
- Border Terrier
- Bull Terrier
- Cairn Terrier
- Dandie Dinmont Terrier
- Glen of Imal Terrier
- Irish Terrier
- Kerry Blue Terrier
- Lakeland Terrier
- Manchester Terrier
- Miniature Bull Terrier
- Miniature Schnauzer
- Norfolk Terrier
- Norwich Terrier
- Parson Russell Terrier
- Scottish Terrier
- Sealyham Terrier
- Skye Terrier
- Smooth Fox Terrier
- Soft Coated Wheaten Terrier
- Staffordshire Bull Terrier
- Welsh Terrier
- West Highland White Terrier
- Wire Fox Terrier

Toys

The Toy Group is composed exclusively of some of the smallest dogs in the canine world—and also some of the most adorable! Many of these cuddly little rascals have been bred purely for companionship and were never intended to be anything other than pets. Some of them come from very obscure backgrounds, but make no mistake—these are dogs.

Yorkshire Terriers are perennially popular—because who can resist them? With their long, silky coats, button eyes and nose, and "I can do anything a big dog can do" attitude, they are at home in all kinds of homes all around the world.

The most amazing thing about little dogs is that they think just like big dogs. They mark territory; they are loving; they are protective; they are great watchdogs; and they will bite, too, if they feel threatened. They do get away with a lot more because of their size and cuteness, and they guard their privileges jealously. They are usually welcome on the couch to sleep in your lap; they're usually allowed in public places and on transportation, where their larger cousins are absolutely forbidden; hotels even sometimes turn a blind eye to them. At the very least, they're so small, they're easier to hide!

FACT

Some of these dogs are so small that many centuries ago in Europe they were called sleeve dogs because ladies of means hid the dogs in their sleeves! If that's not a companion dog, what is?

The popularity of the Pug continues to increase year after year. It seems people can't get enough of their chubby, compact little bodies; curly tails; and one-of-a-kind faces. They are beloved by children and adults alike, and they are quick to return the sentiments.

There are many stories about how loyal these breeds are, belying their size to protect their masters, using shrill barking to warn of danger and persistence to distract danger. Toy dogs tend to be smart and feisty. They can be trained easily for the most part (though housetraining can be a challenge), and many do not require too much exercise. All Toy breeds make good house and apartment dogs. They love attention and they expect to get it. They also require grooming, and they love that, too. The dogs in the Toy Group in the American Kennel Club are:

- Affenpinscher
- Brussels Griffon
- Cavalier King Charles Spaniel
- Chihuahua
- English Toy Spaniel
- Havanese
- Italian Greyhound
- Japanese Chin
- Maltese
- Manchester Terrier (Toy)
- Miniature Pinscher
- Papillon
- Pekingese
- Pomeranian
- Poodle (Toy)
- Pug
- Shih Tzu
- Silky Terrier
- Toy Fox Terrier
- Yorkshire Terrier

Non-Sporting Dogs

The dogs in this group all have one thing in common, and that is that they don't really "fit" into any of the other groups! While some of them were working or sporting dogs in their early development, their "jobs" have been so long outmoded that they have primarily been companion dogs for almost a century, in some cases longer.

The Boston Terrier is an all-American breed, developed on these shores to be a well-mannered, distinguished-looking dog-about-town. He is always dressed for any occasion—and always welcomes being part of the crowd.

In this unique group, you have some very popular if disparate dogs. There is the Poodle (originally one of Europe's finest hunting dogs); the Bulldog (used to bait bulls centuries ago); the Bichon Frise (a companion dog too big for the Toy Group); the Schipperke (a Dutch boatsman's dog in another century); and many more.

FACT

The Löwchen is one of the newest members of the Non-Sporting Group. He has an outgoing personality in a medium-sized, compact body. He is clipped to resemble a lion, complete with a long, flowing mane.

The Non-Sporting Group is a good one from which to choose a versatile companion, as its members are so unique. The all-American Boston Terrier is becoming more and more popular as a small—but not too small—dapper dog-about-town, as is the French Bulldog. You can't describe the dogs in this group as focused on a particular thing, like retrieving or fetching or chasing or herding or protecting. Rather, they are multifocused, and as such, make for pleasant all-around dogs. The members of the AKC Non-Sporting Group are:

- American Eskimo Dog
- Bichon Frise
- Boston Terrier
- Bulldog
- Chinese Shar-Pei
- Chow Chow
- Dalmatian
- Finnish Spitz
- French Bulldog
- Keeshound
- Lhasa Apso
- Löwchen
- Poodle (Standard and Miniature)
- Schipperke
- Shiba Inu
- Tibetan Spaniel
- Tibetan Terrier

So thoroughly associated with courage, strength, and resolution is the Bulldog that he is the mascot of numerous sports teams and—of highest distinction—the United States Marines.

Herding Breeds

The Herding Group is relatively new, having been established in 1983. Herding breeds were originally part of the Working Group, but when it became so large as to be unmanageable, the breeds were subtracted from it, and the Herding Group was established independently. Some of the oldest breeds we know of today got their first job guarding and managing their humans' livestock.

Among all the breeds of dogs, these are some of the smartest, most trainable, and hardworking. It is important to remember that these dogs have been bred to do a job—a demanding job—herding and protecting what they perceive as "theirs." This means that while you are walking down the street your Shepherd will want to keep you gathered in—especially if you are with a family member or close friend. The bigger the crowd, the more they want to form you into a cohesive entity. They can be determined to get their way.

FACT

The "classic" German Shepherd Dog is black and tan, but there are also German Shepherds that are all black and all white! In fact, the White German Shepherd is considered a unique breed with a following all its own. To see these beautiful dogs, go to *www.wgsdca.org*.

The German Shepherd Dog has remained popular around the world in part because of his amazing intelligence combined with his impressive athleticism. He has demonstrated exceptional talent as a war dog, police dog, service dog, therapy dog, shepherd, guardian, obedience competitor, and of course, companion. His history is written right alongside so much of ours.

The Herding Group tends to have some dogs in it that are persistent barkers; their instincts are to communicate verbally to alert you to anything suspicious or worthy of attention (in their opinion, not necessarily yours). Herding breeds are generally happiest in homes with large yards and should be given plenty to do. In general, they are very active, so you need to be able to keep them busy. These dogs really, really want to work; they have the bodies and minds to do jobs and do them well. That's why you find so many Herding breeds taking home top honors in competitions like obedience, agility, herding, flyball, and freestyle—not to mention their ranks among police, military, and service dogs.

He has sometimes been misnamed a "miniature Collie," but the Shetland Sheepdog is no such thing. He is his own dog, distinctive in so many ways—and prized for his sweet and affectionate nature, protective instincts, and good looks.

Not all the Herding breeds are suited for novice owners. In fact, many were developed to think on their own or do the bidding of their human counterparts. With some of them, when you are unsure, either you will fill them with confusion or they will make decisions for themselves. You need to be their fair leader—and if you are, they will follow you to the ends of the earth. The AKC Herding breeds are:

- Australian Cattle Dog
- Australian Shepherd
- Bearded Collie
- Beauceron
- Belgian Malinois
- Belgian Sheepdog
- Belgian Tervuren
- Border Collie
- Bouvier des Flandres
- Briard
- Canaan Dog
- Cardigan Welsh Corgi
- Collie
- German Shepherd Dog
- Old English Sheepdog
- Pembroke Welsh Corgi
- Puli
- Shetland Sheepdog
- Swedish Vallhund

There's More!

As if this selection of breeds isn't enough to choose from, the American Kennel Club also designates others in a couple of other categories: the Miscellaneous Class and the Foundation Stock Service (FSS). This is because the AKC will not officially "recognize" a breed and place it into a Group until there is a large enough demonstrated interest in and veritable sustainability of a particular breed. Recognition is achieved when the AKC Board of

Directors concludes, in working with the parent club for the breed, that all the necessary criteria have been met.

Until they are recognized—at which time individual dogs and litters may be registered with the AKC and the breed may compete in all AKC-sanctioned events—the breeds are accepted for recording in the FSS, and if they reach a particular benchmark, are considered part of the Miscellaneous Class. MC breeds may compete in select AKC events until they achieve full recognition. Visit *www.akc.org* to learn the status of a breed you might be interested in. The FSS breeds (which include some MC breeds) are:

- American English Coonhound
- Appenzeller Sennenhunde
- Argentine Dogo
- Azawakh
- Belgian Laekenois
- Bergamasco
- Berger Picard
- Black and Tan Coonhound
- Bluetick Coonhound
- Bolognese
- Boykin Spaniel
- Bracco Italiano
- Cane Corso
- Catahoula Leopard Dog
- Caucasian Mountain Dog
- Central Asian Shepherd Dog
- Cesky Terrier
- Chinook
- Cimeco dell'Etna
- Coton de Tulear
- Czechoslovakian Wolfdog
- Dogue de Bordeaux
- Entlebucher Mountain Dog
- Estrela Mountain Dog
- Finnish Lapphund

- German Spitz
- Grand Basset Griffon Vendéen
- Icelandic Sheepdog
- Irish Red and White Setter
- Kai Ken
- Karelian Bear Dog
- Kishu Ken
- Kooikerhondje
- Lagotto Romagnolo
- Lancashire Heeler
- Leonberger
- Mudi
- Norwegian Buhund
- Norwegian Lundehund
- Perro de Presa Canario
- Peruvian Inca Orchid
- Portuguese Podengo
- Portuguese Pointer
- Pumi
- Pyrenean Shepherd
- Rafeiro de Alentejo
- Rat Terrier
- Redbone Coonhound
- Russell Terrier
- Schapendoes
- Sloughi
- Small Munsterlander Pointer
- South African Boerboel
- Spanish Water Dog
- Stabyhoun
- Swedish Lapphund
- Thai Ridgeback
- Tosa
- Treeing Tennessee Brindle
- Treeing Walker Coonhound
- Xoloitzcuintli

CHAPTER 4

Preparing for Your Dog

You've actually picked a dog and the arrival date is near. Now comes one of the most important parts: preparing for your new family member. This is a super-exciting time for everyone, comparable to getting the nursery ready for a new baby. There are things your family needs to know to make the homecoming happy and smooth; things you will need to do to your home to be sure it is safe for your dog; things you will need for your dog to help care for him on a daily basis; and more far-reaching considerations, like selecting a veterinarian.

4

Preparing Your Family

If you have children, no matter their ages, they will be extremely excited about the arrival of the family dog. Dogs are sensitive to the emotions of the people around them, and your family's nervousness and excitement are going to have an effect on the new dog.

Getting Your Puppy

For most puppies, being picked up by you and taken to your home is the first big change in their very young lives. For you it's the greatest thing ever; for them, it's confusing and scary. Everything they've known so far will be gone—their mom, their brothers and sisters, the people who've been caring for them, the smells and sounds they're used to. With this in mind, a puppy will certainly welcome your family's loving attention. Be aware of what "loving attention" can be, though. Handling the puppy gently, speaking calmly and soothingly, allowing the puppy to do some exploring on her own while still keeping an eye on her, making sure she has a quiet and comfy place to nap—all of these are ways to help your pup feel secure and loved.

It's okay for everyone to come along when you pick up your puppy, but think about how you want to position her for the ride home. Your children will all want her to be on their lap and may want to pass her around during the trip. This could lead to arguments over the puppy, pulling the puppy, or accidentally mishandling the puppy. If the puppy should have an accident in the car, the kids may not handle it well. All of these scenarios lead to major distractions for the driver as well as a negative experience for the puppy. If you're traveling with another adult who can sit quietly in the passenger seat, allow her to hold the pup on her lap during the trip home. Place an old towel or blanket on her lap for extra comfort and in case of an accident, and have some paper towels handy, too.

If it's just you and the kids picking up the puppy, bring along the pup's crate and bring him home in that. Make sure there's a thick, soft towel or blanket for him to lie down on, and secure the crate on the front seat or in the back of the car. The pup may cry in the crate, but at least you'll know he's safe.

Getting Your Older Dog

Depending on your dog's circumstances, you could be one of several new places he's been lately. You are just another change of scenery for him at first, and it will take some time for him to warm up to and trust you. You may think that you're giving him the greatest home ever, but he may still be mourning a past caregiver or finally feeling used to his most recent situation. Whatever his past holds, your dog is leaving everything he knows to come to your home, and just as you would respect that change for a puppy, you need to appreciate it when it comes to your new, older dog.

FACT

For the most part, dogs are amazingly adaptable and resilient. Expect that a young puppy or new dog will need time to get used to you, and be accommodating without being overly indulgent. As you all get to know each other and settle into your routine, you'll see your dog's true personality emerge, and you'll feel your bond deepen.

The loving attention your older dog needs is similar to that of a new puppy: be gentle with him, allow him to explore under your watchful supervision, don't pester him, and don't overwhelm him.

Whether you are bringing home a puppy or an older dog, make sure you already have all the supplies you'll need to care for a dog. If you have those ready when he arrives at your house, you won't need to stress him by going for yet another car ride to another strange place.

Preparing Your Home

Take a look around your home and ask yourself what you need to do so that your puppy or dog doesn't destroy all your family's prized possessions, or hurt herself chewing on something that could be harmful. Think about where your dog will sleep. What will she eat, and out of what? How will you take her outside? These are the considerations that affect what kind of equipment and other supplies you'll need to make sure you and your dog get off to a good start and for you to provide a safe and secure home for her.

Puppy-Proofing

The first thing you want to do with a puppy is limit the amount of space she has to run around—especially when you're not home. Many people confine the pup to a room or group of manageable rooms in the beginning. Choose a room in which there's a lot of people traffic so your puppy doesn't feel isolated. Pick a room that's fairly easy to clean, with an easily washable floor surface. The room should be light and airy. The kitchen or washroom are good first choices, whether you're crate-training your puppy or not.

There's no way around it—if you're getting a puppy and you want to limit her space, you need a baby gate. She will not be in her crate all the time, yet she might not be trustworthy enough in her housetraining to have free run of other rooms.

FACT

Baby gates do a good job of setting up a solid barrier while allowing the puppy to see into the other room and also smell what's going on in there (very important to a dog). Another nice thing about baby gates is that they're portable and removable.

Once your puppy understands what's expected of her with regard to housetraining in the kitchen and the den, for example, you can expand the area she's allowed in, still using the baby gate(s) to keep her from rooms that are off limits.

Confining Your Dog

Why do you want to confine your puppy (or new dog)? It's for his benefit and yours. When you're not home, it limits the amount of damage he can do to himself or the house to just one room. Before you leave, if you're not going to be crating Junior, it's easier for you to look around one room and either move or put away things that might cause him harm.

Once you've put the baby gates up, you need to look around the room and ask yourself the following question: If you were a dog, what would you chew on? The usual answer: everything. If there are exposed wires, cover them up. If the chairs around the kitchen table are wood, consider putting them in another room while your pup's alone. Are all bottles and cans securely put away? Are all cleansers and other potentially toxic substances safely locked inside child-proofed cabinets? And don't forget: hide the garbage. As far as a dog is concerned, everything wonderful to eat is in the garbage. Dogs are persistent, and simply having a can with a lid that automatically closes is not enough.

You should dog-proof your house for an older dog in much the same way as for a puppy. You're not really sure what a new dog will do in a strange new environment. Better to take precautions. Sometimes they adapt quickly and easily with few problems. Other times, they're unsure of themselves and become nervous, resorting to destructive habits to deal with anxiety. The right mix of confinement, appropriate chew toys, exercise, nutrition, and TLC should make things right.

Small kitchen cans need to be behind securely closed cabinets; large kitchen cans should be behind a closed door. Not only is finding the contents of your garbage all over the floor annoying, knowing your dog or puppy ate something that could make him ill is even worse. Beware and prepare!

What can't be moved—especially anything that's made out of wood—spray with a chew-deterrent product such as Bitter Apple. These sprays leave a very bitter taste on things so that if your dog puts his mouth around it he'll get the terrible taste and leave it alone. Because you'll be removing everything that your pup or dog would normally find interesting to investigate or chew on, it's critical that you provide appropriate toys and chew items.

Preparing Your Yard

While you were thinking about what kind of dog to get, you no doubt had to decide what to do about your yard so that you could properly exercise your pooch. It is not safe or smart to let your dog out and expect that she will do her business and then return to you. A fenced-in yard protects your dog from running off and protects her from other dogs or animals that may want to run onto your property. Even a small fenced-in area allows you to at least let your dog out when she needs to relieve herself without you having to join her—this is especially helpful in inclement weather.

Beyond the consideration of a fence, you should take a look at your yard or property and think about what might be on it that could harm your pup or dog. This could include any kind of debris or junk that's been allowed to decompose in any way. It could include old wood that might have nails or splinters. It could include gaps in the fence line where your dog might be able to slip out or, with a little digging, get out. Remember, better safe than sorry! Clean up or remove anything that could be potentially dangerous before you bring home your dog, or pay the consequences once she's at your home. It's easier and cheaper to take care of this before your dog is at your home.

Fencing

If you don't have a fence yet but are thinking about getting one, you have several options. Cost will undoubtedly factor into your decision, though practicality and aesthetics are very important, as well. If you think about it, the fence you install should last many years, so an expensive choice that best suits your situation will be better than a cheaper option that doesn't quite fit. There are wire fences, wooden fences, and fences made of synthetic materials.

Think about whether the breed you're interested in is particularly territorial, how close you are to other houses and the street, and how much time you think he may spend outside. If he can see through the fence and may spend a fair amount of time outside, you may end up with a dog who barks at and runs alongside the fence—a tough habit to break.

Leashes, Collars, and Identification

These are some of the essential items you have to have for your dog. There are many types to choose from, however, and understanding the differences will make it easier when you get to the store.

You'll need an all-purpose leash for walks around the block and most training sessions. Leashes or leads come in a variety of colors, textures, and styles. There are leather leashes, nylon leashes, and even chain leashes. The best (and also the most expensive) is a six-foot-long leather leash. You should have this leash for a long time if you take care of it. Leather is strong, wears well, doesn't stink, and is comfortable in your hand.

Nylon leashes are also strong and come in a huge assortment of colors and patterns. They come in handy when you have to walk your dog in the rain and you don't want the leather to get wet. If you have to give your dog a bath, a nylon leash can get wet while providing some restraint. They dry quickly and don't shrink or crack. But they're not comfortable to hold; in fact, some may give you a rope burn if they get jerked out of your hand.

FACT

Chain leashes are decorative but quite impractical. They're hard to hold, and can hurt you or your dog if they get pulled against your skin.

Flexi-leads are just that: flexible leashes that allow you to extend or shorten the leash like an adjustable clothesline. The idea is that it lets the dog have some freedom to roam, but when she comes nearer to you, the line automatically withdraws and recoils. There is also a button that can stop the flow of the line at any time, so if you need to keep your dog close to you, you can limit the amount of line you let out. These leashes provide you with the opportunity to run your dog with greater freedom in open spaces where dogs are not allowed off-leash.

The only problem is that if your dog circles you or someone nearby with the leash, the cord may cause a burn against your unprotected skin. When using a Flexi-lead, you must be alert to any changes of direction or sudden activity on the part of your dog. Overall, though, they're a handy way to have control and still let your dog run.

QUESTION?

Can I use a harness?

Many people dislike having to pull on a collar that presses up against their dog's trachea. Owners of smaller dogs and toy breeds need to be especially sensitive to this. For such owners (and their dogs), a harness is a practical way to safely go for a stroll. The harness goes over the dog's head and around its front legs and chest, securing with a clasp. There is a ring hook on the top where a leash is attached. Harnesses are now made in a variety of materials, colors, and patterns, often with matching leashes.

Collars

Like leashes, collars come in a huge variety of materials, styles, and colors. Unlike the leash, however, one size does not fit all; you will need to buy a collar to fit your dog at her current size. Collars should fit snugly but not be too tight. You want something that goes around her neck comfortably and won't slide off the head, but you need to be able to insert two fingers between the collar and the dog's neck. Don't pull on the collar to make the space. It should be slack enough that it happens without creating too much tension.

There are four basic types of collars: traditional buckle collars; choke chains; the pronged collar; and electronic collars. The traditional buckle collar is recommended as your dog's first collar and the one he'll wear almost daily. These collars come in leather or nylon and have the traditional buckle or clasp fastener. They are adjustable, so your puppy should be able to grow into her buckle collar (though she will definitely grow out of at least one!).

FACT

You can get a buckle or clasp collar in whatever color or style you want, from a conservative but elegant rolled leather, to black leather with metal spikes, to bright pink, to monogrammed, to decorated with ducks, hearts, or flowers. There are even buckle collars that glow in the dark! Your dog's collar can be a true expression of how you feel about her.

Other Collars

The **choke chain** (now often referred to as a slip collar) is a metal link collar that is primarily used for training. Basically, this is a slip-knotted smooth metal chain that comes in different sizes. The idea is that as the dog pulls harder, the collar "chokes" him, pinching his skin slightly or impairing his breathing. To relieve the tension and breathe easier, he has to stop pulling. Used properly, this kind of collar can save years of wear and tear on your arms and shoulders and teach your dog not to pull. Your dog's trainer can demonstrate the correct way to put the collar on and how to use it for maximum efficiency.

This collar should be used only during training and should not be the collar you use all the time. Because the collar has two big rings on either end, it can get caught on things. If your dog catches his collar on something while you're not with him, he could easily choke to death trying to free himself. If you properly train your dog in the beginning, eventually you won't need this collar—though he will always associate it with training, which might help him pay attention to you.

The **pronged collar** operates like a choke chain in that it tightens around the dog's neck as she pulls harder. But the pronged collar has dulled metal prongs that poke her in the neck as she pulls. Many people use this collar when walking dogs that are very difficult to control or for whom a smaller choke chain is not effective. If you think you need this kind of collar for your dog, you must be instructed in its proper use. Speak to a trainer or your breeder about whether it's the collar you need and how to use it. Additional training classes are probably in order, too.

You will also find a number of **electronic collars** in your pet supply store. There are electronic collars to stop your dog from barking, electronic collars to keep your dog within your property, even electronic collars to be used as training aids by hunters and people who work their dogs at great distances. The most commonly used are the bark collar and the collar that works with an "invisible" electronic fence. All work by "zapping" your dog with a burst of electricity when she barks or tries to break the barrier of the fence, or when you need to get her attention. All should be used in conjunction with more humane training methods of teaching the dog to shush, mind her property, or respond to a whistle or voice command. They can definitely be abusive in the wrong hands.

Head halters are essentially harnesses that slip over and around a dog's head, like the halters used on horses. The theory is that a dog can be led more easily by the head than by the neck (which is usually a very strong part of a dog's anatomy). These halters are very effective. But they have some drawbacks. First, they look like a muzzle, making poor Spot look like the canine version of Attila the Hun, ready to bite at the slightest provocation. Many people think they are cruel because they make your dog look more dangerous because she's being muzzled. It takes some dogs a while to get used to head halters, too, as they can feel strange at first. But if you have a dog who pulls no matter what, you should consider using one.

Identification for Your Dog

One of the most important things that your dog could ever have is proper identification in the form of an ID tag, in addition to a more permanent tattoo or microchip. This is because he could become lost quickly and easily, and it's important that when he does he has a clearly visible piece of identification on his body.

Most pet supply stores large and small have in-store kiosks where you can make tags for your dog's collars. The tags come in all kinds of fun shapes and sizes and the machines are easy to use. The tags are inexpensive. The information that's critical to put on the tag is the dog's name and your phone number(s). List whichever phone you use most frequently first—nowadays that's typically a cell phone number. Then list your home phone and even your work number. It's not necessary to list your address. Someone who finds a dog with a tag will call the number, not take it back to a street address (what if no one is home?).

Permanent Forms of Identification

As necessary and important as an identification tag is on your dog's collar, it can come off or be removed. To further protect dogs, they can be tattooed or microchipped. Many people tattoo their dogs with the animal's American Kennel Club or other registering body's registration number. The tattoos are applied on the inside of the back leg where they are hard to see unless you're really looking (shelter and animal control staff know to look for them).

An identification tag attached to your dog's collar is an essential piece of equipment. It is the first thing anyone will look for should your precious companion become lost. Tags come in many shapes, styles, and colors these days, so they can also serve a decorative purpose.

Even more popular and standardized today is the implantation of a microchip—a rice-sized capsule that contains a computer chip with a unique number. These tiny microchips are injected between your dog's shoulder blades into the muscle mass there where it won't migrate to another part of the body. The injection looks worse than it is—it doesn't hurt your dog at all. These chips are permanent for the life of the dog and are easily scanned. Ask your veterinarian about getting a microchip for your dog. Once chipped, your dog receives a tag to go on her collar alerting anyone who finds her to call an 800-number where the chip numbers are registered. Should the tag be lost, animal shelters, animal control officers, and veterinary offices are equipped with scanning machines.

Bowls, Beds, Crates, and Toys

So many things to shop for! Because every dog needs these things, there are lots of them to choose from. What's great about the large selection you'll find is that it means you can really personalize your dog's things. Another bonus is that you can find things that complement the overall décor of your house—while being practical, comfortable, and easy to care for.

Bowls for Food and Water

There is one simple rule with dog bowls: Make sure you buy bowls with wide, heavy bases that are hard to tip over. Especially with puppies, bowls can become playthings. You want to avoid letting this happen. With smaller dogs, obviously, you don't want to have too small a bowl. With larger dogs, make sure the bowl is not just bigger, but also a little heavier. Another consideration when buying bowls is what they're made of. You'll find stainless steel, ceramic, and plastic bowls, all in a variety of shapes and sizes.

Stainless steel is the easiest to clean. Ceramic is another excellent choice, and it can complement your home's décor. A plastic bowl can come in handy while traveling, but be advised that it can be easily chewed, and the materials it's made with can possibly leach into your dog's food or water. For safety and sanitary reasons, ceramic or stainless steel are best.

FACT

You will need two bowls for your dog: one for water and one for food. Clean the food bowl after each use and set it aside. Clean the water bowl once or twice a day, and be sure to keep it filled with cool, fresh water.

Beds, Glorious Beds

No, not yours, hers! Let's get this right out in the open: Your puppy should not sleep on your bed with you. You may want to comfort her and have her near you, but it's not a good idea for several reasons. When a dog sleeps on your bed, you're confusing her. Sleeping in your bed (or one of your kids' beds) with you tells her that she's an equal member of the pack, and that she has as much say about things as you do. Dogs who sleep on the bed with human family members often become possessive and territorial of the bed. As the pup grows or the older dog feels more comfortable and starts to stretch out and hog the bed, she may not accept your request that she get down. This can lead to aggressive behavior and result in a child who becomes afraid of the dog in his bed.

This certainly doesn't mean you should banish your puppy to the basement to "keep her in her place." But a cozy dog bed or crate placed in the bedroom with you or in one of the kids' rooms will be comfortable for your dog, and better for you to maintain the hierarchy. You need to be the Top Dog in your puppy's or new dog's eyes, especially in the beginning.

There are a number of well-made dog beds available, so you won't have to look long or spend a lot to find one that suits your tastes and your dog's needs. Like collars, there are many types of beds to choose from. They're filled with different materials, covered with different fabrics, designed for arthritic dogs, big dogs, tiny dogs, spoiled dogs. This is another area where you can have fun shopping for Fido. Beds are better than folded blankets or towels or carpet remnants. Remnants can't be cleaned as thoroughly, and folded blankets may end up being a play toy and will require your constant folding. The only recommendation about doggy beds is that the bed you choose should have an outer shell that can be removed. Many have zippers. Unzip that shell and toss it into the washing machine whenever it starts to get dirty or stinky.

All about Crates

Even today many people still think crate training is cruel for a dog. Despite it's "cagey" look—which is evolving—the crate is one of the most popular training tools, and rightfully so. Training a dog to use a crate gives the owner a way to control her dog. With a crate, the dog gets his own private "room" in the house. Let's consider some things. First, the dog is a den animal by nature. He likes a closed space that offers him protection and, when he wants, isolation. Dogs will also typically not eliminate where they eat and sleep, which is in their den or crate. This is why crates are such useful housetraining aids.

Proper crate-training starts with the right crate, correctly appointed. You want to buy a crate that will be big enough for your adult dog to stand up and turn around in. There are two main types of crates: wire and plastic. The wire crates fold down and can be carried. The plastic crates are typically referred to as airline crates because they're the ones that are used to transport animals on airplanes. The wire crates are open and airy so your dog can see, hear, and sniff everything that's going on around him. Airline crates have only a front opening and some air holes for ventilation; they are much more denlike. One way that owners can make a wire crate more protected is by draping sheets or, in cold weather, blankets over the top of the crate. This shuts out light and drafts.

ALERT!

You might consider having more than one crate for your dog if you want a permanent crate for her in the kitchen as well as one to serve as her bed upstairs with you. That way you won't have to worry about transporting the crate several times a day. You can also decorate each crate differently to fit into its respective room.

Whichever kind you choose, if you have a puppy and you've bought a crate that will fit him when he's full grown, he is going to have a lot of room in it. This is not good because he will be able to eat and sleep in one end and eliminate in the other, which defeats all your housetraining efforts. To reduce the amount of room your pup has in the crate, create a divider to put in it so that the space is cut down to about half. As your puppy grows, you can move the divider until he doesn't need it anymore. You can use anything from stiff cardboard to plywood as a divider. Just make sure it's securely positioned so your puppy can't grab an end to chew on and devour it.

Once you've selected a type of crate, you want to create the perfect den inside it. The best thing to do while housetraining your pup is to line the crate with a thick layer of old towels or blankets—ones that can be easily washed. This way if he spills food or water or has an accident, it's no big deal. Help your puppy associate the crate with good things by feeding him in his crate. The first time you want him to go in, put his food dish just past the opening and let him eat from it. After you've taken him out after his meal and played with him, toss a toy or treat into the crate so he scampers in after it. Close the door behind him, tell him what a good doggy he is, and leave him. He will probably cry, but you have to be strong. If you let him out while he's whining or crying he'll learn that making that sound brings you to his rescue. Instead, wait until he stops for at least a minute, then let him out while he's quiet. He will soon learn that good things happen when he's behaving himself in the crate.

Once your puppy or dog is crate trained using a more traditional style crate, you can shop around for ones that are more fashionable. These include collapsible crates made in a variety of materials, from a combination of wire and hard plastic to mesh and nylon.

Toys—Oh, Joys!

A trip to your local pet supply store will reveal that there are almost as many toys for pets now as there are for children. This makes choosing some for your dog a lot of fun!

Kongs are cone-shaped rubber pieces that are seemingly indestructible, and dogs love the way they bounce. They are also hollow, and trainers recommend stuffing them with different dog-friendly foods to keep your dog interested in the Kong and not your kitchen cabinets. Frisbees are a lot of fun, too. But most Frisbees, while they feel pretty strong, are made out of a plastic that just can't take the pounding that a dog's teeth can dish out. That's why the Nylabone Frisbee is the best. Your dog can play Frisbee with you all day long and not puncture it. It also has a bone-shaped handle on the top, which makes it easier for your dog to pick it up. And of course, if your dog has a passion for fetch, you'll want tennis balls, which are also handy because they float in water.

There are all kinds of toys with squeakers in them, even ones that make particular animal noises. These are designed to tease and interest your dog. Just be sure the toys don't rip apart too easily; you do not want your dog to swallow the squeaker!

Toys that are *not* appropriate for your dog are those meant for children, including action figures, plush animals, any plastic object with a liquid center, footballs, basketballs, soccer balls, kickballs, baseballs, and anything made of glass or twine.

ALERT!

As dogs chew things they have a tendency to swallow pieces. If the pieces are big, they may become stuck in the dog's throat, or they can cause intestinal damage. Supervise your dog with some toys to see how she chews. Some dogs will rip almost anything apart; some will simply sniff, nibble, and carry a toy around. Ask the people in the store for help selecting what's best for your dog once you see what kind of chewer she is.

Edible Chews

Many toys for dogs are edible, such as Greenies, some Nylabones, chew hooves and other smoked or dried animal parts, and rawhide. These should only be given to your dog while you're there to supervise so you don't risk your dog choking on small pieces. Rawhide, in particular, can become gummy when softened, and dogs can rip off and ingest fairly large chunks of it. When provided correctly, though, they make great cross-overs between treats and toys.

Finding a Veterinarian

Studies prove that veterinarians are the first people most pet owners turn to for help with a variety of problems, from health to behavior. Like your child's pediatrician, your dog's veterinarian can and should be an invaluable resource for you. The relationship will only work, though, if you trust and respect each other.

It might seem easy to find a competent and caring veterinarian with whom you can develop a great relationship around caring for your dog. The truth is, even when a veterinarian is recommended to you, if you don't feel comfortable around him, you may not seek or receive the proper care for your dog.

If you're bringing a puppy into your life, you will need to take her to a veterinarian within the first couple of days of her homecoming to get a thorough health exam and get you started on a course of routine care. It's nice to know from the very beginning that you have chosen someone you really like.

To find the veterinarian that's best for you and your dog, ask several dog-owning friends as well as your pup's breeder or other breeders near you for some recommendations. Make a point to visit the offices of all the recommendations. See how you're greeted when you come in. Take note of how crowded the waiting room is. Do the people working there seem to enjoy their jobs? If possible, ask to meet with the veterinarian. Without an appointment she may not have time, but with an appointment she may be on her best behavior. Also, if you get a bad feeling from the office, you may not want to bother to meet the doctor. If you find yourself in an office with a friendly staff surrounded by people who seem content to be there and you can see the veterinarian, let her know what you're doing and schedule your puppy's first visit.

CHAPTER 5

Feeding Your Dog

Pet owners have long believed that large pet-food manufacturers make the dinner decisions for dogs easier and healthier. All a good owner needs to do for the well-being of his dog is to feed her a balanced, commercially prepared food. But today's pet food market is so flooded with products that it's hard to know what to choose. Increased awareness about food sensitivities and allergies only compounds the problem, and the massive pet food recall in the spring of 2007 heightened owners' anxiety about what to feed their pets.

Understanding Dog Food

Pet food started to become commercially available a little more than 100 years ago. The idea that a commercial product had everything a dog needed for optimal nutrition took hold of pet owners. So prevalent was this attitude that people were told not to feed table scraps, as these could upset the nutritive balance (as well as the tummy). Supplements and additives were discouraged. It was truly believed that feeding a dog anything besides what was manufactured as being a food for dogs was simply spoiling a dog or risking making him sick.

Recent years have seen a reversal of this theory, and there is no greater proof of it than the pet-food recall scare of early 2007, in which many manufacturers of dog and cat foods had to take their products off the shelves after pets died from eating them. The source of the problem? Tainted wheat gluten from China. It didn't seem like something like this could happen in the wake of a virtual revolution toward healthier pet foods since the 1990s.

FACT

Pet food is a billion-dollar industry, and competition is fierce. Confused by manufacturers' claims, disheartened by pervasive health problems, and aware of the ills of their own diets, dog owners have begun to take a closer look at what they're feeding their animal companions. After all, if people are being told to eat fewer processed foods and more fresh foods, then wouldn't it make sense that pets should benefit from that advice as well?

It does make sense, and capitalism has benefited our canine friends, who overall now have a healthier, better-tasting, and wider variety of foods than they've ever had before. It is possible to marry convenience with sound nutrition, and as this chapter will explore, there are many options available to dog owners seeking to provide such a diet for their dogs.

Necessary Nutrients

Fortunately, it's easy to find out whether your dog is getting the correct amount of nutrients. Health and safety regulations do require that dog foods list their ingredients and their nutritive values on their labels. You can learn a lot about the quality of the food by looking carefully at the label on the package.

You're looking for some basic factors that must be present for sound nutrition: proteins, carbohydrates, vitamins, minerals, and fats. The ingredients are listed in descending order by weight—that is, how much of the ingredient is actually in the product. Therefore, if a pure meat source like chicken, beef, or lamb is right up there at the top, you can be sure you're buying a protein-rich food.

Proteins

Proteins are present in all kinds of meat and meat by-products, such as chicken, lamb, beef, or chicken meal. These are the best sources of protein for your dog. Many foods use vegetable proteins such as soy. These are harder for your dog to digest, so although you will invariably find them in his food, make sure they aren't a sizable source of that food's ingredients. A dog's need for protein varies depending on his age, size, and activity level. You'll see that puppy foods have high levels of protein, whereas senior foods contain lower levels.

FACT

Dogs need a total of twenty-two amino acids, but their bodies can only synthesize twelve of them. Essential amino acids include arginine, histidine, isoleucine, leucine, lysine, methionine, phenylalanine, threonine, tryptophan, and valine. Good health correlates to the consumption of the proper amino acids.

Carbohydrates

Carbohydrates, which are necessary for energy, also make up some of the primary ingredients in dog food. Their sources are typically rice, corn, or some other grain, though more and more frequently vegetables such as sweet potatoes are being used as well. Wheat and soy can sometimes trigger an allergic reaction in dogs, which is why more and more formulas use rice as their starch. Some dogs aren't affected at all, however, so it's always wise to monitor your dog's overall health.

Vitamins and Minerals

Dogs need vitamins and minerals to keep their bodies functioning, just as we do. A lack of iron means not enough hemoglobin to pick up red blood cells in the lungs, which means a less energetic dog. A lack of vitamin E can result in brittle skin. Vitamin C has been called a wonder vitamin for its curative powers. Several commercially available foods on the market now already add special vitamins to the food to compensate for certain conditions. One of the most popular is the addition of glucosamine and chondroitin in foods for senior dogs, as these vitamins promote joint health. If you're not sure what a particular vitamin's function is and you note that there's a lot of it in your dog's food, do some research and, most important, observe your dog for the potential side effects (hopefully good ones).

Fats

Fat is a necessary part of any dog's (or animal's) diet. Fat is what keeps the skin supple and the coat shiny. Too little fat, and your dog will end up with a dry, brittle coat and dry skin; too much fat, and you'll end up with an obese, well-greased dog. Fat is extremely palatable to dogs, so manufacturers need it for nutritive and taste values. This can lead to problems with storage, as fats tend to oxidize and go rancid when exposed to air or heat. They must be preserved in order to hold.

What about preservatives in the food?
Manufacturers use preservatives to maintain freshness, taste, and texture. In the 1980s, dog breeders raised concerns about the adverse effects of a common chemical preservative, ethoxyquin. Ethoxyquin and the chemicals BHA and BHT were thought to contribute to numerous health problems. Now these are rarely used, though it's important to check for them. Instead, most manufacturers use natural preservatives—tocopherol, a form of vitamin E, and ascorbic acid (vitamin C).

Canine nutrition is a hot topic. The bottom line is how well your dog does with the food you feed her. If you select a premium brand and feed according to the guidelines in this chapter, your dog should show all the signs of being healthy: clear, shiny eyes; soft, supple coat; pink gums; normal stool and urine; and appropriate energy level. If she doesn't seem healthy to you, speak with your veterinarian and research a dietary change.

All-Important Water

No discussion of what to feed a dog is complete without mentioning water. This is a nutrient as important to dogs as it is to other living things. Dogs can go longer without food than they can without water. To stay hydrated, and to cool off, dogs need a constant supply of fresh, clean, cool water.

ALERT!

Don't let your dog drink out of the toilet. This is not a substitute for a water bowl, and in fact could be contaminated with bacteria that could seriously harm your dog.

It's absolutely necessary to leave out a clean bowl of water at all times for your dog. Dogs can't tell you when they're thirsty, so it's vital that you leave water for them at all times. That way, when they're thirsty, they'll drink. Change the water in your dog's bowl a few times a day, and clean the bowl thoroughly once a day. Attention to the water bowl may also alert you to any changes in how much—or little—your dog is drinking, which can be an indication of a more serious medical condition.

Feeding a Commercial Diet

Commercially prepared pet foods come in three standard forms: kibble (dry food), canned (wet food), and semi-moist (burger-type foods). If each claims to be nutritionally complete, do you feed one instead of another or combine them?

This dog is eating a commercially prepared kibble. Fortunately for today's dog owners, kibbles are increasingly more nutritious and are even formulated to address a dog's growth stages or specific nutritional needs. They are tasty and economical as well, making them a common staple of a dog's diet.

Again, think about and look at what's in the foods. Kibble is the most economic food choice, but it is also the least palatable. Canned food, on the other hand, is quite palatable, but it can't provide the hard crunchiness that benefits a dog's teeth and gums. Semi-moist, burger-type foods are the most comparable to human "junk food." They're loaded with extra sugars and preservatives.

ALERT!

It's important to store kibble in as airtight a container as possible to help ensure freshness. You will find a variety of containers at your local pet supply store. When you bring a new bag home, open and pour it into the airtight container as soon as possible. Also, buy the appropriate-sized bag for your dog or dogs. Don't think you'll be saving a lot of money if you buy the giant bag when you're only feeding your Chihuahua a cup a day. Freshness is more important.

If you're confused about whether to feed kibble or canned, ask your pup's breeder what he feeds. After all, he will have spent years developing a feeding plan that works for that particular breed—what a great resource! But it doesn't mean you have to stick with his recommendation. Many owners feed their dogs a mix of kibble and wet food that's approximately three-quarters dry and one-quarter wet. Both these foods are formulated to provide your dog with the same types and mixtures of proteins, fats, carbo-hydrates, vitamins, and minerals. While dry food contains the same thing canned food does, it's different because all the water (and often blood) has been taken out of it.

Many breeders and dog experts feed their dogs commercial, name-brand dry dog foods and supplement those foods occasionally with canned food and fresh foods. There's no denying that canned food provides great flavor and a little added meat, which dogs love. The dry food is nutritious and hard and crunchy. This causes your dog to chew more, and eating the kibble helps clean her teeth by scraping off bits of accumulated plaque or tartar. Wet food, like our soft foods, can accumulate along the gum line and between teeth, contributing to poor oral health.

Feeding an Alternate Diet

Many pet nutritionists and pet owners firmly believe that a raw diet comes closest to what dogs and wolves eat out in the wild. The diet includes everything from raw chicken, pork, and beef bones to frozen or freeze-dried nuggets that combine meat, fruits, and vegetables. Popular ingredients include beef hearts, broccoli, romaine lettuce, and carrots.

Proponents of raw diets say their dogs exude good health—no allergies, no chronic conditions, few parasites, fresh breath, healthy joints, and so on. Critics claim the raw meats carry potentially dangerous bacteria, and the bones pose a choking hazard.

For owners who don't want to risk the potential ill effects of a commercial diet, there is the option to feed a homemade diet. Again, there are many books detailing what to include in the meals. Dogs do have nutritional needs that are different from ours, and simply giving leftovers from the family's table will not provide for all of them. A successful homemade diet needs to contain the necessary proteins, carbs, vitamins, minerals, and fat that a dog needs. The nice thing is that these proportions are under your control when you make your dog's food. Typically owners who feed homemade diets prepare large batches and freeze portions, often adding fresh ingredients as the individual meals are prepared.

Supplementing Your Dog's Diet

For years, all the advice recommended against supplementing your dog's commercial food in any way, claiming that the supplements could cause harm, from the seemingly inconsequential—giving your dog diarrhea—to potentially deadly—such as causing debilitating growth spurts or disrupting the overall balance of a food.

While these fears can be valid, canine nutritionists, veterinarians, breeders, and pet owners have come to find that not only does smart supplementing do more good than harm, it can actually significantly improve your dog's health. Note the word "smart" before supplementing. That's the key. Your dog's bowl shouldn't be a garbage can for every leftover you have in your refrigerator. At the same time, there are lots of things you and your family eat that are really good for your dog. Some of these are fresh veg-etables; fresh fruits; plain, organic lowfat yogurt; organic meats; fresh fish; omega-3 oils; and other fresh and natural foods.

ALERT!

If your dog stops eating his dog food because he's waiting for you to give him something tastier, it's time to take a step back. Unless you want to research how to feed a nutritionally sound homemade diet, your dog needs the nutrients that are in commercially available foods. His kibble should make up 95 to 98 percent of his meal. Cut out the supplements until he is eating his dog food again, and proceed with caution.

It's critical to understand what you're supplementing your dog's food with and why. For example, if your dog is taking an antibiotic, you should add some plain, organic lowfat yogurt to his meals. Antibiotics can destroy the beneficial bacteria in the intestine, and the live, active cultures in yogurt can help reestablish a healthy balance. If your dog has itchy or dry skin, add an omega-3 oil such as fish or flaxseed oil. Adding steamed fresh vegetables to your dog's food provides the same benefits from an excellent source of carbohydrates and fiber as it does to your diet.

FACT

One of the best books written on understanding the health benefits of supplements and what types and quantities to feed is *The Goldsteins' Wellness & Longevity Program: Natural Care for Dogs and Cats* by Dr. Robert Goldstein and Susan Goldstein.

Besides the health benefits of certain supplements, your dog will appreciate the variety that supplements can provide. The key to feeding human goodies to your dog is moderation and consideration. Excessively fatty, over-processed foods aren't good for us, and they're not good for dogs. But small pieces of pizza crust, the last slice of lunch meat, the occasional potato chip—these will not hurt your dog in moderation. You just have to use common sense.

When and How Much to Feed Your Dog

As always, there are no hard and fast rules about how many times a day a dog should be fed. The idea is to maintain a desired body weight—not too heavy, not too thin. It's the amount of food they're eating that remains the most important thing. Other indicators of a happy and healthy dog are the brightness of the eyes, the shininess of the coat, and the activity level of the dog.

Timing

Dogs by nature are worse than humans: many of them would eat to the point of bursting. Because they get such enjoyment out of mealtime, many experts believe that two meals a day is both more satisfying and more nutritionally sound for dogs. Some dogs pick at their food, while others gobble it like it's their last meal. Smaller portions are better for both types of eaters, as the pickers have less to get through, and the gobblers won't overdo it.

Feeding two meals a day will give you an additional opportunity to see how your dog is feeling. If your normally healthy eater is picking at her food and turns away from her bowl, you'll know something is wrong. Even a fussy dog shouldn't want to miss mealtime entirely. If your dog is off her food at either meal, you'll need to keep a close eye on her for signs of an upset stomach or worse.

ALERT!

Free-feeding your dog is not recommended. Simply pouring his kibble in one bowl and leaving him fresh water in another as you race out the door to get on with your day is not the way to maintain a healthy dog. Just as monitoring what your children eat contributes to their good health, the same is true for your dog.

Your dog's mealtimes can be conveniently scheduled around your own. Typically, she should get her morning meal after she's been taken or let out to relieve herself. That leaves enough time for her to eat, you to have a cup of coffee with breakfast, and both of you to get ready for the rest of the day. That should include letting her out at least once more and making sure she has cool, fresh water and any favorite toys—and that she's safely confined—before you leave to do what you need to do.

The second meal can be given in the late afternoon or early evening—preferably before you sit down to eat with the rest of the family. If her tummy's full she'll be less inclined to be interested in your meal, and you won't feel sorry for her and possibly give her treats.

Part of monitoring your dog's food and eating is giving her a set amount of time in which to finish what's in her bowl. Fifteen minutes should be plenty. Whatever she hasn't eaten in this time, pick up and save for later (if it won't spoil) or throw it away. Your dog needs to know that "it's now or never," so she won't develop fussy habits. If she isn't finishing her food and comes begging to you, don't feel sorry and give her yours. That is her way of training you to feed her something other than her regular food. Unless she's sick (which should be considered), she'll eat if she's hungry, and it should be her food first. If she shows no interest in the food and seems sluggish or ill in any other way, call the veterinarian.

How Much to Feed

How often you feed your dog is one thing. How much you feed your dog is another! Some dogs by sheer weight require smaller amounts. You wouldn't feed a Shih-Tzu the same as you would a Labrador Retriever. Nor should you feed a senior dog the same amount as a puppy. So where does that leave you?

Your best bet is to ask your puppy or dog's former caretaker how much he was feeding your dog. If you like the condition your dog is in or if you're getting a puppy, you can continue following this protocol. Also, dog foods include feeding instructions on their packages. You could use them as a guideline, too. The other thing to consider is your dog's life stage. You may need to feed more or less depending on how your dog is doing on the food at his particular stage of life.

All dogs are individuals, so you need to gauge what's right only for your dog. You want a dog who looks trim, has the appropriate energy level, and radiates overall good health. If that describes your dog, your feeding regimen is on track. If you're feeding too much, your dog will lose his waistline, look more portly all around, and have less energy. If this happens, you should immediately cut down on his rations. If he's too thin, increase his portions. Any unusual weight variations should be discussed with your veterinarian.

Feeding for Different Life Stages

Part of the difference between the dog foods available today and those of the previous generation is that scientists now understand that bodies need different nutrients at different ages and for different energy needs. A growing puppy or a dog nursing pups both have greater nutritional needs than a senior dog whose routine consists of getting up to go to the bathroom and napping. This is another way feeding your dog properly is made easier: Feed a puppy a puppy formula, an allergic dog a hypoallergenic formula, a working dog a protein-rich formula, and so on.

Puppy Food

Puppy foods are specially formulated to help develop strong bones and good muscle mass. If you read the ingredient panel, you'll see that puppy foods tend to offer more protein and vitamins than normal dog foods and are formulated for excellent health at this very important developmental stage.

When your dog is old enough, you should switch her to a food more appropriate for her next life stage. When this might be right for your dog is something you'll need to gauge. Talk to other owners of your breed, and especially with your dog's breeder. You want to gradually wean your puppy from a puppy food to a maintenance diet.

Maintenance Diet

This is the stage that includes the largest percentage of the dog population, as it's typically what's fed between the ages of ten to twelve months and six to eight years (before switching to a senior food). There are many formulations in this category, and each has its own claim to quality: there are high-protein formulas, natural formulas, lamb and rice, chicken and rice, beef, liver, and so on. The truth is, every dog is an individual, as is every dog owner. You need to prepare and feed something that works for both of you.

"Lite" Foods

Today, many foods for humans have been manufactured to reduce their overall calorie count, and the same is true for dogs. If you suddenly find that Rover looks like a barrel with four legs, you should consider switching to a lite formula dog food to help get her back into shape.

ALERT!

Always consult with your veterinarian before switching from a maintenance to a "lite" food. Your vet is your ally in helping to get your dog's weight down so he is in better health, and the two of you should work together on the problem.

Lite foods are developed to deliver the same amount of vitamins, minerals, and proteins as other dog foods but with reduced calories. They tend to contain more fiber, which helps your dog feel full after a meal. Follow the directions and don't overindulge your dog with treats.

Even if your dog is not obese, you may find switching to a lite formula is better for him. Middle-aged dogs (from four to seven or eight years old) that don't exercise too frequently may be ideal candidates for a lite diet. After all, they don't need the protein and calories their more active friends do, but they still enjoy eating and want their regular, healthy meals.

Senior Formulas

When does your dog become a senior? That's a good question that's sometimes difficult to answer. It ranges from breed to breed and from dog to dog, though there is a general understanding that dogs aged seven or older are considered "seniors." Some breeds, however, don't even reach that age, and are considered to be seniors before then. Your dog's breeder, your veterinarian, and other owners of your breed can help you determine when switching to a senior food would be right for your dog.

Aging means the loss of vigor and ability to perform feats once thought normal during the adult years. Seniors can't run or walk as fast. They sleep more. Their systems begin to deteriorate just as ours do. Senior dogs need a food that gives them as much energy as possible without making them heavier and slower. Many senior formulas contain the extra vitamins older dogs need, like glucosamine and chondroitin or extra vitamin C.

Hypoallergenic or Therapeutic Diets

If your dog's diet doesn't seem to be agreeing with her—her skin and coat are dry and itchy; she has loose stools; her energy level is off—work with your veterinarian to determine if she might be allergic to any of the ingredients in her dog food. Foods are being made with a variety of protein and carb sources now, including lamb, rice, fish, and sweet potato. A switch to one of these may dramatically clear up her condition.

A particular, recurring health concern may lead your veterinarian to prescribe a therapeutic diet for your dog. Several manufacturers now make these diets, which are prescribed by veterinarians to assist in the treatment of problems associated with particular organs or body systems and conditions.

Feeding Treats and Bones

From organic cookies cut in fun shapes to beefy chewsticks and beyond, dog treats come in every size, shape, color, and flavor imaginable. There are even smoked and freeze-dried animal parts (ears, noses, feet) in the treat bin, and dogs love these. In a nutshell, there are so many treats because dogs love them and people love to spoil their dogs. As much as your dog will love you for giving him treats, remember: everything in moderation!

FACT

Unlike you, your dog cannot feed himself. So, if he develops weight problems due to overeating, especially with treats, only you are to blame. Let's be honest—the urge is incredibly strong to give lots of treats to dogs, especially puppies. However, weight gain is a problem for dogs just as it is for humans and may cause all kinds of illnesses. Treats are not as nutritionally balanced as they are tasty.

Like us, dogs are happy to receive food treats. When considering what kinds of treats to feed, think "healthy"—nothing too fatty or loaded with artificial ingredients—and remember to incorporate the calories into the dog's overall daily allowance; otherwise, the treats contribute to obesity. Sound familiar?

Moderation

One way to reconcile the amount of treats you like to give with how much you should feed your dog is to incorporate regular treats with the overall amount of food your dog gets in a day. In other words, take out a half-cup of kibble if you know your dog's going to get your leftover Chinese food and a biscuit every time she does her business.

Treats are especially useful during training of any kind, whether it's the simple sit/stay or something more difficult, such as housetraining. Treats are a wonderful way to get your dog's attention and encourage good behavior. They also convey a simpler message—your affection for your dog.

What About Bones?

One of the defining images of dogs is of them gnawing on a big bone. As scavengers in the wild, the bones may sometimes have been all that was left for dogs to eat, so they made the most of them. Today's pampered pets don't need to raid the garbage can to find the scraps they need to survive on, but that doesn't stop them from enjoying a good bone. Chewing on a bone is a simple pleasure your dog should not miss out on, but there are right and wrong ways to do it.

For the occasional gnawing bone, these are the safety guidelines you should follow:

- Never give a cooked bone that could splinter as your dog eats it. This includes most poultry.
- Never give your dog a cooked bone with a sharp edge that could be swallowed and cause internal damage. This includes the bones from steaks and chops.
- Do give your dog a bone that's been presterilized. These are available at most pet stores. They come in all different sizes to accommodate all different dogs. To make them more enticing, spread some soft cheese or peanut butter on the inside edges where it will be a challenge for your dog to lick it out.
- Do consider giving your dog the special treat of a frozen beef marrow bone. These are available in different shapes and sizes in the meat department of the grocery store. If you have a large dog, buy the larger bones. If you have a small dog, buy the ones that are sliced thin. Put the package in the freezer, and when it's frozen solid, give it to your dog. He will spend as long as it takes working the bone so that the marrow and scraps of meat thaw while he chews on the bone. Heaven!
- Do supervise your dog while he's eating any bone. A cooked bone is hard and sharp and if anything unusual happens can certainly injure your dog. Take it away if it breaks in any way.

Bones are fun for your dog to chew on, and they provide the added benefit of allowing him to scrape the plaque off his teeth.

CHAPTER 6

Exercising Your Dog

There's a great saying to keep in mind when you think about dogs and exercise. It goes, "A tired dog is a happy dog." Why? Because when your puppy or dog is sleeping soundly at your side (or in her crate or bed), she's not getting into any trouble. Dogs who pace, whine, cry, dash around the house, get up and down frequently, bark for no reason, or constantly run to the door to be let out are not happy dogs. While some of that restlessness may be the result of their breeding or a lack of effective training, another part is a lack of sufficient exercise.

Why Exercise Is So Important

It's a fact for dogs and people alike: exercise is just plain good for you all over. It keeps your weight in check; it helps maintain all vital organs, especially the heart and lungs; it keeps muscles healthy; it creates endorphins, which stimulate a more positive attitude—it's a win-win endeavor.

FACT

Dogs who don't get to go out, who don't get to stretch their legs, use their noses, explore their world, or play with others—in short, dogs who don't get to be dogs—literally go crazy and in turn drive their human companions nuts. It's a sad scenario that is so easily avoided!

Think about your life and your dog's life for a minute. Maybe you have a job that keeps you busy for eight or more hours a day. Maybe you have kids to look after and they take up a lot of time and energy. Maybe you travel a lot. All of the things we do to earn a living and make a life for ourselves are necessary for our survival. Our canine companions in our ever-more-hectic lifestyles are typically just along for the ride. Unless we need them to help us herd cattle or serve as a service dog, most dogs don't have "occupations" that keep them busy and satisfied (well, at least busy).

Our house-bound dogs depend on us for everything. They are not stuffed animals that can be propped on the sofa for the day until it is time for them to greet us at the door when we return from our stressful jobs. They can't watch TV, read magazines, chat on the phone, or use a computer to connect to the outside world. What they are is extremely sentient beings who need the stimulation of the outside world and the interaction of those around them as much as we do. Without it—through little fault of their own—they find other ways to explore and interact with their world in ways that satisfy them. Those ways include chewing, barking, pacing, crying, excitable behavior, and other things we tend to dislike—especially when we're tired.

How Often and How Much to Exercise

If you asked your dog how often he should be exercised and how much, he would probably say, "always, and lots!" Unless he's a working farm or service dog, that simply isn't going to be possible. What are some working guidelines that the average dog owner can follow to help her companion get in a decent amount of exercise?

Assessing Your Dog's Energy Needs

Being individuals like us, the truth is that every dog has his own level of exercise that would be best suited for him. You can own several dogs of the same breed and soon learn that while some of them may be able to go all day, others are more content to lounge about. That said, there is some truth in stereotyping certain breeds and their exercise requirements. Chapter 3 profiles some of the more popular breeds and whether they are considered "high energy" or not.

The Parson Russell Terrier, the Border Collie, the Doberman Pinscher, and the Golden Retriever can all be considered high-energy breeds. Originally bred for demanding jobs that included keeping the home free of vermin, watching over family and livestock, and locating and bringing in food for the family, their bodies and minds still need that kind of stimulation even though they don't have these responsibilities in most places today.

Dogs like Cocker Spaniels, Shih Tzus, Great Pyrenees, Cairn Terriers, or Beagles could be considered of average energy levels. Their original jobs weren't as demanding as some others, but they still had them. For many of the toy breeds, being "on" for attention was a job, and it was one they took seriously. These dogs are always eager for their outings.

On the lower-energy scale are breeds like Greyhounds and other sight hounds, who were bred for short bursts of speed, or larger dogs like Mastiffs, whose jobs were to be more of an intimidator than a hunter. The Basset Hound may not move quickly, but her nose never stops.

Walks—a necessary part of every dog's day, no matter her size—should be enjoyable times for both of you. Train your dog to walk nicely on her leash, and you'll enjoy going everywhere together. These walks can provide not only exercise, but bonding experiences as you share the wide world.

Ask your breeder about your pup's potential energy needs, or be sure to ask the previous owners of an older dog you adopt how energetic that dog was. At least this knowledge will help prepare you for making the adequate exercise needs of your dog a priority.

Just Do It!

Regardless of the overall energy needs of your dog, she will require a *minimum* of two walks a day as an older dog, and several more as a puppy. "Walks" mean outings of at least a half-mile, during which your dog should be allowed to sniff and investigate things along the way.

If you are an active person with a breed that is suited for it, you and your dog can enjoy jogging together. Start slowly to avoid injury, and be careful not to run when conditions may be dangerous for either of you.

As you will learn in Chapter 7, Housetraining, it's important to teach your dog to eliminate at the start of the walk so the exercise becomes the reward. If your dog figures out that you bring him in immediately after he goes even when he wants to stay out, he may hold it so that he gets to walk a while first.

In order to schedule at least two adequate or better walks a day, most owners take their dogs out in the morning and the evening (around their work schedules). Knowing that your dog may be alone for several hours in between, the morning walk is one during which you want to help your dog release her energy and satisfy her need to connect to the world through sniffing, exploring, and greeting others. If you're forced to keep your dog on a leash during this time, use a long one so she can at least get some scampering or running in or feel like she can explore more freely. Reel the leash in when you need the control. Let it out if you don't.

As a young pup, your dog will need more frequent but shorter walks as she builds up her bones and muscles. As an adolescent, your dog will need frequent and longer walks, ideally with a solid period of off-leash running and playing time included.

Vary your walks by starting off in different directions, changing the streets you go down, using different sides of the sidewalk, etc.—anything that provides some extra stimulation. Plan on being out for twenty minutes or longer.

As your dog ages, you will get to know the signs that tell you to cut back on the duration or intensity of exercise. Nothing will kill her spirit more than being deprived of her walks, but where her exuberance may lead, her body might not follow. Be sensitive to her overall state so she can get the full benefit of her walks.

Don't skimp on the evening walk because you're tired or overcommitted. If you can't do it, hire a dog walker. After being isolated and obeying your house rules for several hours, it's your dog's time to "hit the streets." Depending on your schedule, you may want to give her a short walk just when you get home from work, and then a longer walk later when you've taken care of some other things. Dogs are creatures of habit, and if this is something you do fairly regularly, your dog will anticipate (and need) the longer walk. Even if it's the last thing you feel like doing, it's the best thing you can do.

Obeying Rules of Common Courtesy While Out and About

No matter where you live and will be walking your dog, you are responsible for his actions. That is why there are leash laws, waste laws, nuisance laws, and so on. Here are some guidelines for you to follow:

- Clean up after your dog. You may think it's not that important, but what if everyone walking dogs felt the same way? Soon our streets and parks would be covered in you-know-what. Every scoop makes a difference. It may seem gross, but you get used to it fast. Use a plastic bag to cover your hand, pick up the offending matter, turn the bag inside out so the waste is securely inside it, tie up the bag and toss it in a trash can.

- Keep your dog on a leash. This is necessary for people who live in cities and suburbs, and even owners of country dogs should have a leash handy when walking their dogs. Even if your dog is responsive and reliable off-leash, you never know what might happen. See the section below on Letting Your Dog Off Lead for more on this subject.

- Keep your dog under control. If you're walking with your dog and you can see that someone is walking toward you who appears uncomfortable at the sight of your dog, be kind and courteous, reel your dog in, and hold him while the person passes. No one likes a dog—even one on a leash—who approaches enthusiastically and tries to sniff or jump up on them. This can become a rewarding habit for a dog, and it's your job to make sure it doesn't.

- Be mindful of trouble. While happily walking your young dog with whom you are totally infatuated, you may think that every other dog must be like her—friendly, playful, cute, and sweet. Hopefully you'll meet many dogs like this on your jaunts around the neighborhood and wherever you travel with your dog, but don't expect it. Dogs get excited about meeting other dogs. Their greeting behavior can often include pawing or spinning to try to sniff each other and find out what they want to know. This can verge on aggressive behavior, and sometimes quickly escalates into aggressive behavior. You are responsible for your dog. Use common sense and only consider approaching strange dogs if they appear calm. When you're a safe distance away, ask the other owner if his dog is okay with other dogs. Approach slowly and be ready to pull your dog away if necessary. If you know your dog starts trouble with other dogs, don't let others approach her. Be nice about it, but keep your distance.

- Be mindful of street signs and traffic patterns. Be sure that oncoming traffic has a stop sign before you begin to cross. Pay attention to pedestrian signals in large cities.

Letting Your Dog Off Lead

When you think about it, restricting a dog's experience of the world to walks on a leash is tantamount to animal cruelty. Imagine if someone did that to you! Dogs need to run and play. They need to be able to go off and explore scents as they waft over to them. Dogs who love the water should have the experience of swimming and fetching; dogs who love to dig should get to really go at it—it's what makes their hearts and souls sing.

Unfortunately, many conscientious and caring dog owners live in places that make it difficult to allow this. Certainly someone living in the heart of a large city can't let her dog off leash; even the parks in most suburbs have leash laws; and with countryside being gobbled up by developers everywhere, even rural dog owners need to fear that a car could come barreling along even the most remote road at any time.

Because of this, a movement started years ago to set aside special dog parks and dog runs that would provide safe, enclosed space for dog owners to gather and let their dogs run free. There are now typically many such dog parks in large cities like New York, Chicago, and San Francisco. Large parks in the suburbs often designate times that allow dogs to be off-leash (typically early mornings and evenings). Sometimes you can find playing fields or tennis courts that are fenced in. Even these provide some space for your dog to cavort at will. Beaches also post signs alerting dog owners as to when they are welcome.

FACT

For a list of dog parks across the United States and in Canada, visit *www .dogpark.com.* There is other information on the site for finding places and ways for more off-leash time, and there is even a resource for forming a dog park in your area should you need to or be interested in doing so.

Giving your dog this kind of free time is one of the greatest gifts ever. If you aren't sure how reliable your dog is when he's off leash, be sure you stay in a securely fenced or enclosed area. Your gift of freedom could lead to a tragic loss, and that is just not worth it. If you have any doubts about whether your dog could escape or get into harm, keep the leash on! And don't forget that the rules of common courtesy apply here, too.

Hip, Hip, Hooray—Exercise Is Play!

If the mention of exercise makes you think of long, boring walks around the same blocks day in and day out, it's time for a change in your thinking and in your routine! Giving your dog the exercise she needs needn't be limited to those morning and evening ritual walks or the scheduled visits to dog parks or other places you take your dog to stretch her legs (though those are certainly worthwhile for all involved, even if they seem monotonous to you).

Your dog (and you) can get in some beneficial exercise without ever leaving home. How? By playing games together. There are lots of games you can play with your dog to get her heart rate up, her body moving, and her mind in gear. There's fetch, hide-and-seek (with objects and people), catch, and dance with me, just to name a few.

Get Ready for Fun

Another great thing about playing games with your dog is that you bring a different kind of energy to the interaction—usually a more up-beat and engaging energy. Your dog will pick up on that and feed off of it, resulting in her being more receptive to what you want to do. Don't delay: Here's how to get started.

Playing fetch may come naturally to your dog—or it may not. Begin by getting your dog interested in a ball or toy by teasing him with it and making playful, engaging sounds. If that isn't enough to get his interest, use a toy that can be filled with treats or other food. You can even puncture a tennis ball and put something deliciously smelly in it. When you have his attention and interest, roll it gently on the floor going away from him. You want the first few rolls to be easily retrieved so he stays interested. As you roll the object, say "Fetch."

Dogs often turn fetching something into a game of keep-away. This can provide them with a lot of exercise as they scamper farther off every time you try to reach them, but it's not a game you want to encourage, as it teaches your dog that she's in charge of playtime with you. Fetch should mean getting the ball and bringing it back to you, not stealing it from you.

Should he steal the ball and begin to run off, simply stop playing the game. Ignore him as he runs off. Do not chase after or call him. When he returns to you, calmly put him in his crate or confine him to his normal room of confinement. Go find the ball or toy and put it somewhere he won't be able to reach or get at it. Leave it there until you're ready to initiate the game again, which should be some time later.

If he gets the ball and returns it to you, tell him excitedly what a good doggie he is, put out your hand for the ball, ask him to Drop It while you take it from him, thank him for it, then toss the ball again. Don't overdo this game, but if he's enjoying it, you can play for a while, increasing the distance you toss the ball or toy.

Hide-and-Seek Games

There are all sorts of ways to play hide-and-seek, and they all make for fast-paced and exciting times that definitely give your dog a physical and mental workout. The best way to lay the basics for all hide-and-seek games is with food. Using pieces of cereal or popcorn (things that are small, easy to chew, relatively healthy, and won't make a mess), show them to your dog so she knows you have something good. Ask her to sit and stay. Watching her so she doesn't break, put a piece or two out of her sight but nearby; for example, behind a table or chair leg, or next to the sofa. Without making her wait too long, give her her break word ("OK"), then say "Find It," indicating that she can come and get the goodies. When she finds and eats a piece, tell her what a good girl she is.

Increase the difficulty and challenge of this game slowly and only play a couple of times a day. As she's sitting and staying, put more pieces down and encourage her to find them all. Don't put so many that she doesn't have to sniff them out, and don't put them in places that are too difficult to reach or find, but slowly put pieces farther away from her and in places that may not be quite so obvious.

QUESTION?

What if my dog doesn't stay while I'm hiding the treats?
If your dog gets up too quickly to come looking for the treats, simply lead him back to his spot and reposition him. Stay standing in front of him once you've asked him to sit and stay so he gets the message. Until he's reliable on the stay, make it easier for him. Once he "gets" that he won't be asked to search for the treats until he can hold his sit, he'll do so reliably and you can make the game more challenging.

Another way to play hide-and-seek is with yourself and other family members. When you're first starting, have a piece of food with you so you can reward your dog when she finds you. Ask her to sit and stay in a room where you can hide not too far away. While she's in her sit-stay, tiptoe to your hiding spot. Now shout, "OK, find me!" You should hear her start to come looking for you. As soon as she finds you, tell her what a good doggie she is and give her the treat. If it seems easy for her, play again right away and hide a bit farther away. If she has trouble finding you or gets distracted, choose a spot that's closer to where she's in the sit-stay.

Eventually, you should be able to ask your dog to sit and stay while you sneak as far away as upstairs and into an unusual hiding place like the bathtub. Once she understands the game, she will continue to look for you. If it's challenging and you sense she's getting frustrated, call out "Missy, find me!" in an excited voice from your spot to redirect and refocus her. Remember, make it simple enough so it's rewarding for her but challenging enough that it's fun and exciting.

Dancing as Exercise

Some people think this is so much fun that they participate in the sport of Canine Freestyle, which is essentially doing dance routines with your dog. Maybe you and yours will be the next Fred Astaire and Ginger Rogers of the doggie dancing scene. For the purposes of this chapter on exercise, all you need to know is if you and your dog enjoy it, do it!

Dogs respond in all kinds of ways when people dance. Some bark and want to be in on the action. Some watch and wonder. Some like to have their paws held and moved to the beat. Don't get too rough with your dog or put him in positions he can't hold or that might put undue stress on his joints, but if he likes to move around with you while you dance, encourage him. See if he has a favorite song. This is a great way to take a heart-healthy break and just have fun with your dog.

CHAPTER 7

Housetraining Your Dog

The first thing every new owner should know before bringing a dog into the house is how to teach him where to relieve himself. The good news is that all dogs can be housebroken. The bad news is that a dog rarely becomes housebroken just by being let out several times a day. This comprehensive house-training plan requires dedication—but it's simple and foolproof if you follow it carefully.

The 7 Essentials for Housetraining

Things sure are easier to understand when they have a set of rules to go by! It's the same with housetraining. To make it easier for you, there are seven "essentials" which, if you follow them, should get you through housetraining successes—and failures. This way, when things work, you'll know why. Also, if something goes wrong, you should be able to tell where you made a mistake. Here goes:

1. Crate your dog when you can't watch her so she won't relieve herself (if you prefer, use another type of confinement, as long as it accomplishes the same goal).
2. Supervise (umbilical cord or shadow) your dog when she is out of her crate.
3. Feed her a high-quality diet at scheduled times (no treats, people food, or edible toys such as pig's ears).
4. Teach her to eliminate on command.
5. Clean up her accidents immediately (remove debris or moisture, then treat with neutralizer and cleaner).
6. Never correct her after the fact.
7. Keep a log of her habits (when and where she pooped or peed, and when and how much she ate and drank).

Using a Crate

Until a dog is perfectly trained, he needs a safe place in which he can do nothing wrong. This goes for puppies and older, unreliable dogs. When you can't keep your eyes glued to your dog and monitor his every move, confine him to a place where inappropriate behavior—soiling, stealing, shredding, chewing or scratching—isn't an option. Crating is suggested because it eliminates the risk that he'll damage woodwork, flooring, wall coverings, or cabinetry.

Assuming you ultimately want your dog to enjoy freedom in the house, crating is almost a necessity when your puppy or dog first comes to live with you. Crating is widely accepted by behaviorists, dog trainers, veterinarians, and knowledgeable dog owners as a humane means of confinement. Provided your dog is properly introduced to the crate, you should feel as comfortable about crating him in your absence as you would securing a toddler in a highchair at mealtime.

Whether the enclosure is a room, hallway, kennel, or crate, it should be:

- The right size. It should be large enough that the dog can stand without his shoulders touching the ceiling of the crate; however, if he soils the area, it's probably too large for him.
- Safe. Homemade enclosures may save you money, but you would feel awful if he poked himself in the eye, stabbed or choked himself, or swallowed wood splinters or material such as wallpaper or blankets because you overlooked potential dangers. Make sure there are no protrusions or sharp edges and no ingestible components.
- Dogproof. If he is prone to chewing, scratching, or jumping up, prevent access to any woodwork, linoleum, furniture, counters, garbage, or windows so your home doesn't become a victim of your puppy's destructiveness during his training period.

Using a crate that both you and your dog are comfortable with will get you off on the right paw. There are many types of crates available, from large wire crates to airline-approved plastic crates to collapsible crates. The types are explained in Chapter 4.

Familiarizing Your Dog with the Crate

To create a positive association from the very beginning, allow your dog to dine in her new crate. Place her and her food inside and sit with your back blocking the doorway of the crate. Read a book until she's finished eating, then take her out. For her next meal, prop the crate door open and sit at the opening with your dog and her food. Place a few pieces of kibble at a time inside so she is walking in and out to eat. If your crate has a metal bottom, place a mat on it to provide good traction and reduce the noise caused by the dog's movement. To encourage your dog to go in more readily, arrange a barrier on both sides of the crate so she is channeled inside.

This puppy has a beautiful crate that's large enough for him to move around in comfortably but small enough to reduce the chances of him soiling it. He has a comfy bed to lie on and a toy to keep him occupied. Should his owner want to give him more privacy, a sheet can be placed over part of the crate. Without a covering, he is able to observe and be part of what is going on around him while enjoying his own space.

Next, teach your dog to enter and exit on command. Put her paws right in front of the opening. With one hand on her collar and the other pointing into the crate, command "Bed." Pull her in by the collar as you place your hand under her tail and behind her rear legs to prevent her from backing away. If necessary, lift her in. Immediately invite her out by touching her chin and saying "Okay," and then try five more quick repetitions. Practice several repetitions of this routine three or more times every day so she goes to bed on command—without being enclosed. If you shut her in and leave her every time she is put in the enclosure, she may develop a bad association with crating. But when she learns to go in the crate on command as a result of frequent practice, she is more likely to accept being enclosed.

Loving—and Hating—the Crate

If you reserve his favorite toy for the times he spends in the crate, he may actually look forward to crating as an opportunity to play with it. Leave food and water out of the crate; dogs don't need it in there and most will dump or scatter it instead of eating or drinking. If you've chosen a metal crate with lots of openings, create a peaceful environment by covering it with a sheet or, if his tendency is to pull it in, surround the crate with a couple of stiff panels for a more enclosed, denlike atmosphere. Avoid leaving a TV or radio on because your puppy may become a victim of unsettling and noisy programming and advertisements. Replace that cacophony with white noise; the gentle whir of a fan puts dogs at ease.

Sometimes a dog will bark, yodel, whine, or howl when crated. Unless he is trying to tell you he has to go potty, ignore any noise he might make. Most dogs will quiet down if you completely ignore them. That means no eye contact or other body language that may show him you're aware of him. If your dog doesn't quiet down and you or your family members are losing sleep or sanity, startle him into being quiet. Startling him does not mean hurting him, it means catching him by surprise. Do this by throwing an empty soda can containing a few pennies at his covered crate, or clap your hands sharply twice. Don't use your voice, as your dog may simply think you're trying to talk to him, which will encourage him to talk back.

You can also create an earthquake by attaching the leash to his crate and giving it a jerk as he barks. If he's keeping you awake at night, move the crate close to your bed. This way you won't have to get up to administer a correction. If you're using a leash jerk, attach the handle to your bedpost for easy access. Once he's learned to sleep quietly through the night, gradually move the crate back to the original location.

Let him know he's behaving the way you want by giving him positive attention once he is quiet. For example, if you clap and he settles down, give him a minute, then go over and speak to him in a kind and assuring voice, letting him know that he's a good boy when he's quiet. If your attention gets him worked up again, turn it off by walking away and ignoring him, only returning to praise when he's quiet.

Umbilical Cording

A crate-trained dog is not housetrained. Your dog is likely to attempt naughty behaviors when loose, and therefore she needs plenty of supervised exploration to learn the house rules. If your dog is out of her crate, keep your eyes glued on her or, better still, umbilical cord her so when you can't follow her, she'll follow you. This gives you the opportunity to cut short misbehaviors before they become habits.

FACT

Umbilical cording is a fantastically simple technique and an important training tool, which every able-bodied household member should use. You can even umbilical cord two dogs at once. Or when one pet is trained and the other isn't, you can cord the untrained dog while giving the reliable one his freedom.

To do this, tie her leash to your belt on your left side. Give her only enough slack to keep her at your side without your legs becoming entangled. If she attempts to jump up, chew, bark, or relieve herself without your approval, you'll be able to stop her instantly by giving a quick tug on the lead. This should get her attention, at which time you can correct her behavior. With your dog this close to your side, you'll be able to train her as you tinker, work, or relax at home.

The Importance of Schedules

Most dogs leave their canine family to enter their new home at about two months of age. At this age, pups eat and drink a lot. They have limited ability to control their elimination and no idea that it might be important. Feeding and potty times should be adjusted to help the puppy reach his potential in the housetraining department as quickly as possible.

Diet and Feeding

Feed specific amounts of high-quality puppy food at specific times. If your dog eats on a schedule, she's more likely to potty at regular, predictable times. Pups should be fed three times a day up to three or four months of age, and after that can be fed twice daily for the rest of their lives. If your schedule requires you to be gone for six or more hours at a time, feedings can be disproportionate. Consider feeding a larger portion when you will be home for a few hours and will therefore be able to give her the opportunity to relieve herself.

A high-quality diet can make a huge difference in the effectiveness of housetraining, as a higher digestibility leads to less and more compact stool. Look for signs that the food you've chosen agrees with your dog. Gas, loose stools, constipation, itchy skin, bald patches, or listlessness indicate a problem that may be diet-related. Investigate possible solutions by consulting with your veterinarian.

ALERT!

With pups who urinate frequently, you might try restricting water. Before doing so, tell your veterinarian about your plans. He might want to perform some diagnostic tests beforehand to rule out bladder or urinary tract problems. In severe cases where, despite a clean bill of health, the pup still continually urinates, offer water only before taking her out to relieve herself. With pups who just can't seem to hold it throughout the night, withhold water for three hours before putting them to bed.

Dogs experiencing difficulty with housetraining will achieve greater control sooner if they're fed a single, totally consistent diet. Therefore, avoid giving your dog treats, people food, or edible toys such as pig's ears, rawhides, or cowhoofs. Additionally, dogs who are not nutritionally indulged are less likely to become overweight or aggressively possessive when food is near.

Eliminating on Command

Understand how much your puppy needs to go potty, and teach him to do it on command. At two to four months of age, most pups need to relieve themselves after waking up, eating, playing, sleeping, and drinking—perhaps as often as every 30 to 45 minutes, depending on the type and amount of activity. At four months, the dog may be developed like an adult internally, but expect him to behave like a puppy. Most adult dogs can gradually and comfortably adapt to three to five outings per day. When active rather than resting, you will notice a significant increase in the frequency of elimination.

Puppies and dogs can—and should—be taught to eliminate on command. This comes in extremely handy when it's dark or raining, as well as when you need your dog to do her business on an unfamiliar surface (such as a city sidewalk). It also ensures that your trip to the potty spot meets its goal!

Teach your dog to eliminate on command. This lesson is handy both when he is too distracted and won't potty or when he's on a surface that he's inclined not to potty on—for example, a kennel run, wet grass, or where other dogs have been. Others will go potty only if they're in a particular area or taken for a walk. By teaching your dog to eliminate on command, you can get him to go where you want and when you want and simplify the housetraining process. Here's how to do it.

ALERT!

Many owners make the mistake of continually taking a dog out before he really needs to go. Although they do so hoping he won't soil the house, they are actually preventing him from developing the capacity to hold it. Since housetraining is a matter of teaching the dog to control his bladder and bowels until he has access to the outdoors, taking the dog out too frequently slows the housetraining process. When you think he doesn't need to go out but he does, try umbilical cording or crating him for a half-hour before taking a walk.

Leash your dog and take her to the potty area. When she begins the sniffing and circling ritual that immediately precedes elimination, start chanting a phrase like, "Potty, Hurry Up." What you say is unimportant, but it should sound melodic and should always be the same phrase. Use the same words for defecation and urination. As soon as she does her business, praise her like you would your child's first home run—effusively. She should understand that she has done something that really pleases you. Also, leave the area as soon as she is finished. An additional reward will be to go explore somewhere else. After a week of chanting while your dog is relieving herself, begin the chant as soon as you enter the potty area.

Only give your dog a few minutes to potty. If you give her twenty minutes, she is likely to demand thirty next time. After a couple of minutes, put her back in her crate long enough to make her thankful for the next potty opportunity you give her. Have your dog earn playtime by pottying first and playing afterward. Potty breaks will be much less time-consuming if your dog learns to associate the initial act of walking outdoors with the act of going potty, not playing. Finally, avoid praising or rewarding with food, since anticipating those things may actually distract her from her primary goal. Besides, the sensation of going potty is a reward in itself.

QUESTION?

Why does he forget to relieve himself when he is outdoors but goes as soon as he's back in the house?
If this happens frequently enough, it indicates that he is overly distracted when you're outside. Leashing your dog during potty breaks will enable you to keep your dog moving and sniffing within the appropriate area, and thus speed the process of elimination. If you sense your dog is becoming distracted from his duty of looking for a potty spot, use a light, quick tug on the leash as you slowly move about the area yourself.

How to Handle Messes

No matter how careful you are, occasionally inappropriate elimination happens. If your dog has an accident:

- Never correct the dog after the fact. Do scold yourself by saying, "How could I have let that happen?"
- Startle him by tossing something at him or picking him up in midstream and carrying him outside to stop him in the act.
- Clean up messes immediately. Remove debris and blot up any moisture, then use a cleaning solution, and finally treat the soiled area with an odor neutralizer.
- Keep a diary. Write down the amounts and times you feed your dog, and any unusual consistency of his stool. If you later encounter a training or health problem, your notes may make the solution apparent. Also, make note of when you are taking your dog out and what he is doing. Document any accidents so you are alert to the potentially problematic times and can make needed adjustments. Take inventory of when your dog isn't going, because at least 90 percent of the time he should go potty when you take him out.

A truly housebroken dog is repulsed by the notion of going in the house. Every consecutive hour your dog spends wandering the house, sniffing and exploring without an accident, brings you closer to this ideal, but anytime he uses the house as a toilet, previous good behavior is usually canceled out. Consider the experiences of these owners:

Jay's Bullmastiff, Rollie, had been housebroken for two years when he began lifting his leg on the corner of the bed. The neutered male's marking made Jay furious. Each time he found it, he would yell and go looking for Rollie, who was invariably parked in the kitchen awaiting Jay's entrance. Jay would grab his collar and try to drag the 130-pound canine watering pot to the bedroom; Rollie would brace himself and stare at Jay, daring him to repeat the familiar scolding, until finally he bit his owner.

Penny considered her Maltese, Angel, to be an ideal companion. Imagine her surprise, then, when a visitor hesitantly inquired about the strange odor in the living room. Embarrassed, Penny thought about those occasions once or twice a month when she would discover a pile, attributing it to having left Angel too long. Penny, offended by the visitor's comment, said, "The house doesn't smell. You probably just don't like dogs."

Months later, Penny replaced the carpeting throughout the house. Upon removing the old carpet, the installers discovered urine stains—the result of many years of accidents. Because small dogs have small accidents, the urine usually dried without being detected. Penny never realized her Angel was not fully housebroken.

As Jay discovered, after-the-fact corrections didn't stop Rollie's marking, but they certainly made him defensive and untrusting. Penny, on the other hand, was unaware of habitual little accidents; she needed to face the fact that her ignorance had allowed a bad habit to take hold.

Housetraining problems are frustrating, but can be solved by treating the dog as totally untrustworthy, just as you would an eight-week-old pup, and doing daily vigorous obedience training so the dog is accustomed to taking direction from you. If your dog has been in your house less than six months, it's likely he's been insufficiently supervised and confined, and you need to follow the plan outlined in this chapter.

When is housebreaking over?
Although your dog may be flawless for days, weeks, or months, any dog can backslide under certain conditions. Plan on it taking a year or more to complete the housetraining process. Seemingly benign events can cause housetraining regression.

Dogs can become upset by all sorts of things, and may regress in their housetraining because of them. If your dog is making mistakes, consider the following possible causes:

- Changes in diet can disrupt normal elimination patterns.
- Weather changes (too hot, cold, or wet, or noisy thunderstorms) can make outings unproductive potty times.
- New environments (vacation homes, new house, or friend's house) may be treated as an extension of his potty area rather than his living quarters.
- Some medications (like allergy medications) and certain conditions (like hormone changes associated with estrus) can cause more frequent elimination.

Paper Training

Owning a small dog offers lots of advantages. One of these is that if you don't want to have to walk her outdoors, you can teach her to eliminate on papers indoors. To start, get full-sized newspapers (not tabloids) and a sixteen-square-foot wire-mesh exercise pen, available from dog supply catalogs or a pet shop. Place the pen on an easy-to-clean floor and line the bottom with newspapers opened flat out. For one week, keep your dog in the fully papered pen anytime you aren't supervising or exercising her. Then, put a bed in the pen and gradually reduce the papered portion to one full-sized newspaper, overlapping five sheets to ensure proper absorption.

Once she is pottying on the paper, open up the pen within a small room or hall. When she consistently soils on the paper, gradually give her access to the house, room by room, when you are able to supervise her. Shuttle her over to the papers if she attempts to go elsewhere. If she begins missing paper to any degree, follow the confinement and umbilical cording procedure described for outdoor training, except take the dog to the paper rather than outdoors to eliminate.

Once trained, some paper-trained dogs only go on their papers; others prefer the outdoors but will use papers if necessary. You can paper-train a previously outdoor-trained dog and vice versa, but you'll avoid extra work by deciding what you want up front.

Crate Soiling

Although dogs normally won't mess in their crates, some do. Occasional accidents shouldn't concern you, but if it happens every other day or more, try these suggestions:

- Remove all bedding in hopes he'll be repulsed by having nothing other than his body to absorb the mess.
- Use a smaller crate so he only has enough room to turn in place.
- Teach him to enter and exit his crate on command.
- Put his food and water in the open crate to encourage a better association about being in there; remove it when he's enclosed.

Identify and halt rituals that precede soiling. Barring physical problems, crate soiling is always preceded by a ritual such as whining, barking, pawing, digging, chewing on bars, or circling, turning, sitting, standing, or lying down repeatedly.

To correct these rituals as soon as they begin, confine your dog when you are home. Stop noisemaking (barking, howling, or whining) and destructive behavior (chewing, digging, or pawing) by using a leash tug or shaker can. By concentrating on the most pronounced behavior first—barking before whining or chewing before pawing—you'll find that minor noisemaking and destructive behaviors will decrease, too. As a result, the dog will relax, rest, and not soil.

CHAPTER 8

Grooming Your Dog

Grooming your dog is very important. Why? Because the more time you spend taking care of your dog, the happier, healthier, and (you hope) longer her life will be. Does Rover like getting a bath? Not always. Does Spot like getting her toenails clipped? Not likely. But both things are preferable to having stinky, matted coats that are infested with fleas or toenails so long they curl under and pierce the foot pads! These are extreme examples of lack of grooming, but things like this happen. Not to your dog, though.

Elemental Grooming

This chapter includes brushing, bathing, the importance of toenail clipping, and ear and eye care. These are grooming essentials for all dogs, even if your dog has very short hair. Grooming is not just about making Fido look pretty (do you think he cares how pretty he looks?)—it's about health maintenance. Why do you brush or wash your own hair? Because eventually, if you don't, it feels oily and dirty and unkempt.

FACT

A well-groomed dog will be happier—and you'll be happier—because not only will your dog be cleaner, your vet bills will be smaller. With an overall grooming routine, you'll be defeating problems before they arise.

Most dogs are very resistant to baths, ear cleaning, and toenail clipping. They sulk through it at best and can actively protest at worst, causing you to throw down the nail clippers in complete frustration. To prevent this, approach grooming with a positive attitude and a ton of patience, and train your dog to enjoy grooming. It can actually be a great bonding experience when the two of you have a positive experience.

Brushing Your Dog

Why do you suppose many dogs stand by you all day long and let you pet them, but then won't let you brush them for a few minutes? Well, maybe you're doing it wrong! More often than not the average owner is using the wrong comb or brush, especially in the beginning. Remember—a puppy has sensitive skin, and a spiky brush or hard comb wielded by an overenthusiastic owner can hurt! So be gentle and use a brush that's appropriate for your breed's coat type.

Brushing is a great thing to do. It helps keep the coat in good shape by removing dead hairs and releasing protective oils in the skin, which also promotes healthier skin. Brushing also exposes things like burrs or mats in the coat so you can get them out right away, and it will alert you immediately to the presence of fleas.

It will take more time to brush a long-haired dog, but it's time well spent. With so much hair it's harder to see things that might be happening with the skin, like sudden bumps or cuts. It's also important to keep longer feathering—such as that found on ears, legs, and tails—tangle-free. Best of all, regular brushing contributes to overall good health as well as good looks.

Brushing is also a way to observe your dog's coat and skin more closely. If there are inconsistencies, infections, bumps, or rashes, you'll see them a lot more quickly and be able to do something about them much more effectively. In many cases, brushing is the time when many owners find out about things much more seriously wrong with their dogs, such as tumors (usually in older dogs) or melanomas.

Unless you have anything but a very large or heavy breed, you should consider investing in a grooming table. Available through catalogs and in pet stores, grooming tables are collapsible tables with a rubber mat on them and an arm to which you can secure your dog's lead. It provides a safe, comfortable surface for your dog, allows you to use both hands, and keeps dirt and hair in one place.

Brushing a Puppy

When you're ready to brush your puppy, keep in mind that her attention span is short and she will likely squirm and fuss. You'll need to work quickly yet patiently, keeping in mind that it's better to quit while you're ahead so that your pup's experience is a positive one. You can start working on the grooming table, but until she understands that she should stand still on it you should keep the leash in one hand so she won't accidentally fall off and possibly hurt herself.

With your puppy on a short (but not tight) lead, brush or comb her in long, even strokes with a soft bristle brush, working from the base of the neck toward the tail. Stroke down from the top of the front shoulders toward the feet. Stroke from the bottom of the jaw to the deepest part of the chest. Brush the hairs on her belly (softly!) and on and around her back legs. Don't forget to brush her tail. During these sessions, make as many happy cooing noises as possible. You're teaching your puppy to enjoy and welcome being brushed. If you enjoy it, chances are she will, too. When you're finished, give her a yummy treat.

The same philosophy applies to brushing adults as to brushing puppies: be firm, be gentle, enjoy it, and make it enjoyable. Use the right equipment, and cover all parts of the body.

Brush Types

There are several types of brushes and combs that are specific to dogs with different kinds of coats. Short-haired breeds are most effectively groomed with a hound glove, which has short nubs on it to massage the skin while loosening dead hair. This should be followed by a soft bristle brush. For longer-coated breeds, a slicker brush is best. This is a rectangular-surfaced brush with tiny metal bristles pointing in one direction. They help loosen and separate a long-haired breed's fine outer hairs. For double-coated breeds that have wooly hair underneath their longer outer hairs, a rake-type brush helps gently secure and remove that thick undercoat. In fact, during times of peak shedding, you may be able to spend hours going over your dog with a rake first before using a bristle brush to finish her.

ALERT!

Include a flea comb in your arsenal of brushes. These are metal combs with very closely spaced teeth. When run through the dog's fur, the teeth are so close together that they snare fleas in between them. Should you trap a flea in the comb, immediately dip the comb in a glass container of rubbing alcohol to stun and remove the fleas, then flush them down the toilet.

Short-coated breeds are easier to brush, but still need the regular attention. Here a French Bulldog shows how enjoyable the sensation of a bristle brush is for her. Grooming time is often bonding time.

Bathing Your Dog

Dogs react differently to water in different situations. Bathing your dog may not be one of the most pleasant experiences, but it doesn't have to be that bad if you employ patience, perseverance, and firm kindness. Though giving your dog a bath outside might work on a warm, sunny day, most of the time you'll want to bathe him inside in the tub or the sink, depending on how big he is. Once he gets used to this, it's best to stick with the routine. Follow these steps and both of you should come out of the experience maybe not loving it, but not hating it.

1. First, brush your dog before you wash him. Any matted hair will become impenetrable once it's wet.
2. Prepare the place where you plan to bathe him: have enough towels on hand, be sure there's a pitcher to fill with water for soaking and rinsing, make sure you have the shampoo and conditioner ready, and run the water until it's warm so you don't have to wait once your dog is in the sink or tub.
3. Use a cotton or nylon collar so it won't be damaged if it gets wet. Take it off once your dog is in the tub or sink.
4. If you're going to bathe your dog in the tub, bring him into the bathroom and close the door before you get started so he can't escape far and can't do too much damage should he get out of the tub.
5. Put your dog in the tub or sink. Speaking soothingly but convincingly to him, begin to run the warm water. Use a temperature that's on the cool side but still warm and not cold.
6. Wet his body with a shower attachment or by filling and pouring water from a pitcher on him. Be sure not to spray or pour water on his face. Work from the neck down, wetting all parts of his body.
7. Pour some shampoo onto your hands or onto his back and begin to lather him up all over—again, avoiding his face.
8. When he's soapy all over, begin to rinse. Don't skimp on rinsing, as residual shampoo can irritate the skin and dull the coat. Remember to rinse his belly, between his legs, under his tail, and all the way down to his feet.
9. When he's rinsed, take a washcloth, wet and squeeze it out, and use it to rub his face clean.

10. Turn off the water, let the tub or sink drain, and run your hands over your dog like a squeegee to remove excess water.

11. Grab a thick towel and begin to rub your dog all over. Then put him somewhere he can shake himself off—in the bathroom when he jumps out of the tub or on the kitchen floor if you've washed him in the sink. Let him shake and tell him what a good doggy he is. Continue to rub him with towels until he's fairly dry. Then let him loose and let him enjoy scampering about, rolling on the carpet, and helping himself air-dry.

12. If you have a longer-coated breed, you may want to use the blow dryer on him to dry him completely. Use a low setting so you don't accidentally burn his skin, and fluff and dry him as best you can, using a brush to help. For a more professional look, put your dog on the grooming table and carefully blow out his coat so he looks "mahvelus, dahling." You can even put a bow or a bandana in his hair to complete the picture.

Ear and Eye Care

Just as you pay special attention to your face, so too should you make sure your dog's face is as blemish-free as possible. That includes her ears, eyes, and teeth. With regular attention, this is a simple process that becomes a very healthy habit.

Cleaning Ears

The first thing you need to know is that dogs with floppy ears tend to need more attention than dogs with cropped or short ears. Why? Because there is less natural air circulating there, and the warm, moist conditions are perfect breeding grounds for bacteria and ear mites. Signs of ear problems include repeated shaking of the head; frequent scratching or pawing at the ears; and a foul odor when you lift the ear flap (sometimes you don't even need to look in the ear to smell it).

If your dog is showing (or emitting) any of those signs, then it's time to clean the ears *and* have them checked by your veterinarian. Preventive care is intended to keep infections from forming, which is ideal. The easiest way to incorporate ear-cleaning into your routine is to do it every time you brush your dog.

As with everything else, there's a right way and a wrong way to do this. The wrong way is to pry into the delicate ear canal with a cotton swab. The right way is to go to your nearest pet store and find a good ear-cleaning solution. Soak a cotton ball with the solution, lift the ear flap, and start to gently swab the inner folds of the ear. Don't go too deeply into the ear. Just swab between the crevices of the outer ear canal. It might take three or four cotton balls before you're able to clean her ears out completely.

After you've cleaned the outer ears, squirt a small amount of the solution into the ears, hold the ear flap against the side of your dog's head and rub the ear around a bit to work the solution in. Swab off one more time with a cotton ball and if she wants to, let your dog shake her head to help displace any residue. With regular cleaning, your dog's ears should stay clean and fresh and you'll avoid costly veterinary bills from having to deal with ear infections. However, any time your dog's ears seem to be troubling her, it's best to have your vet take a look. There are different kinds of things that can infect the ear and each needs its own medicine.

FACT

It's important to note that dogs who suffer from problem ears tend to be repeat offenders. In other words, if your dog has had ear problems once, they are more likely to recur. Keeping your dog's ears clean will keep recurrences to a minimum.

Cleaning Eyes

The most important thing about the eyes is that they are the windows to your dog's soul—and his health. Your dog's eyes should always appear alert and clear (unless he's very old). In terms of hygiene, it's always important to wipe away the crust that builds up in the corners of your dog's eyes. While you might not think it bothers him, it does indeed. Left unchecked, it often is a source of irritation, or worse, may instigate an infection. Make sure to wipe your dog's eyes whenever possible using a special cleaning solution that won't irritate the eyes or simply by using a clean, warm washcloth (no soap). This is best done after his regular brushing and ear inspection.

Some breeds have large, protruding eyes that are especially prone to getting dirt and dust in them and to potential abrasion and infection. These include Boston Terriers, Chihuahuas, Shih Tzus, Bulldogs, Cocker Spaniels, and others. Some breeds, such as Bloodhounds, have droopy eyes. All these dogs need extra-special eye care.

Brushing Teeth

Healthy puppies and young dogs have bright white teeth and pink gums. It is possible to keep your dog's teeth looking almost as good as they did when she was a pup. This requires regular brushing, proper feeding and chew toys, and inspection for problems. Get your dog used to having her mouth handled by regularly lifting her lips and gently opening her mouth. Look at her teeth and gums. Is the gum line red or swollen? Are the teeth white all the way to the gums? Do you see any chipped teeth?

You should brush your dog's teeth several times a week. To do this, you can purchase one of several types of doggy toothbrushes on the market. Some even come with their own doggy toothpaste that's specially flavored so dogs like the taste. Remember, never use human toothpaste on your dog. He won't like it, and it's bad for him.

If you don't want to try the special toothbrushes and paste, you can wrap a small strip of gauze or cheesecloth around your finger to use as a scrubber. Use a paste of baking soda and water as the dentrifice. To brush, lift your dog's lip and brush or rub against the teeth with your finger. Try to get the brush or your finger all the way to the back of the mouth to reach the molars. Open the mouth and move the brush or your finger along the inside of the teeth along the gum line. Work quickly, gently, and thoroughly. The whole process should only take a few minutes. When you're finished, reward your dog with a crunchy snack—dogs love those miniature carrots!

Clipping Toenails

Keeping your dog's nails short is another part of keeping her in the best of health. Nails that are allowed to grow out can curl under and even pierce the pads of the dog's feet. They can cause the toes to stretch apart, disfiguring the foot and crippling the dog. They can get stuck in between floorboards or in thick carpet, potentially breaking and causing severe pain. For all these reasons, it's necessary to keep your dog's nails trimmed.

Being able to clip your dog's toenails shows a great deal of courage and skill on your part and a great deal of trust on your dog's. There are few dogs who naturally enjoy having their paws fiddled with. What's worse, inside each toenail is what's called the quick—the inner, fleshy part of the nail, where blood flows and there are nerve cells. If you snip into the quick by mistake, not only is it quite painful for the dog, but the bleeding can be profuse. For dogs with white nails, you can see the quick (it's the dark shading about halfway up the nail). With black nails, you need to guess. That's why when you're clipping it is better to err on the side of not cutting enough than cutting too much.

When clipping nails, you have to be patient with your dog. You have to train him to accept the process, and the only way to do that is to make it as pain-free as possible. The idea is never to get too aggressive about cutting the toenails or you can accidentally cut off too much, causing pain and bleeding. You just want to clip off the end, no matter how long the nails are. Even if they still look long after cutting off just the tips, don't worry. Repeat the process a week or so later and keep snipping away. As you cut the toenails, the quick recedes.

ALERT!

If you accidentally cut the quick, you'll need to get the bleeding under control. A styptic pencil, purchased at a pet supply store, is the best way to do this. If you don't have one, get a bar of soap and press the nail against it. The soap should stop the bleeding in a few minutes. If you just nicked the quick, the scary episode will be over quickly. However, if you did some real damage, get your dog to the veterinarian immediately.

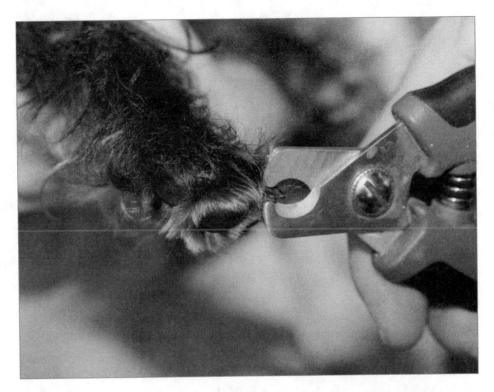

Accustoming your dog to having his nails trimmed is something you can do over time. Be gentle, patient, and clip off only small pieces of nail (but do it more frequently) so you won't cut into the quick. Reward your dog for enduring this ticklish and awkward process.

Training to Accept Clipping

The best way to clip is to use a powerful distraction the first few times you want to handle her feet. With your dog in her grooming spot, place the clippers innocently on the table so she can see and sniff them. Go through your normal grooming routine. Then, cut up some cheese sticks or lean lunch meat into small pieces and, as you hold them near your dog's nose, reach for and try to hold a paw.

When you have the paw in your hand, give her a treat and praise her. Touch each of her feet and, if she doesn't fight you, give her a treat. Do this every day for a week before you even pick up the clippers. She should feel quite comfortable with you touching her paws. Work the same way while introducing the clippers. Take a paw in your hand and quickly snip off the end of one nail. Give her a treat. If it goes well, do the entire paw at that session. Then stop. Do another paw the next day, and so on. Giving a tasty reward for accepting this touching should make things okay for your dog. Oh, and when you're done, give yourself a reward, too. You earned it!

When to Use a Professional Groomer

Especially if you own a longhaired breed or a breed that needs a particular look—such as a Schnauzer, a Poodle, a Shih Tzu, a Bichon, or a coated terrier—you should find a professional dog groomer to work with. You will still need to regularly brush and examine your dog, but it can take years to develop the techniques necessary to give some breeds their well-coiffed "looks." Make it easier on yourself and your dog and let someone with that experience do it for you. What a pleasure it is to pick up your dog from the groomer and have everything be done and your dog looking like the distinguished Airedale Terrier you see at dog shows.

Treat Yourself

Even for owners of short-haired breeds it's a treat to take your dog to the groomer's every once in a while. A groomer can give him the royal treatment—bathing, drying, cleaning eyes and ears, trimming nails—while you take care of something else. There is no shame in leaving your dog with a groomer. You can't possibly know the many trade secrets they've learned from their years of experience and network of mentors and friends.

User Beware

You know from experience that finding someone you trust to cut and style your hair isn't always easy. It can take several tries—even with referrals from friends—to find someone you really like. Then you just hope they stick around! The same can be true with dog groomers. In your search, you will hear plenty of stories of West Highland White Terriers coming home looking like Miniature Schnauzers, Bichons erratically trimmed, or Yorkies with no top knot. Some groomers will trim your dog's nails so short that her feet may hurt and she will become very defensive when you try to handle her paws. Because you're not there while they're grooming your dog, you have to trust that they'll treat your dog kindly and with the greatest of care.

Groomers who are confident in their abilities will willingly give you the names of their clients so you can call to get their opinions. Be suspicious of groomers who seem reluctant to do so or who try to win you over so you bring your dog before really learning what the groomer is like. When you find someone good, tip him well when you pick up your dog and talk to him about any concerns he has about your dog. Like your veterinarian, your groomer can become one of your dog's best friends outside your family. Value his opinion as well as his skill.

CHAPTER 9

Socializing Your Dog

Congratulations on this great new addition to your family! Now, make sure you show him off. Not for your sake, but for his. This eminently important process is called socialization. When the socialization of puppies is neglected, they never reach their potential. They're less adaptable, harder to live with, and less happy.

Why Socialization Is So Important

A dog who's received frequent and early socialization thrives on environment changes, interactions, and training procedures. She is also more likely to tolerate situations she's accidentally exposed to—such as kisses from a pushy visitor or a Big Wheel riding over her tail.

Usually, the socialization process consists of providing a safe environment for your dog to explore. Concentrate on four areas: socializing your dog to people, places, things, and other animals. In unpredictable or potentially unsafe situations, keep your dog leashed. That lets you prevent a wobbly youngster from trying to pick her up, and you can keep her off the sidewalk as a skateboard zips by. Socialize her to people, making sure she gets plenty of experiences with both genders and a variety of races and ages. Go to the park, a parade, the beach, or outside a shopping center.

Occasionally, leave your puppy in the care of a trustworthy, level-headed friend for a minute, an hour, or a day. Your objective is to teach the pup to be self-assured in your absence; therefore, don't say goodbye or hello to the puppy. Treat the situation as a nonevent so your puppy is less likely to experience separation anxiety.

Perhaps your veterinarian advised you against exposing your puppy while her immune system is developing, but you fear the risks of neglecting her socialization during this critical period. Though you may not be able to walk her around the big city, you can start a socialization program at home. Consider the following:

- Desensitize her to noises by letting her play with an empty plastic half-gallon or gallon milk jug or big metal spoon.
- Accustom her to walking on a variety of surfaces such as bubble wrap, big plastic bags, and chicken wire. Put a treat in the middle so she gets rewarded for her bravery.

- If her experiences with meeting new people will be limited, meta-morphose using costumes. Wear hats, masks, and capes, and walk with a cane, or limp, skip, and hop.
- Think about items people carry and equipment they use. Expose your dog to key chains, pocketbooks, vacuum cleaners, wheel-chairs, canes, bicycles, lawn mowers, Big Wheels, and roller skates, to name just a few.

How and Where to Socialize

Take your puppy as many places as possible so he becomes a savvy traveler who is accustomed to elevators, stairways, manholes, and grates. Acclimate him to walking on a variety of surfaces such as gravel, wire, sand, cobble-stone, linoleum, and brick. Because some dogs prefer to eliminate only in their own backyard, teach him to eliminate on command in different areas, so weekend trips and the like won't be a problem. If you want to foster enjoyment of the water and your dog isn't a natural pond puppy, walk him on-leash on the shoreline. Once he is at ease with that, venture into the water. Gently tighten the leash as you go, encouraging him to swim a couple of feet before you let him return to the shoreline. Never throw any dog into the water.

Let her get to know other animals—dogs, cats, chickens, horses, goats, birds, guinea pigs, and lizards. Often, upon meeting a new species, a puppy is startled, then curious, and some become bold or aggressive. For her own protection and for the protection of the other animal, always keep her leashed so you can control her distance and stop unwanted behaviors by enforcing obedience commands.

Be Prepared

Whatever you are socializing your puppy to—animals, objects, or people—approach in a relaxed manner and avoid any situation that would intimidate the average puppy, such as a group of grade-schoolers rushing at him. Be prepared for three reactions: walking up to check it out and sniff, apprehensive barking with hackles raised, or running away. No matter his response, remain silent. In the first—and by the way, best—scenario, he is thinking rationally and investigating his environment. Don't draw attention to yourself by talking, praising, or petting. Allow him to explore uninterrupted. This good boy is entertaining himself and being educated at the same time.

If your puppy lacks confidence or displays fear, don't console him, because this will reinforce his fear. Use the leash to prevent him from running away. If he is still slightly uncomfortable, drop some tasty bits of food (such as slivers of hot dogs) on the ground. Most puppies will relax after a nibble or two because the uncomfortable situation has been positively associated with food.

Things That Go Bump

If loud noises frighten your puppy, desensitize her by allowing her to create a racket. Offer her a big metal spoon with a little peanut butter on it. Give her an empty milk jug with the cap removed and a bit of squeeze cheese in the rim to bat around. It won't be long before she is creating hubbub and loving it. Of course, if the clamoring drives you nuts, feel free to limit her playtime with these items.

Supporting Your Dog's Socialization

As you get out into the world and investigate new places and meet new people and animals, your puppy or dog will have "out-of-the-box" experiences that may elicit different responses. It's not always easy to determine when you should console and when you should encourage. So that you don't inadvertently foster negative or fearful reactions, consider attending puppy kindergarten and get to know a dog's fearful stages.

Puppy Kindergarten

Puppies have so much potential, curiosity, and intelligence. That's why puppy training begins the moment your dog comes into your house—whether you want it to or not. Soiling, biting, jumping, barking, and running are natural behaviors; as a new puppy parent, it is up to you to show him where and when those behaviors are appropriate and, more importantly, where they are inappropriate. Begin teaching and socializing your puppy as early as eight weeks of age if he is properly vaccinated and his good health is confirmed by your veterinarian.

FACT

How do you go about finding a puppy kindergarten? Start by finding a local trainer who you trust and ask her if they run one or can recommend one. If you aren't sure how to find a trainer, the Association of Pet Dog Trainers has a database of trainers across the United States that you can search. Try *www.apdt.com*.

Like kids, dogs love to get together and play. Puppy kindergarten classes, dog parks, and friends, family, and neighbors with trustworthy dogs are all excellent opportunities for your dog to mingle and play. You'll have as much fun watching a game like this one as the dogs have playing it.

The best place to begin is in a puppy kindergarten class, so named because it serves as preschool for dogs. These classes emphasize socialization and early, informal training that evolves out of the puppy's behavior. By working with a professional dog trainer, you'll get the benefit of his perspective on your pup's temperament and overall personality. By working in a group with other puppies and their owners, you'll get the benefit of seeing that your puppy is a lot like the others—sweet and cuddly one minute, a ball of mischief the next. You'll learn by watching others' successes and failures as you all begin to use basic training principles to teach your new family members what you expect from them. And you'll leave with a pup who's been positively stimulated and had a chance to expend some energy in a constructive manner.

Overcoming Fear

For your dog's sake, ignore your natural desire to console a fearful dog. Whether her phobia involves inanimate objects such as garbage cans, loud or strange noises, other dogs, children, or places like the veterinarian's office, hallways or stairwells, reassurance only reinforces fear.

Her fright will diminish if you insist she concentrate on something else. Give obedience commands in rapid-fire sequence for two minutes or until she is relaxed, or at least responding automatically to "sit," "down," "stay," and "come." Then initiate playtime by running, nudging, patting the ground, or talking silly. Continue rapid-fire commands if she seems preoccupied by her fear. Practice first in situations in which she's only slightly uncomfortable— and certainly not panicked—then gradually progress to greater challenges.

QUESTION?

My dog is frightened of the stairs. How can I teach her to go up and down?

If possible, begin practice on no more than a half a flight of stairs or use a very wide stairway with good traction. Leash your dog, grip the railing, and progress up or down one step at a time, looking straight ahead to convey confidence. Ignore her balking and expect the first step to present the biggest challenge. By holding her leash short and tight you'll prevent her from losing balance if she begins scrambling. Repeat methodically and mechanically until your dog takes stairs without hesitation.

Trouble-Free Car Rides

Good car-riding manners ensure safety for both driver and dog. A dog who sticks his head out the window exposes his eyes to injury, and if you swerve or brake abruptly he may fall out of the car. His movement can obstruct your view and that, along with barking or whining, can distract you. Reduce the chance your dog will develop bad habits like vocalizing and lunging by containing him during car rides.

A trip to the pet store or a search through a pet catalog will reveal many choices for keeping your dog safe and secure in a car. The most obvious is, of course, his crate. If you crate-trained your pup from the beginning, he will have no fear or hesitation about settling into his crate for a car ride. If you use a crate, be sure that it, too, is positioned in the car so it won't slide around or be thrown if there's an accident. You can also try a dog seat for smaller dogs, or dog seat belts for larger dogs.

By making sure your dog is a secure passenger like everyone in your car, you can minimize the chances that in the unfortunate event you have an accident, he won't be thrown about the car or escape through a broken window and run into traffic.

Veterinary, Groomer, and Kennel Visits

These experiences are more pleasant if your dog is under control. Test and improve her obedience by using calm control as you invite her out of the car, walk around the grounds, and enter the building. Hand her over to caretakers without fanfare and expect her to remain somewhat composed when she's returned to you. Especially when you venture away from home, treat the outing like a training session rather than a vacation from obedience.

Socializing as Your Dog Grows Up

Puppy parents can be so attentive in their desire to make everything as wonderful—and correct—as possible for their "baby." As the pup grows and settles into the family routine, though, the attention to detail tends to fall off. One area where this happens is socialization. With a pup who may have gone to puppy kindergarten and even a beginner's obedience class and who is now used to riding in the car and visiting other friends and family members, you might easily feel that the dog is adequately socialized. But you would be wrong.

If new experiences and encounters aren't introduced on a regular basis, your dog may become rigid. Spending more and more time with his immediate family and less and less time out in the great wide world can cause him to be more suspect of strangers and new environments. Meanwhile, his constant proximity to you and your family may bring out defensive or territorial behavior when someone new comes along.

Providing a change of scenery is good for your dog and usually for you, too. Get out an area map, find a new park to explore, and pack your dog and your kids in the car to go check it out. Be sure to pack water for everyone.

Find out what time the local elementary school lets out and take your kid-friendly dog there for a walk. You'll see the kids will be more than happy to come say hello and pet your dog. Go for a stroll along the sidewalks of a small shopping area where people of all types are coming in and out of stores with packages and carts. They will gladly take a break to say hi to your pooch. Every such opportunity is a good one.

Life Changes and Your Dog

As part of your family, your dog will feel the stresses of changes in the lives of everyone in the family. Grown children heading to college, the passing of close relatives, contentious holidays—your dog will sense the emotions surrounding these occasions. Take care to reassure her that she is a valued member of the family no matter what, and consider lifting both your moods by going for ice cream or a long walk on the beach when you're feeling blue.

In the end, the concept is simple: The more friendly and positive experiences your dog has with a variety of people, places, and things, the more confident and calm he'll grow up to be and remain.

Unsocialized Older Dogs

By reading this chapter you will understand how critical adequate socialization is, and you will probably recognize older dogs who have not been socialized. In fact, you may have adopted such a dog not realizing that many of her issues are the result of this very thing.

If you recognize that your older dog is inadequately socialized, don't assume that since she's older she can handle things more quickly. You're working against habits that have been reinforced over time—at least a puppy has fewer experiences upon which to base her reactions! An older dog may already be convinced that men are scary, evil creatures, or that young children will hurt her, or that strange dogs should be warned to back off.

ALERT!

A dog's fear and stress levels can range from moderate to severe, and there's the risk that the fear can escalate to aggression. If your dog is so afraid of something that he will bite or attack to avoid it, he needs professional help. Seek it immediately.

These established ways of reacting to perceived threats are a challenge to overcome, but it's certainly worth a try—especially if the dog is basically good-natured. What you'll need to do is identify the things that frighten or stress her, and begin to introduce them in nonthreatening ways. This will take time and ingenuity on your part. Read this chapter several times, and consult with a trainer if you need to. Getting another perspective and having someone's help will benefit everyone.

Socialization Dos and Don'ts

To summarize, there are many positive ways in which to broaden your puppy's or older dog's horizons to help him become a more confident and secure member of society. There are also some things you shouldn't do, because forcing your dog may backfire and cause him to be even less secure in the face of certain distractions. Keep these things in mind:

Some Socialization Dos

1. Wear different kinds of clothing around the house and interact positively with your dog. For example, wear floppy hats, baggy pants, perfumed scarves, gloves, sunglasses, high heels that clatter, and so on. When you're wearing these things, approach your dog normally and reassure him by speaking in your regular voice.

2. Let your puppy or dog explore strange things in your house—shiny pots and pans, the vacuum cleaner, buckets, crinkly grocery bags. Supervise him to make sure he doesn't ingest anything inappropriate, and move the object around once he's sniffed it.

3. Make it a point to take your dog to different places at least once a week for a long walk, preferably public places like parks, small towns, or even pet-friendly stores or the vet's office.

4. Include touching him all over as part of his socialization. Remember that strangers like to pet dogs, so yours should be accustomed to being reached for and touched. Be sure to pick up his feet, look under his tail, tug gently (gently!) on his ears, hold his muzzle between your hands, tickle his tummy, and so on. Do this in a gentle, loving way and make it fun and positive.

5. Be sure to visit areas where your puppy or dog will encounter children. Take him to an area school when the kids are getting out of class. To get them even more interested in saying hello, put a bright-colored bandana or bow on your dog's collar.

Some Socialization Don'ts

1. If your puppy or dog appears overly frightened or unsure, don't coddle or comfort her. If you do, you're rewarding the fearful response. Instead, without showing emotion, remove her from the situation or take away the object that's frightening her and make a note to yourself that you will need to work on building her confidence around that experience or object.

2. Don't expose your pup or dog to dogs that may be untrustworthy. If there are too many strange dogs in the dog park, don't let her run around with them yet. If a strange dog is pulling her owner down the street to try to get to your puppy, chances are his over-exuberance could frighten yours. Greet her some other time.

3. Don't allow your dog to go somewhere that looks dirty or has been used by other strange animals if she hasn't had all her shots. The last thing you want is for her to contract a disease.

4. Socialize regularly, but don't overdo it. Puppies especially need lots of sleep and downtime. More frequent but shorter adventures are better than ones that overstimulate her.

5. Don't force a situation. If she's truly afraid of the vacuum, don't think that confining her in the room while you work around her is a good way for her to get used to it. Where there are strong reactions, go slowly. Get her used to being around the vacuum when it's off, then gradually work up to turning it on when she's around.

CHAPTER 10

Basic Training

Even though you may love your puppy or dog more than you ever thought possible and think of him as your child, it's important to remember that a dog is not a person. Their genetic makeup dictates that they respond to things differently—after all, you wouldn't get to know your neighbors by sniffing around their toilets. But for a dog, the scents that are released from other dogs are key communicators about how they interact. This is just one example of how dogs are very different from us. What's wonderful is that we have learned to live together as two different species sharing the same world. That's because dogs are responsive to our signals, and we can train them to behave in ways that are acceptable to us.

Training for Good Manners

Chapters 12 and 13 explain how to take basic training to the next levels—more advanced training and activities you can do together. Some people really get into training and want to challenge themselves and their dogs to do everything from walking nicely by their side to high-speed agility to amazing pet therapy.

FACT

Dogs who end up in shelters are there not because they weren't loved by their owners, but often because their behavior became uncontrollable. Don't let this happen to you! Training is easy and fun and so rewarding for both of you. Start early and keep it up to enjoy a great relationship with your dog for many years.

This chapter deals with what the majority of dog owners are interested in: training for good household manners. What does that mean? It means a dog who listens and responds to your requests. It means sharing your home with a dog who respects the house rules—just as your children or guests do. It means teaching your dog what you expect from him, as it is unfair to think that because you love him and he loves you that he will simply do what you want him to do.

Good manners start with a thorough understanding of the basics: sit, stay, down, and come. They grow to include requests like heel (walk nicely by my side) and household manners requests like off, drop it, quiet, and wait. This chapter will guide you through the basics and give you examples of how to use the requests around your house to enforce (and reward) good manners (behavior).

What You'll Need to Get Started

There are some general rules for teaching sit, down, and come commands: Use a buckle-type collar; give commands only when you can enforce them; never repeat commands; praise your puppy before releasing her from duty with a "chin-touch okay" (step forward as you gently touch her under jaw and say "okay" as an invitation to move).

Since dogs thrive on consistency, ideally one person should be the trainer. But if the puppy is a family pet, she can adapt to a multiple-trainer system and feel a special connection to everyone who works with her. If family members aren't committed to learning the proper skills, agreeing on rules, and working with the puppy, the person with the most interest should take responsibility.

You'll need the right equipment to train your puppy or dog. This includes a well-fitted collar, a 6-foot leather leash, and a 15-foot longe line. Additionally, when working toward off-leash control, you'll need a tab (a short nylon rope) and a 50-foot light line.

Collars

When you begin training, use the collar your dog wears around the house. It should be well made and properly fitted. If it's not, or if he doesn't wear a collar, start with a snug-fitting flat buckle-type collar. Consider switching to a slip collar, a prong collar, or a head halter if you've used the procedures recommended in this book but, because of his size or strength, you would like an extra measure of control.

- **Slip chain collars:** When using this type of collar, take advantage of the quick slide-and-release action of a slip chain with flat, small links. It should be only ½ to 2 inches larger than the thickest part of your dog's skull so it will fit easily over her head when you put it on. Although collars this small can be difficult to slide on and off, snug collars deliver timelier corrections. This type also stays in place better when properly positioned—high on the neck, just behind the ears, with the rings just under the dog's right ear.

  So the slip collar will loosen after corrections, make sure the active ring (the one the leash attaches to) comes across the top of the right side of your dog's neck.

- **Nylon slip collars:** Nylon slip collars offer the slide-and-release action of a chain, and deliver stronger corrections than buckle collars. As with any collar, the nylon slip should only be tightened momentarily while correcting; constant tension means the dog isn't being told when he's doing well and when he's doing poorly.

- **Prong collars:** Strong or easily distractible dogs may benefit from the use of a prong or pinch collar. The prongs come in an array of sizes, from micro to extra large. The length is adjustable by removing or adding prongs. Since some brands of these collars can fall off without warning, when you're working in open areas, consider fitting your dog with a buckle or slip collar in addition to the prong, and attach your leash to both.

Cruelty or kindness isn't linked to whether a dog wears a prong collar, but rather to the way it is used. If you want to use one, have an experienced trainer show you how to properly fit and work with it.

Some people think prong collars look like instruments of torture. If you're turned off by the appearance of the prong collar, look for another tool to aid you. However, it's actually a very humane tool when properly used. Ironically, some harsh trainers abhor them and some soft trainers embrace them.

Leashes and Lines

To teach commands and mannerly walking and to umbilical cord your dog, use a 6-foot leather, Beta, or Biothane leash (see examples at *www .tackatack.com*). Use a ¼-inch width for dogs up to 15 pounds; use a ½-inch width for dogs 16–45 pounds; use a ¾-inch width for dogs 46–75 pounds; and use a 1-inch width for dogs over 75 pounds.

Many exercises, including sneakaway and advanced distance stays, are done on a 15-foot nylon cord called a longe line. Since many pet stores don't carry them, just go to a hardware store and buy a swivel snap and 15 feet of nylon cord—¼-inch diameter for a medium-sized dog, and one-eighth-inch smaller or larger for small or large dogs, respectively. Tie the snap on one end and make a loop for your thumb on the other.

The tab is a piece of ¼-inch diameter nylon rope, approximately 18 inches long. If your dog is tiny or giant, adjust the length and width. Tie the ends of the rope together, then slip the unknotted end through the ring of the collar and, finally, thread the knot through the loop. The knot will keep your hand from slipping off the tab as you enforce commands. But when you're not holding it, it will be dangling on your dog's chest, which means he may be thinking about mouthing it—in which case, you can't use it. So if he takes it in his mouth, tell him, "Drop it." If necessary, enforce your command by saturating the tab with a chewing deterrent spray like Bitter Apple.

When you're working with the tab and lightline, wear a form-fitted gardening glove to ensure a better grip and to prevent rope burn.

The lightline is a 50-foot nylon cord. Use parachute cord for large dogs, Venetian blind cord for medium or small dogs, and nylon twine for tiny breeds. The lightline is tied to the tab and used as you make the transition to off-lead work.

Using Treats to Train

Most trainers want their dogs to obey out of love rather than because they were beaten or bribed. But since most dogs love tasty treats, food has long been used as a training aid. There are basically three ways to use food: (1) as a lure to get the dog to perform a task, (2) as a reward for completing an already learned task, or (3) as reinforcement for behaviors offered by the dog (click and treat training).

Most people use treats and body language as a lure because it is the fastest way to entice the dog to perform a task. But beware: there is a huge gap between following a lure and obeying a command. To bridge that gap, learn how to enforce your commands with your hands, leash, and praise. This will also prove invaluable if your dog isn't interested in the treat because she's full or distracted. If you are reluctant to build your training foundation using a food-based approach or prefer not to use treats, don't. You, too, are likely to find it simplifies and improves your communication with your canine.

Clicker and Treat Training

Clickers were once used almost exclusively for training service and trick dogs to learn more complicated requests than those required of the average pet or even obedience-trained dog. However, today clicker training is much more mainstream, and trainers are applying it to everything from introductory dog training to advanced horse training.

How does it work? Simply put, when the dog does something desirable, he is given a signal (the click made by a plastic clicker) that the behavior is right, offered a food reward, and, eventually, taught to do it on command, possibly without the food. For instance, if the objective is to teach a dog to sneeze, the trainer would wait for him to do that, click the clicker and offer a treat or other reward. Because of the power of association, soon the dog reacts to the sound of the clicker with as much delight as to the treat. Therefore, if the dog is working far away or retrieving and can't be given a treat, the clicker communicates that he is doing a great job. Of course, many people do the same thing with the word "Good" instead of the clicker. With animals who are unresponsive to verbal praise—such as rodents and farm animals—the clicker is an invaluable training tool, but a variety of methods are equally successful when teaching basic dog obedience. If you are interested in clicker training, investigate the resources offered by Gary Wilkes at *www.clickandtreat.com*.

Training with Patience

Dog training is an adventure of sorts: never predictable, sometimes elating, and sometimes tedious. Be optimistic about your dog's potential, but expect his progress occasionally to be slow or nonexistent. Don't, however, abandon your original goals and settle for meager results. Shoddy, half-learned obedience can cause annoying problems or allow them to fester. Many owners give up on training but later decide to give it another try—this time approaching it with far greater determination and achieving far better results.

ALERT!

Whether this is your first time around or your last-ditch effort, recognize that a degree of frustration is part of the learning process. If frustration or doubt strike, keep training. You may be five seconds from a learning breakthrough. Don't let your frustration or impatience get the better of you!

Finally, learning anything new—including how to train your dog—is challenging, so show yourself compassion. You will probably make mistakes when training. Follow the philosophy that if you attempt to train, you may make a mistake—but if you never try, you'll never have the dog you really want. Your goal: Decide what kind of behavior you want and pursue it with patience and kindness.

12 Ingredients to Teach Any Command

This is a great list to keep handy and review before and after you work with your dog.

1. Decide what you'd like your dog to do.
2. Decide what clear visual or auditory signal you will use to initiate the desired action.
3. Give verbal commands using the right tonality, inflection, and volume (don't plead, mumble, or shout; rather, use a more excited tone of voice, as you would to get the attention of a toddler).
4. Preface verbal commands with the dog's name. The name and command should sound like one word ("Busterheel," rather than "Buster . . . heel"). Just one exception: Don't use her name in conjunction with the "Stay" command, since hearing her name implies she should be attentive and ready to go.
5. Say the command only once.
6. Make an association: While teaching, give the command as you make the dog do the action (for example, say "Sit" as you pull up on the collar and push down on the dog's rear).

7. Give commands only when you can enforce them—otherwise, you risk teaching disobedience.

8. Decide on reinforcement: How are you going to show the dog what to do? Unlike the other eleven steps, this will change depending on your dog's stage in training.

9. Show your appreciation with precisely timed praise—like fireworks: full, but brief.

10. End every command by releasing with the "chin-touch okay."

11. Test your dog's understanding by working him around distractions before progressing to the next level.

12. Don't take obedience for granted. Dogs forget, get lazy, become distracted, and inevitably fail to respond to familiar commands. Especially if he rarely makes a mistake, correct him so he understands the rules haven't changed and neither should his behavior.

Just as important as the cue you use to start an action is the one you will give to end it. Release your dog with a word like "okay" or "all done." Pair this with an outward stroke under the dog's chin—the "chin-touch okay." Dogs who rely on a physical and verbal release cue are less inclined to "break" their commands. For the first three weeks, step forward when you deliver to make the dog move from his previous command on cue.

Basic Skills: Sneakaways

Use the sneakaway as the foundation for teaching commands and solving problems and to teach your dog to walk nicely on lead. This mesmerizing exercise teaches your dog to be controlled and attentive despite distractions. Even without specifically addressing problem behaviors, you may find they magically disappear as your dog learns her sneakaway lessons. At the very least, you'll find sneakaways improve her general trainability and therefore greatly reduce your workload.

Walking Sneakaways

The sneakaway is simple: When your dog goes north, you go south. When he is thinking of things in the west, you head east.

To begin (Step 1), put your dog on the longe line (the 15-foot nylon cord). Then take your dog to an obstruction-free area. Put your thumb through the loop of the line and your other hand under it. Plant both hands on your midsection to avoid moving them and jerking your dog. She may get jerked during this exercise, but it won't be because of your hand movement.

As you stroll with your dog, watch him closely but inconspicuously. If he becomes distracted or unaware of you, immediately turn and walk briskly in the opposite direction. The line will tighten abruptly if he isn't following as you move away.

After an hour of practice, split up any way you like over the next two days, your dog should be keeping her legs tangle-free, be aware of your movements, and be willing to be near you.

Remember these key points when practicing sneakaways:

- Keep your hands steady so you don't use arm movements to jerk your dog.
- Don't allow your dog to hear you move or stop, or see you with his peripheral vision. Avoid tricks like scuffing your feet, or inching, bowing, or arcing away; instead, always sneak directly away, with conviction, so your dog will learn to pay attention to you rather than your tricks.
- Move at a constant rate until your dog is following you, then stop dead.
- Use momentum to your advantage by heading away from your dog while there is still generous slack in the line. Calculate your departure so you'll be able to take two running steps before the line tightens.

Although most dogs will be strolling along cooperatively after an hour of sneakaway practice, a rare dog may continue to display odd resistance such as refusal to move or biting at the line. Although this is unusual, it, too, can be remedied by creating an umbilical cord for her by tying her leash to your belt. For two days, make her walk by your side as you perform your daily activities around the house and yard. After a few hours of umbilical cording, staying near you should be second nature. Now practice sneak-aways again, using a slip chain or prong collar. If you do so for a total of three hours over the course of a week, she is likely to be following happily.

Running Sneakaways

In step 2, instead of walking away, pivot and run when your dog's attention wanders from you. Once he's begun running after you, stop dead. Also, take inventory of your dog's personality, desires, and fascinations. These may include noises, smells, certain activities, food, toys, different areas, or other animals and people. From now on these will be known as distractions. Each time you practice, run a little faster as you sneak away and use more challenging and irresistible distractions.

Leash Walking

Begin step 3 once your dog is content to be near you no matter what distractions are around. This step teaches her to walk on a loose leash at your left side. Attach the 6-foot leash to her collar and put your right thumb in the handle. Enclose your fingers around the straps of the handle below. Hold the midsection of the leash with the right hand so your left hand is free. The leash should have just enough slack to touch the middle of your left thigh when your right hand is at your hip—unless you are very tall and your dog is short, or vice versa; the taller the handler and shorter the dog, the lower on your leg the leash will hang.

If your dog forges ahead, open and close your hand to release the slack, then grip the handle as you pivot and run away. Do this when her shoulder is only inches ahead of your leg, rather than waiting until she is tugging at the end of the leash or lunging frantically ahead. When your dog is running after you, pick up the slack in the leash again and stop dead.

If your dog runs right past you, pivot once again and sneak away before she bolts ahead. If your dog is a charger, watch her body language closely so it becomes easy to anticipate when to do multiple, direction-changing sneakaways. If, on the other hand, your dog attempts to lag, reduce the slack by tightening the leash a bit—about 1 to 5 inches—as you briskly walk forward. Use your left hand to pat your left thigh as you continue moving briskly. Praise her by saying, "good, good, good" so your dog knows you're happy with her.

The dog may bump into the back of your legs for the next few steps, but that, along with the fact that the leash tightens against your left thigh with every step, will encourage her to return to your left side. Remember to keep your left hand off the leash so nothing interferes with your thigh pulling into the leash.

Priorities change when a dog becomes distracted. She might never think of disobeying—unless food is being prepared, leaves are blowing, people are laughing, or rabbits, cats, birds, or squirrels are present. Prevent distractions from rendering all your obedience training useless by making fascinating temptations a part of every training session.

ALERT!

Do sneakaways to get control, and then give commands to teach listening skills. Your dog's dignity will grow in proportion to her obedience, so she'll be more relaxed in those social settings even when she's not been commanded.

Sneakaways teach your dog to watch you in anticipation of your speedy departure. As a bonus, your dog will enjoy the sneakaway if she likes running with you. Being astute observers of human behavior, it's easy for your dog to avoid the correction by "catching you" before the line tightens. So sneakaways not only teach your dog to walk nicely—she'll also watch you, have fun, and never be the victim of an unjust correction.

Sneakaways teach your dog that when she is attached to a line that you're holding, she is expected to control herself even though she isn't under command. This lesson in self-control is the foundation that makes everything else in dog training—problem solving, command training, and off-lead control—easy.

Teaching "Sit" and "Sit-Stay"

To teach the "sit" command, put your dog on your left side, hold his collar with your right hand, and put your left hand on his loin just in front of his hip bones and behind his rib cage. Ask him to "Sit" as you pull upward on the collar and with authority rather than dominance, push downward on the loin in one fluid motion. It's important that you project confidence to your dog. Praise him, then release him with the "chin-touch okay."

Practice a few times, but don't overdo it—especially with a young puppy. You want him to come away from the experience having been praised for doing what you've asked, not with you upset about something he can't understand.

As your puppy learns what "sit" means, go ahead and begin teaching him to hold the position in a "sit-stay." In a nutshell, teaching the sit-stay involves the sit command, teaching sit-stay from one step away, then advancing to teaching the leash-length sit-stay.

Teaching Basic Sit-Stay

Talk, pet, and praise, but don't let your dog move. When necessary, smoothly and instantly reposition her by pushing her back into the sit as you tighten up on the collar. If she is rigid and won't budge, move her forward and walk her into the sit. After a few seconds, release with a "chin-touch okay."

After three days with no sign of resistance, command "Sit" and wait for a response. To reinforce your command, push downward on the loin and give a quick upward jerk on the lead as you praise. Release with the "chin-touch okay."

Here are some basic guidelines for teaching your dog to stay:

- Just before leaving your dog, use a hand signal along with your "stay" command.
- Use distractions—people, places, movements—to test your dog and confirm that she's learning.
- Be acutely attentive. Move in to correct the instant your dog begins leaving the "stay" position; otherwise, she'll wonder what the correction was for.

This Fox Terrier is in a perfect position for the sit-stay. He is responding to the request with a hand signal, which can be used in conjunction with a verbal request when you're first teaching the dog, but can eventually be used by itself. Notice the dog's full attention on the trainer.

- Correct silently. If your dog didn't listen the first time, repeating yourself will only cause further confusion or disobedience. Use the leash, your hands, and praise to guide her into the appropriate response.
- Leave instantly after the correction. Avoid lingering next to or slowly moving away from your dog after correcting her; instead, immediately return to where you were at the time the dog made the mistake.
- Adjust the strength of your correction to your dog's size, level of training, reason for moving, and her level of excitement or distraction.
- Finish all stays by returning to your dog's right side, giving lavish praise, and using the "chin-touch okay" release.

Teaching the Sit-Stay One Step Away

Before you begin, your dog should be able to sit on command and wait to be released with a "chin-touch okay." To practice, hold the leash taut over the dog's head. Command "Stay," then step in front of him and act busy while producing distractions—use many distractions, return to praise frequently, and finally release with "chin-touch okay." Moving the head and wagging the tail is acceptable, but you should curtail attempts to scoot forward, rotate, or stand with a light, snappy upward jerk and praise.

If your dog tries to lie down, tighten the leash enough to prevent him from lowering comfortably into the down position and praise warmly as he realizes he doesn't have enough slack to lie down. Loosen the lead and prepare to repeat this sequence many times during the next week of training if your dog is one who is inclined to recline.

Teaching the Leash-Length Sit-Stay

To practice, command "Stay" and walk out to the end of the leash, holding its handle. Use distractions such as stepping side to side, bending down, pulling forward lightly on the leash, or dropping food or toys in front of your dog. This teaches her that no matter what your preoccupation or what activities surround her, she stays put. Frequently tell her she is a good girl. Stop movement immediately by (1) sliding your free hand down almost to the snap of the leash as you step into your dog, (2) quickly maneuvering your dog back into place without saying a word, (3) jerking upward, and (4) moving back to the end of the leash.

Enforce sit-stays while you (1) address a postcard, (2) read the headlines, (3) pop in a video, (4) empty the garbage, (5) download your iTunes, (6) tie your shoes, (7) wrap a gift, (8) get stuck on hold, (9) weed a flowerbed. When you no longer need to allow spare time for corrections, your dog has mastered the sit-stay.

Teaching "Down"

Start with your puppy or dog in the sit position. To teach "down," follow the same procedure as described for "sit," except use the command "Down." Gently pull downward on the collar as you use the palm of your left hand to push down on his shoulders or neck. When he lowers his body to the ground, pet his tummy. If he rolls on his side or back, continue rubbing his belly, then release him with the "chin-touch okay." If your dog braces and won't lower his front end to the ground, lift the paw that is bearing most of his weight as you push downward on his shoulder blades. If his fanny stays up as his front end lowers, simply keep your palm on his shoulder blades and praise him until he relaxes his rear legs and lies down so you can give him a tummy rub. At a glance, teaching the down-stay involves using the down command and teaching the down-stay.

The Down Command

This exercise introduces your dog to and reinforces the "down" command. To practice with just a push, position your dog again on your left side. Place your left thumb and index finger behind your dog's shoulder blades and on either side of her backbone. Command "Down" as you push. Practice by scratching her tummy, and then release her with a "chin-touch okay."

If your dog braces, use your right hand on her collar to pull her front downward as you push and give soothing praise. Another option is to push as usual with the fingers of the left hand as you use your right hand to lift the front paw that is bearing most of her weight. If you still simply can't get her down, discontinue work on the down and concentrate on perfecting the sit command around distractions; rare is the dog who resists the down after becoming completely cooperative on the sit.

To practice with a jerk-and-push combination, which teaches your dog to lie down without the two-finger push, first enforce "down" by simultaneously using a two-finger push and a bouncy and light jerk. Jerk diagonally toward your dog's right rear foot by holding the leash close to the snap while you stand facing the dog's right side.

The goal of the "machine-gun down" is to teach your dog to "down" without a hand signal or touch by practicing thirty downs a day in quick succession. To do this, practice rapid-fire downs by commanding "Down," giving praise, and releasing with a "chin-touch okay." Repeat the sequence for one minute, three times per training session. You should be doing ten to seventeen downs per minute for optimal results.

This Border Collie knows what's required: palm facing down means get in the down position facing me and wait for the next request. Once your dog understands this, you can start working from farther and farther away, asking for a long down-stay.

Exceptional dogs may learn the verbal "down" command in a week. With an average of twenty repetitions per day, most dogs will "down" 50 percent of the time after one month.

Test whether your dog really understands what you're asking by trying these things:

- Eliminate body language by putting your hands in your pockets and evaluating yourself in front of a mirror. Your mouth is the only part of your anatomy that should move when commanding "Down."
- Whisper the "Down" command.
- Turn your back and look over your shoulder at your dog to give the command.
- Stand in the shower (without running the water), sit in your car, and lie on a bed or sofa. See if your command still has authority.

Working on Down-Stays

Use this request to ask your dog to lie down and stay for grooming and examinations, during meals, or as guests arrive, or simply to calm your dog.

FACT

Before you start going for long down-stays, your dog should be able to do a leash-length "sit-stay" around distractions and should "down" on command.

To practice, ask your dog to down and then command "Stay." Examine his ears, eyes, teeth, and paws. Correct movements such as crawling, rolling, or getting up. Praise him frequently when he cooperates. Return to his right side to praise and then release him with the "chin-touch okay."

Teaching "Come"

Simply put, to teach this, leash your dog and wait for her to get distracted. Call "(Dog's name), come" and reel in the lead as you back up and say "Good, good, gooood!" Kneel down to celebrate her arrival and release her with the "chin-touch okay."

A great way to teach your pup that it's very rewarding to come when she's called is to play a game called "Pass the Puppy." Get your family to join the program by leashing the pup when at least one other member is present. Have one person hold the leash while the other holds the pup.

When the person holding the leash calls "Buddy, come," the other lets go so the pup can be reeled in as the person with the leash backs up slightly until the pup gets to her. After praising and petting the pup, that person then holds the pup and gives the lead to the next person. This exercise can be practiced daily for up to fifteen minutes; if you all habitually use the same, consistent training techniques, the puppy will learn to respond to everyone in the family.

Here are some basic guidelines for teaching "come."

- Don't put your authority at risk by calling "come" when your dog may not obey and you know you can't enforce.
- Standardize your voice, always using the same enthusiastic tone which suggests urgency to say, "Buddy, come!"
- Appeal to your dog's chase instinct and help ensure a faster recall by moving away after calling "come."
- Praise enthusiastically while he approaches. If you wait until he arrives, your lack of commitment will reduce his commitment to the process, too.
- Squat to acknowledge his final approach and arrival.

Perfecting the command so that your dog will listen to you while you're walking or otherwise distracted demands more work. First, leash your dog and take him for a walk. If he begins sniffing something, gazing around, or meandering off, call "Buddy, come!" Immediately back up quickly as you reel the leash, praising enthusiastically. Kneel down when your dog arrives, using verbal praise only. Release with a "chin-touch okay" and continue practicing the sequence.

After doing this about twenty times, your dog is probably running toward you faster than you can reel. Now see if he'll leave distractions when you stand still and call "Come." If he doesn't respond promptly, use a light piston-type horizontal jerk toward you as you praise and back up. If he does respond to your command, praise and back up.

When your dog responds to your command around strong distractions 80 percent of the time, you can start working on asking him to come from a distance. Arm yourself with a glove and a long, lightweight line to do this (the glove will prevent the line from hurting your hand should it get pulled).

Attach the line to your dog's collar. When he's distracted, position yourself over the line and call him. Praise him during the entire recall, from the time he begins taking his first step toward you until you release him with a "chin-touch okay." As he arrives, squat down and release with the "chin-touch okay." If the dog ignores your command, correct him by grabbing the line and using "wrap, run, and praise"—wrap the line around your hand twice just above where your thumb attaches to your hand, make a fist around the line, and anchor your hand on your waist as you run away from your dog, praising all the way. Release with the "chin-touch okay" when he arrives.

CHAPTER 11

Common Behavior and Training Problems

Always remember, dogs will be dogs. Like small children, they do what comes naturally, and what's advantageous—and pleasurable—for them. Behaviors like jumping up, chewing, and barking are all hard-wired into dogs as effective means for them to communicate. Problems don't appear out of nowhere, but their sources can be hard to pinpoint. If your puppy or dog is doing something you aren't happy about—raiding the garbage, jumping on the furniture, begging excessively—part of solving the problem and changing his behavior is understanding it and applying a commonsense approach.

A Holistic Perspective

Giving a puppy or untrained dog freedom in your house can be deadly. Natural curiosity and boredom could make her chew electrical cords, ingest toxic substances, or destroy valuables. When dogs are given too much freedom too soon, those who don't accidentally execute themselves often become homeless after causing damage to the owner's home or possessions. To make sure this doesn't happen, it is your responsibility to eliminate any dangers and prevent any damage. Dogs are opportunists. This doesn't mean they are bad; it just means humans are foolish if they leave goodies unattended on the coffee table and truly believe a dog would never even think about touching them.

If you don't know where your puppy is, she is probably into something she shouldn't be. Save your valuables, your sanity, and your puppy by watching her every move, umbilical cording her, or confining her to a safe, destruction-proof area.

Remember, too, that dogs were bred to behave in certain ways, so while you may love the look and size of a Shetland Sheepdog, if you can't stand her barking you may be taking on a problem that will be particularly challenging because, for them, barking is a genetic trait. A breed's original purpose will certainly manifest itself in its behavior, as will its individual temperament.

Environment can affect her behavior. Maybe one of your kid's friends is being rough with your puppy and she finally snaps, or she is confined for so long during the day that she is mischievous when you are home. What you feed your dog affects her behavior. Additives and preservatives can cause imbalances that exacerbate certain behavioral tendencies. Feeding too much or too little food will bring on certain behaviors.

Are You Guilty?

There are so many contributors to behavior. Here are some common mistakes people make that solicit or encourage unwanted behavior. Do you recognize any of them?

- Impassioned hellos promote hyper-excited greetings.

- Feeding your pup while you're cooking, eating, or snacking encourages begging, possessiveness, or an upset stomach.
- Putting strong-smelling items in the waste basket or leaving any trash can easily accessible invites garbage raiding (remember, a dog's sense of smell is much keener than ours).
- Not securing clothing, children's toys, and linens encourages stealing.
- Repeating commands teaches the puppy to ignore them.
- Lack of exercise and meaningful activity forces the puppy to look for outlets—such as digging and barking—to relieve her boredom.

Problem Prevention Strategies and Steps

Doing your best to prevent problems from occurring is one of the simplest and most effective of strategies. Included here are three key problem prevention strategies—basic prevention, channeling his energy, and correction—along with the steps that can be taken to put them into effect. Start implementing these strategies and steps from the moment your puppy or dog comes to live with you, and your problems will be minimized.

1. Basic prevention
   - Confine your dog, and confine properly. Every dog needs a place where he can do no wrong in your absence. Kennels and crates are best suited for this purpose.
   - Use the umbilical cord to control your dog around the house. Tie your dog to your belt with a short leash so his legs won't tangle and neither will yours. Your hands will be free so you can do what needs to be done and train your dog simultaneously.
   - Make calm entrances and exits. Though your dog may greet you with enthusiasm, remain emotionally detached and don't return the affection until you've been in the house with him at least fifteen minutes. Remain emotionally detached when leaving, as well.
   - If it's tempting, get it out of his reach. Common offenders include paper, garbage, personal belongings, and paraphernalia such as remote controls and eyeglasses.

- Close off areas with problem-making potential: shut the kids' bedroom doors so he can't confiscate their toys, for instance, or block off the living room so he can't see or hear the mail carrier's approach.

ESSENTIAL

Consult your veterinarian to confirm there is no medical reason for the problem your dog is experiencing. There is no sense in wasting time trying to change a behavior when it might be due to a physical ailment. Knowing your dog is in good health can keep you focused on the real problem.

2. Channel her energy
   - Increase her activity by providing vigorous aerobic exercise for a minimum of fifteen minutes, at least three times a week. Try jogging your dog on foot or alongside a bike, or having her continuously retrieve or swim.
   - Exercise her mind, too, by continually teaching her new tasks—tricks, obedience, or specialized work (hunting, herding, etc.). Develop a better relationship by pursuing challenging and stimulating goals.
   - Encourage her to play with a toy to curtail attempts to chew woodwork or dig in the garden.
   - Enable yourself to stop inappropriate behavior instantly by attaining one-command control around all distractions. Stop barking, jumping up, or nipping by giving obedience commands in rapid-fire succession.

3. Correct every attempt to misbehave
   - Act immediately: If your dog tries to jump on guests, stand on his leash; if your dog tries to grab the leash, spray Bitter Apple on it; or if your dog barks at you for attention while you read the paper, without missing a beat, put a leash on him and toss a toy. If he ignores the toy and barks again, correct her for barking but don't give a command.

Taking your dog to a professional dog obedience class can give you a safe place to work with him as well as the opportunity to watch other owners with their dogs. You'll see that all dogs have their quirks and that there are many ways to arrive at a solution that works for both of you.

- Concoct a situation that would cause your dog to attempt a misbehavior. This allows you to be physically and mentally prepared to stop him.
- Distract your dog as he contemplates or actually begins to misbehave by tossing shaker cans (empty soda cans with eight pennies inside), clapping your hands together sharply, spraying a water pistol at your dog, or blasting a boat horn.

- Set "traps" that will correct your dog remotely when triggered by his misbehavior—for example, strategically placed shaker cans or electronic "scat mats."
- Use a Bitter Apple spray correction, but only while your dog is misbehaving. Hold the collar and/or the back of your dog's neck as you press the nozzle of the spray bottle against his lip, then spritz. Never let your dog see the bottle in your hand unless you are actually correcting.
- Jerk the leash: Snap the leash quickly in the direction opposite to his misbehavior.

FACT

Professional dog trainers and behaviorists have years of experience working with many kinds of dogs. Their perspective and recommendations can be the difference between solving problems and making them worse. If you feel overwhelmed by your dog's problem(s), find a professional to work with.

Naughty or Nasty Behaviors

In this section you'll find ways to cope with the most common problems of dogs—barking, chewing, digging, jumping up, and so on. They're described as naughty or nasty behaviors because they are considered such in a human household, where the rules are quite different from those a dog would use to survive in the wild. "Naughty" dogs and "nasty" behaviors can be remedied with persistence and patience—and the help in this chapter.

Barking

Out of respect for other household members, neighbors, tenants, and anyone with a low tolerance for barking, correct this problem—otherwise, you may be forced to get rid of your dog or face eviction. Don't worry that your dog will stop barking altogether. Teaching barking inhibition increases her value as a watchdog because when she barks, you'll know it's for good reason.

To correct barking, even if it is only a problem in your absence, teach the dog to be "quiet" on command when she's standing next to you. If your dog will obey the "quiet" command without making you raise your voice or repeat yourself, no matter what the distraction, barking in your absence will usually subside. If it doesn't, you may be unintentionally reinforcing excessive barking—you may be attempting to silence a dog by petting her or giving her a toy, or you may be letting her be vocal without consequences.

If you use the "quiet" command and never tolerate barking or try to appease her, but she continues to vocalize in your absence, find out exactly when and why she is barking. Record her with a tape recorder when you leave, ask a neighbor about her habits, and spy on her. If she isn't barking at outside noises, separation anxiety is probably the problem. Read and follow the suggestions in the section later in this chapter on "Separation Anxiety."

If she is barking at outside noises:

1. Teach her not to bark at outside noises when you are home. Keep her leash attached and periodically knock on the walls to create strange sounds. Say nothing as you run over to correct with Bitter Apple. Alternately, you can give her a series of rapid-fire commands to distract her from the noise and, in turn, stop her barking. An added benefit to this approach is that both her obedience and self-control will improve.
2. Keep her in a covered crate in a noise-insulated room with a fan or other generated white noise in your absence. Occasionally crate her when you're home to confirm that she's peaceful when confined.
3. Although rarely necessary, investigate these options as a last resort:
   - Antibark collars automatically emit a warning buzz when the dog vocalizes. The collar will deliver a timely correction if the dog continues to make noise after the warning. The two most popular collars correct by delivering a mist of annoying citronella at the dog's muzzle or a mild electric shock.
   - Antianxiety medication. See your veterinarian to find out if your dog is a good candidate and to discuss benefits and risks.

Begging

It often takes only one tidbit for your clever dog to be convinced that your meals are better than his and that you're willing to share if he begs. If you've fostered this bad habit, it can be broken, but you probably can't be cured. On the other hand, if you've acquired a dog with a begging habit, keep him out of the room when food is near, enforce the "down-stay," or teach him to go to his bed.

In addition, follow these feeding rules: feed him dog food in his dish and never share goodies or feed him from your hands or a plate. Finally, when you eat or prepare food, completely ignore him.

Chewing

Here's the lowdown on the things you should be giving your pup to provide for her needs and reduce the chances of her putting her teeth around the wrong things:

To avoid problems, give your dog only toys such as hard Nylabones, sterilized bones (from a pet shop, not a grocery store), rubber Kongs, or squeaky toys and balls of the proper size and durability for your dog. These are solid, chewable items. Encourage your dog to chew on them by smearing a tiny bit of peanut butter or spreadable cheese on them or—better still—inside, if the item has a hole.

Be aware that certain items can increase problems with inappropriate chewing, soiling, or guarding behavior. Avoid giving your dog personal items to chew on, such as slippers, socks, gloves, or towels. If she is attracted to the family's stuffed toys, don't allow her soft dog toys that are made of fleece or are stuffed. If she's attracted to rugs or tassels, don't provide her with rope or raglike toys.

Edible products such as rawhide, pig's ears, and cow hooves increase your dog's thirst and can upset her stomach and even get lodged in the intestines—a medical emergency. Some dogs get defensive and possessive around edible items. If your dog is having house-soiling problems or gets tense in the presence of these edible items, get rid of them. Of course, if you want to give them and they keep your dog busy without causing side effects, consult your breeder or veterinarian.

In addition to providing dogs with proper toys and exercise, it is best to keep intriguing items out of reach—eyeglasses, remote controls, laundry, plants, dried flowers, and so on. Allow her to drag a leash or tie it to your belt as an umbilical cord so you can correct her if she begins exploring the wrong thing, then direct her to play with an appropriate toy. If she is off-leash, distract her from inappropriate chewing with a sharp clap of your hands as you say "Hey!" followed by praise and play with an appropriate toy. Smear Bitter Apple cream on tempting woodwork. Confine your dog in a safe place when you can't supervise her, and teach the shopping exercise.

The Shopping Exercise

Teach your dog the difference between his toys and taboo items. Choose a word to mean "get that out of your mouth" (use the same word whether he has a finger, a slipper, or a bone). To do so, place a number of personal items and paper items on the floor and allow your dog to explore them. As he picks up a taboo item, command "drop it" as you jerk the leash, moving away from the item toward one of his toys. Get him to play with the correct item.

If he doesn't drop the taboo item as you move him away, spray your finger with Bitter Apple and slide your finger along his gum line as you command "drop it." If he still doesn't drop it, spray Bitter Apple directly against his lip line and redirect him to an appropriate toy.

Digging

Digging is practically the only problem that cannot be prevented, lessened, or solved with obedience training (although sometimes training indirectly reduces the behavior because it relieves boredom). Dogs don't dig because they are dominant, belligerent, unaware of authority, or out of control—they do it instinctually, to make a cool or warm place to lie down in or to make a nestlike den for their puppies. Interesting smells in the soil and the wonderful feeling of vigorous burrowing and dirt in their toes are hard for any dog to resist. Therefore, monitoring your dog and correcting digging attempts is an ongoing process—you aren't fighting your dog, you are fighting nature.

Your best option is to never leave your dog unsupervised in an area with digging potential, but if you insist on correcting, here's what you'll need to do:

- When you can't supervise your dog, leave her in a run or tied out on concrete, patio block, or a similar undiggable surface.
- Provide a comfortable environment for her. Fresh water and shelter from heat, cold, wind, and rain must always be available.
- Exercise her vigorously and regularly so she doesn't seek aerobic activity from digging.

FACT

Correcting digging requires you to monitor your dog more closely than the Secret Service guards the president. Any time he begins digging, startle him without saying a word. If he is leashed, jerk it, then praise. If he is tied out, attach a second leash, long enough for you to hold and jerk. If he is in the backyard, create a sharp noise, spray him with water, or toss a shaker can at him.

House Soiling

This problem is often the result of optimistic owners wrongly assuming a dog is housetrained after a brief period of appropriate behavior. Hormonal changes, varying weather conditions, diet, and medications can quickly disrupt good potty habits. To prevent house soiling problems from recurring, wise owners do the following:

1. Watch and/or accompany your dog to his potty area. If he is prone to becoming distracted from the task, using a light jerk of the leash will encourage him to do his business quickly. Never assume that because your dog has been outdoors for a lengthy period that he won't soil the house when brought back inside.
2. Supervise indoor activity during "dangerous" times, for example when there is unusual activity in the household, when he has been more

active, eaten anything atypical or consumed a lot of water, or when he's chosen not to relieve himself despite your pleas.

3. Never discipline after the fact. Instead, treat your dog as totally untrustworthy. Crate or confine your dog in a safe place when you can't watch him and set him up to have an accident in your presence. Consider surreptitiously following him during dangerous times, ready to issue a surprising correction. A shaker can works well for this purpose because it is lightweight and harmless but is very startling when tossed at his rear end the moment he contemplates misbehavior.

Jumping Up

Some dogs have no desire to jump up. They're content to let you bend down to pet them. Others jump up either because they are very bold and sociable or because they've been rewarded for doing so with petting and attention. Stop encouraging bad habits by controlling yourself. Greet your dog only after she's settled down. If that's more than you can bear, respond to her jumping by folding your arms, looking overhead and shuffling into your dog until she is forced to walk away. Advise your guests and household members to do the same.

Another way to correct jumping up is to attach a leash to your dog's collar and step on the lead so she has only enough slack to begin jumping but will be stopped before she is able to pounce on someone. Of course, if she's obedience trained, simply tell her to sit when she is excited and release her from the command only when she appears to have more self-control.

To stop jumping up, the choice is yours:

- Shuffle or stumble into the dog as she jumps.
- Stand on the leash so it tightens every time she attempts to jump up.
- Teach the "off" command. Enforce by pulling your dog off her target with the collar or leash if necessary. Praise the instant her feet hit the floor.

Counters and Furniture

Jumping on counters and furniture is the result of giving your dog too much unsupervised freedom too soon. Distract your untrained dog every time he considers looking at the counter or hopping on the furniture: toss a shaker can at him, clap your hands sharply, or jerk his leash even before he misbehaves.

Many people enjoy having their dogs on the furniture. Dogs love it, too: furniture smells like you, it's comfortable, and it usually affords him a better view of what is going on both inside and outside. Once you allow him on furniture, it becomes his domain, so don't expect him to wait politely for the next invitation. If he's sneaking on the furniture despite your consistent disapproval, provide your dog with his own pieces of furniture—several very comfortable dog beds (store-bought or homemade) located in various areas of your home. If you ordinarily allow him on furniture, teach him to get "off" on command.

Mouthing and Nipping

For puppies aged three to six months, mouthing is very common because it is their teething stage. Natural though it may be, you must stop mouthing of flesh and valuables regardless of when it occurs, so that it doesn't become habitual. It can also be scary and painful for children and some adults when a puppy clamps down on them with her needle-sharp puppy teeth. This can lead to unnecessary anxiety and fear around the puppy.

Correct chasing or nipping of children by never allowing unsupervised contact. Always intervene to curtail disrespectful, inappropriate actions from puppy or child. Attach a leash to your pup that will allow you to pull him away as the child says "ouch."

Here are some tips for how to handle a mouthing puppy:

- First, keep your puppy leashed any time mouthing may occur (especially in the house), provide her with plenty of exercise, and encourage play with proper toys such as hard Nylabones and Kongs. Flavor the items by rubbing or filling them with a special soft food treat.

- Offer your puppy clean wash rags that you've wetted, wrung out, and frozen. Chewing on these relieves the discomfort of teething. Replace with a fresh one when it begins to thaw.
- Correct mouthing by either screeching "ouch!" and then pulling the leash so the puppy moves away, then eliciting play with the proper toy, or by using Bitter Apple spray on pup's lip line while gripping her collar with your free hand.

QUESTION?

My puppy won't stop biting when I say "ouch" or jerk the leash. Is there any other way to stop him?

Issue a stronger correction by spraying Bitter Apple on his lip line as he is biting. Make sure to hold his collar with your free hand as you spray to ensure proper aim. Also, only engage in play when the puppy is leashed and you have the Bitter Apple bottle in your pocket. Consider giving and enforcing "sit," "down," "come," or other commands to redirect his energy until he regains his calm disposition.

Stealing and Scavenging

If you were all alone in someone else's house, what would you do when you got bored? Would the thought of looking at their stuff or even rummaging through cabinets, closets, or the refrigerator tempt you?

Now you know how a dog who is left alone for hours at a time feels. He is trapped and bored and has no hands with which to do arts and crafts, but he does have plenty of senses yearning to be indulged. When given too much freedom too soon, he will quickly discover the joys of hunting for household treasures too often left easily accessible by negligent humans. When he is "rewarded" by finding something interesting to devour (for him), he seeks to replicate the experience, which leads to the habits of stealing and scavenging.

Many dogs even steal or scavenge when you're home. They know the only guaranteed way to rouse you from the recliner is to show off the valuables they've confiscated. Police the canine klepto by:

- Incarceration (crating)
- Chain gang (umbilical cording)
- Surveillance (making sure you know where he is at all times)

There are simple things you can do to avoid being a victim of stealing or scavenging, too. Do them diligently, because the one time you forget and your dog discovers he has found his "treasure," it's like winning the lottery and he will keep coming back. The common sense things you must do include:

- Keep the garbage out of reach.
- Close cabinets and closets and put laundry away.
- Teach the "drop it" or "leave it" command.

So that your dog gets the message, dispense justice fairly by:

- Only correcting crimes in progress; never correct stealing after the fact.
- When you discover the infraction, leash your dog, invite him to make the same mistake, and correct it with a leash jerk followed by praise.

Stool Eating (Coprophagia)

So your dog has a thing for poop—her own or that of other animals? Don't be embarrassed. This tendency is so common that virtually every dog training book devotes a section to it. Nutritional deficiency can be the cause for this behavior, so you should first consult a veterinarian. As a rule however, coprophagia is simply a behavioral problem.

Preventative measures are the best solution. Accompany your dog outdoors on-leash and command her to go potty so you'll be able to clean up immediately and stop the habit before it starts. If she prefers to eat other dog or animal poop, the leash will allow you to pull her away from that, too.

Products such as Forbid® can be added to your dog's diet to make the resulting poop less palatable, which therefore may dissuade your dog from sampling it. However, many dogs will instantly resume the behavior once they are no longer fed the supplement. Supervision and attention to cleanliness are the best remedies.

Bad Behavior: Aggression

Aggressive behavior such as biting should always be considered a serious problem. Whether it occurs because a dog is trying to get attention, relieve frustration, or change your behavior, biting is never cute and rarely justifiable.

Unfortunately, some owners appreciate (consciously or unconsciously) a dog's aggression and reinforce it by rewarding it or denying its existence. Most dog-bite injuries and aggressive-dog euthanasia could have been avoided with proper supervision, socialization, training, sufficient exercise, and intervention by an owner who recognized the warning signs and instantly stopped inappropriate behavior. The signs of impending aggression include intense eye contact, stiffening, weight shifting forward, tail out, growling, fast whining, or signs of interest, excitement, or arousal. Whether it's playful, fear-driven, or dominant, A-1 obedience skills are imperative. Aggressive tendencies always diminish as the owner's control of his dog increases.

FACT

Through obedience training, owners have the opportunity to learn how to interpret their dog's mood and body language. It is that astute observation that enables owners to get control of the potentially aggressive dog well before she reaches a highly agitated state. If the owner intervenes too late—when the dog's adrenaline is peaking—the dog will be oblivious to attempts to stop her. Finally, a responsible owner never assumes his dog is "cured" and takes every precaution, no matter how well-trained the dog is.

Playing Too Rough

Avoid rough play such as pushing and pulling, tug of war, and growling. Instead, get down on all fours, swing your hair, and pounce, or play retrieving games, chase, and hide and seek. If games get too rough or out of control, stop the action by saying "Ouch" as you abruptly leave the game. If you choose to resume play, do so only after leashing the dog. That way you can jerk the leash to stop the bad behavior and immediately continue your game.

You should be able to stop the game you're playing with your dog at any time and walk away or ask him to "down." Never use games to frighten your dog or hurt him. If he ever hurts you during play, make sure he knows you don't approve by using the techniques listed under "Mouthing and Nipping."

Anxious Behaviors

These are behaviors that are the result of your dog feeling anxious. Naughty and aggressive behaviors may indeed be triggered by anxiety, as well, but there are some that are specific to a dog not being able to cope in a particular situation. The best-known is separation anxiety, but others include riding in a car and submissive urination. These behaviors can be vexing because when your dog senses that you're upset about what she's doing, it may cause her to increase the very behavior you don't want! Stay calm, be patient, and help her through.

Separation Anxiety

Having to leave a dog alone is worrisome if he gets frantically frustrated when he's separated from his owner. Overly dependent dogs commonly respond to separations by continually barking, whining, and howling, destroying their living space, and attempting to escape by chewing, digging, and jumping over fences and out of windows. In addition to causing expensive damage, many dogs injure themselves. When panicked, they are oblivious to the physical discomfort of laryngitis, bloody-raw gums and paws, broken teeth, self-mutilation caused by chewing and licking, and even broken limbs as a result of jumping out of windows.

Avoid both after-the-fact corrections that increase anxiety and consoling tones or gentle petting that embed the neurosis. Instead, be sure you exercise your dog vigorously and regularly; improve his ability to handle all sources of stress by teaching reliable obedience; and, as you come and go, remain relaxed and refrain from addressing your dog directly.

There are three exercises you can do with your dog that can lessen the effects of separation anxiety. They are described here.

1. Random tie outs: Take your dog to indoor and outdoor areas, familiar and unfamiliar, filled with or absent of distractions. Silently tie his leash short to a stationary object and walk away for a few minutes. Insist that he remain quiet when you leave. Sometimes remain in sight and other times walk out of sight. To correct noise making, toss a shaker can, spray him with water or run over to spritz his mouth with Bitter Apple. Concentrate on the areas that make your dog most uncomfortable. Practice every other day for a half hour until he'll be silent regardless of where you leave him, where you go, and how long you're gone.
2. Out-of-sight sit- and down-stays: At least every other day practice fifteen- to twenty-minute down-stays with lots of distractions.
3. Whirling dervish departures: Dash from room to room grabbing your keys, briefcase, jacket, lunch box, etc. Rush out the door and to your car, then back out of the driveway, motor around the block, pull back in the garage, and saunter into the house. As you put your keys, jacket, and paraphernalia away, completely ignore your dog. After relaxing for a few minutes, repeat the frenzied departure and relaxed arrival over and over for an hour. To thoroughly desensitize your dog to comings and goings, repeat this pattern three times the first week, then once a week for a month.

When at home, make it a habit to periodically confine your dog. Sequester him in a quiet area and place your recently worn sweatshirt or bathrobe on the floor on the other side of the closed door. If your smell permeates his room, he may not even realize it when you finally do leave. Give him his favorite toy only when you confine him. Make the toy more desirable by rubbing it with your scent before every offering. Reduce the agitating sounds of neighbors or delivery people by creating "white" noise with a motorized fan to soothe your dog. This is a better solution than subjecting your dog to TV and radio stations with their unsettling cacophony (bells, whistles, applause, sobbing, screeching, and laughter). Then, when you do actually leave, follow the same routine. Since separation problems can periodically return despite these precautions, reinstate these recommendations as needed.

Riding in the Car

Restraining your dog by crating, tying, or seat belting reduces the chance that she'll act unruly in the car and ensures ease of correction when necessary. Teach carsickness-prone and reluctant riders to enter and exit the car on command. Leash her, open the car door or hatch, and command her to go in as you give her a boost. Immediately invite her out with a "chin-touch okay" and repeat the procedure five times in a row, several times per day. Within a week she should be readily responding on command.

The more relaxed your dog becomes about getting in the car, the less inclined she'll be toward motion sickness. To make the car a more pleasurable place to be, arrange to have her sit in the car with a canine companion who likes riding. Try building the positive association with food. If your dog is a fairly neat chowhound, feed her only in the parked car.

Don't feed your dog for three hours before a ride if he has a tendency to get carsick. Experiment with placing him in different spots in the car. You may find a location that, because of the view, air flow, or smoothness of the ride, doesn't induce sickness. If motion sickness continues to be a problem, ask your veterinarian about using medication.

Submissive Urination

If your dog wets when he greets people or is disciplined, he isn't having a housebreaking problem. Uncontrollable and unconscious leaking of urine is common in puppies and certain breeds. If your dog has been given a clean bill of health by a veterinarian, extinguish this tendency by practicing the following:

- Teach commands so you can give orders that force your dog to focus on his responsibilities instead of his emotions.
- Keep your dog leashed to enable nonemotional, silent correction of misbehaviors.
- Avoid eye contact, talking, and touching during emotional states.

- Make your entrances and greetings devoid of emotion.
- Never yell, strike, or show anger toward him.

Since living with this behavior can be exasperating, consider diapering your dog for the first month so you don't have to continually clean up. To diaper your dog, simply pin a bandana or towel around his privates and teach him not to remove it. Acclimate your dog to wearing the diaper by umbilical cording and jerking the leash if he even sniffs at it. When he is totally uninterested in the diaper—usually after less than a week of umbilical cording—let him walk around the house unleashed as usual, without concern about dribbling.

Avoid vigorous petting, impassioned tones of voice, and strong eye contact. Only interact with a superficial, brief pat, calm word, or fleeting glimpses when his bladder is empty. When he consistently responds without tinkling, test his control after he's had water. Gradually try a warmer approach, but be ready to turn off the affection and issue a command if it pleases the pee out of him.

"All in the Family" Problems

To be most effective, dog training needs to be consistent. That's the only way your dog will learn what you want and not get too many mixed signals. So what can you do if your family consists of difficult, contradictory personalities?

Perhaps one is a wimp who tries to talk you out of doing "nasty" obedience which will ruin the dog's free spirit; each time you enforce a rule, she commiserates with the dog. Maybe another is a loudmouth, giving what he thinks is much-needed training advice, demonstrating his expertise by yelling commands to you and the dog. Maybe there's a talker who is always jabbering and saying nothing, then wonders why the dog treats her like an inanimate object. Or perhaps there's a secret saboteur who watches what you do and then undoes your hard work by feeding table food during meals, letting the dog pull on the leash or hang her head out of the car window, or inviting her on the furniture.

Each family situation is unique, but it's appropriate for you to express and demonstrate your concern for the dog's well-being by taking charge of her training, housing, supervision, and care, including health, exercise, and grooming. Make arrangements for someone trusted to handle these tasks when you are unavailable. Only assign care and training duties with specific details as to how to perform them to interested household members.

FACT

Dog training is a lot like showering. Thinking about showering or complaining about being stinky won't make you cleaner. You actually have to get wet and lather up. Even then, you don't stay clean forever. No matter how meticulously you scrub and how carefully you attempt to avoid getting messy, you will never be free of the need to shower regularly.

Remember, too, that no matter how common your philosophies, no two people will agree 100 percent on how to raise a dog. Hey, it's family. Expect to be annoyed sometimes, and understand that what others do can't sabotage your authority. The dog will learn what you expect from her by the way you react to her behavior in your presence.

CHAPTER 12

Advanced Training

Once you've gotten a taste of how simple and rewarding basic training can be, you'll want to have access to ways to teach your dog other things. This will expand your vocabulary with your dog and improve your relationship. All sorts of things fall under the umbrella of "advanced training," from an everyday instruction like "heel" (walk nicely by my side), to improving household manners, to getting started in more organized activities like the extremely popular sport of agility or the more formal work of obedience training. Enjoy!

Teaching "Heel"

Like the skill and art of dancing, the benefits of heeling stretch well beyond the exercise itself. Dancing is a wonderful form of recreation on the dance floor, but the posture, alignment, controlled energy, balance, and poise practiced in dance movements spill over into everyday tasks.

The Basics

Similarly, the heel command teaches the dog to walk at your left side, regardless of your pace or direction, and to sit when you stop. Gone are the days of her pulling ahead or dragging behind, weaving from side to side, or getting underfoot during walks. As the dog learns to heel and you learn how to teach her to move precisely, a deeper learning takes place for both of you. To remain in position, the dog's awareness, watchfulness, and willingness must grow. Since you need to watch your dog very intently during the process, you'll develop a sense of what the dog is going to do before she does it—otherwise known as reading your dog. Trust and respect develop as you and your canine partner master the art of heeling. This newly formed bond will help you channel the dog's energy more efficiently, no matter what the task, challenge, or obstacle.

Teach your dog to maintain heel position on your left side, with her shoulder aligned with yours, and her body three inches from your leg. The position is the same whether you're moving forward, turning, or stationary. When you stop, your dog should sit automatically.

Before you begin, practice sneakaways for at least one week (explained in Chapter 10), until your dog is attentive to you despite distractions. When you feel comfortable with this, begin to practice heeling. Hold the leash in your right hand with your right thumb through the loop and four fingers holding the slack just as you did during leash-length sneakaways. Command "(Dog's name), heel" as you begin walking. Prepare to stop by grabbing the collar with your right hand and using your left to place her rear end into a sitting position so her right front foot is alongside your left ankle.

As you walk along preparing to halt, control your dog's position using the fold-over maneuver. Grab the leash with your left hand and hold it taut over the dog's head, then use your right to grip the braiding or stitching of the leash just above the snap. Next, take your left hand off the leash and use it to place the dog in a sit in perfect heel position as you halt.

Forging and Lagging

If your dog forges ahead, do a leash-length sneakaway. Drop the slack of the leash, grip the handle, hold your hands at your waistline, and run away. As the dog returns to your side, return to the original leash grip, holding the slack as you continue walking.

If your dog lags behind, say "Good dog!" as you spring ahead by taking a puddle jump with your left leg first. As you do this your left thigh will pull the leash—and your dog—back to heel position. The jump ahead will also prevent the dog from crossing behind to the right side.

Enforcing Household Obedience

Maybe your dog obeys fine in the backyard and at class or in the park but won't listen in the house. That is your cue to leave the leash dragging from his collar in the house so you can stop misbehavior and enforce commands. If he does well until the leash comes off, try this intermediate step: Replace the leash with a tab and a five- to ten-foot piece of light line, and then follow this training routine.

Attach five to ten feet of light line to your dog's tab and give him commands periodically. Tell him to sit in odd places where he is allowed but has never been expected to obey—on the stair landing, or a sofa, or in the bathtub, for instance. Give commands while you wash dishes, fold laundry, wrap a gift, open mail, put on your jacket, or attach a collar and leash (have an additional collar and leash attached so you can enforce). When he is interested in what other household members are doing, or who is in the yard, at the door, or pulling into the driveway or garage, give commands. In all these situations "sit" is practical, but also utilize "down," "come," "stay," and "heel" for variety. Enforce by jerking the tab as you would a leash—jerk the tab up if you want him to sit, downward for "down," and forward for "come" or "heel."

FACT

Remember, obedience isn't supposed to be treasured like a fine crystal vase you admire and display but don't use. Anything you teach your dog should be used constantly and consistently. Wear and tear may not look good on crystal, but the more you utilize obedience, the more it becomes positively ingrained in your dog.

Of course, you'll be using the "heel" command on walks and the "come" command any time you need your dog nearby, and you probably can think of all sorts of times to use "sit," "down," and "stay" commands. Additionally, consider using the sit-stay to stop or prevent jumping up, fidgeting during grooming, or begging. Ask your dog to sit before and during petting to control shyness, apprehension, or enthusiasm, and also if he begins to pester people or other animals, before feeding, when you're putting on a collar or attaching a leash, and at street curbs. During mealtimes, ask your dog for a down-stay on his bed to keep him away from the table.

Manners: Wait, Off, Quiet, and Drop It

It's really helpful if you can teach your dog to understand some variations on the basics of sit, stay, down, come, and heel. For example, when it's time to go for a walk you can call your dog to the place where her leash is hanging and ask her to sit and stay while you put it on. Most dogs are so excited about this part of their day that it's hard for them to stay still. Asking an over-excited dog to sit perfectly still while you put on your coat, get your poop-scoop bags, put on your shoes, check for your cell phone, and so on, may result in your having to reposition her as she moves from the sit/stay several times. Instead, you can ask her to Wait, which means to remain in a specified area rather than in an exact position.

Teaching Wait

As discussed, the "stay" command means freeze in the sit, down, or stand position, and therefore is very restrictive. The "wait" command, though, allows your dog to move about, but only within certain areas. You can use it to keep your dog in the car or out of the kitchen. The only thing "wait" has in common with "stay" is that both last until the next direction is given—20 seconds or 20 minutes later.

The Basics

Teach the "Wait" command at doorways first. Choose a lightweight door and estimate how wide your dog's front end is. Open the door about two inches more than that as you say, "Wait." Stand with your hand on the knob of the partially open door, ready to bump the dog's nose with it should she attempt to pass through the opening. Be sure never to shut the door while correcting. Instead, leave the door open with your hand on the door handle, ready to stop attempted departures with an abrupt and silent bump of the door.

ALERT!

Work with your dog on a leash so that if your attempts to deter her fail and she successfully skips across the border, you can step on the leash and prevent her escape. Practice with lightweight doors until you feel confident that the timing and strength of the tap is appropriate to deter your dog. Then apply the technique at heavy or sliding doors.

Work with your dog at familiar and unfamiliar doors as a helper tries to coerce your dog to leave. Your helper can talk to the dog and drop food, but he shouldn't call your dog. As he remains on the opposite side of the door, engage in lively conversation to teach your dog that even when you are preoccupied, the "wait" command is enforced. When that lesson has been learned, you'll no longer need the leash.

Dogs Who Barrel Through Doors

If your dog waits but bounds through the door when released, mowing down anything in her path and dragging the unfortunate master gripping her leash, obedience is the last thing on her mind. This potentially dangerous situation must be resolved. To alter this behavior, after inviting her through a main door, command "Sit" immediately following her exit.

When she does it on a slack lead the first time through, start doing the same pattern with the leash dragging. If she obeys with the leash dragging, let her drag the light line, and finally try it off-lead. She should now usually proceed through doorways in a mannerly fashion, but surprise her with that "sit" command a couple of times a week to keep her sharp and attentive, and to maintain decorum.

Teaching Off

"Off" is a request that can be confusing for you and your dog. You're sitting on the sofa reading a magazine when your dog comes in and jumps up next to you. Your instinct is to say "Down," while directing him off the furniture. Think about it, though: What should "down" mean to your dog? It should mean "assume a position of lying down until I ask you to do something else." So when you say Down and push him away, you're sending a very mixed signal. That's when you need to remember to use the word Off instead. Off should mean "remove yourself from what you're on" or "get off of whatever you're jumping on." To enforce the Off command, pull him off his target with the collar or leash and praise him the instant his feet hit the ground.

Teaching Quiet or Shush

It's nice when your dog barks at the door to alert you that someone is there. It's not nice when she won't stop barking—especially if your baby is trying to sleep or you're talking on the phone. Fortunately, teaching her to shush is simple. There are three ingredients to teaching your dog to be "quiet" on command.

1. If you've been trying to silence your dog by petting her or giving her a toy, stop. You may not even realize you've been inadvertently encouraging her excessive barking, so the habit can be tough to break.
2. Leash your dog and enforce the quiet nonverbally with one of the methods described in this section. Be on the lookout for opportunities to

enforce—such as when she barks at your neighbor, a noise she hears in the distance, or just because she's bored.

3. When you are confident of your ability to quiet your dog at will, introduce the command. If you start saying "quiet" before developing a strategy, you're likely to get hoarse long before she tires of barking.

FACT

Feel free to praise and encourage your dog for appropriate barking, such as when an intruder is near. There is nothing wrong with a dog barking if you can silence her easily when necessary. But it isn't necessary for a dog's well-being that she be allowed to bark, so if you find virtually all barking disturbing or unacceptable, correct it.

There are a variety of ways to enforce quiet. If you have the leash in hand give it a quick jerk as she barks and briskly turn and walk away. Praise her for following (the leash offers her no other option) and taking her focus off of the thing that caused her to bark.

You can also carry Bitter Apple in a pocket-sized bottle to spritz her lip line in mid-bark. Have your foot on the leash and one hand on her collar to ensure an accurate spray, and praise her afterward. Never threaten her with the bottle. Be unemotional and keep it close at hand—but hidden—between uses.

No matter how you choose to enforce the quiet, follow the correction with a quick series of heel, sit, down, stay, and come commands. Not only will your dog be quite relaxed after a minute or two, her future inclination to overbark will be reduced exponentially.

QUESTION?

How can I make sure not to get Bitter Apple in my dog's eyes?
Never spray bitter apple at your dog. Use it as the dog is chewing or barking, and press the bottle against her lip line before you depress the sprayer. Keep the Bitter Apple hidden in your hand, ready for use, and before taking the bottle out of hiding, grip your dog's collar with your free hand to ensure precise application.

Teaching Drop It

Use the "Drop it" command to teach your dog to release objects from his mouth or not to pick something up. Dogs typically learn this request when it's time to give up the tennis ball during a game of fetch. Once he understands it, though, you can use it to ask him to let go of a child's toy or anything you don't want him to have in his mouth.

Some dogs, and virtually all puppies, like to chew, carry, and mouth anything they can—hands, clothing, the leash, gravel, cigarette butts, landscaping timbers, tissue. Your first reaction may be to pry his jaws open to remove it, but if you do, he'll soon be prowling for another item to grab. Teaching "Drop it" will reduce his scavenging tendency.

When you notice him eyeballing a taboo item, give your command. Accompany the "drop it" command with a prompt jerk of the leash as you quickly back away and offer to play with an acceptable object. If that doesn't work, carry Bitter Apple so you can give a spritz along with your command.

Using Hand Signals or Whistle Commands

Using something other than a verbal request to ask your dog to do something can come in very handy. For example, a snap of your fingers followed by a point to the ground could mean lie down—and wouldn't that help when you want your dog to settle while you're brushing your teeth or in mid-conversation with someone else?

Hand Signals

Teaching hand signals is easy. Always give your hand signal in a distinct way so the dog doesn't assume you are just scratching your nose or grabbing for something. Formal obedience trial regulations allow the handler to use a single motion of the entire arm and hand but penalize any body motion—something to think about! It's imperative to use clear, concise, and consistent commands if you want your dog to understand and comply. The hand signals that will be most useful are those that communicate the frequent requests like sit, down, stay, and come.

Whistle Signals

Whistles are commonly used to train hunting dogs or dogs who need to work at a distance from their handlers. That's because the sound travels so well and serves as the clear, concise form of communication that's necessary for this kind of work. Initially, though, the dog must be trained close to the handler to understand the association between behaviors and whistles. Using the leash, guide the dog in the desired movement following your whistle. As you move your dog into position, she should associate the movement with your verbal command, and because she has felt and seen the same movements, she should understand and follow the guidance eagerly. Generally, one toot of the whistle means sit and stay, and multiple toots mean come into the heel position of sitting by the handler's side.

Tricks as Fun Ways to Train

Teaching your dog a few tricks gives you both a break from the routine of the common requests—and it's a great way to impress your family and friends. Some simple ones are: Jump, Dance, and Shake.

Teaching Jump

Teaching a controlled jump is a fantastic way to burn off your dog's excess energy while bringing a smile to your face (and probably to his). Teaching the jump is easy if you have a hungry dog, a leash, and tasty but tiny treats.

Begin by positioning your dog in a sit, parallel to a barrier like a wall or a couch. Kneel next to your dog at a right angle. The first step is achieving a very low leg jump by extending your leg and putting your foot against the barrier and the floor so your dog has no option except to jump over it. Show him the treat in your far hand, and use it to lure him over your leg. Reward him for his success by giving him a treat. Reverse the process, luring him back over your leg with the other hand. (You may need to put the nonluring hand behind your back or by your side so he won't be distracted by it since it was the source of the preceding treat.) Once he's mastered this low hurdle, raise your leg in two- or three-inch increments until he's actually leaping over it.

Here are a few success-building tips:

- Try to anticipate when your dog is likely to go off course. Use the food lures or leash to keep him on track.
- Don't jerk the leash. Instead, pull it—and praise him lavishly when he responds properly.

As he gains confidence and is performing successfully, begin directing him over your calf . . . and then over an arm. Again, maintain the barrier but raise the height of the jump incrementally. Next, go back to the beginning and repeat the entire process—this time without the barrier. Once he's mastered these component jumps, take your show on the road, practicing in new locations and in the presence of increasingly tempting distractions. (Keep a line on him to maintain control.) Soon you can start mixing it up, combining various leg and arm leaps into a mini canine ballet.

Teaching Dance

Some dogs naturally love to spin, often favoring one direction over the other. Others need some prompting. Either way, here's how to turn this form of canine dancing on and off.

Begin teaching this trick in a corner to limit your dog's working area. With a tasty treat in your hand, hold it by her nose and lure her around in a tight circle. At first, reward her with treats and praise for even a partial turn. Expect a full turn after a dozen or so attempts. With a larger dog, keep your hand low so that she will twist her body around to get the treat.

After a few sessions, begin weaning her off the food, using hand signals and a leash if necessary to get her started. Then add commands, one for clockwise turns and a second for counterclockwise. Unable to contain their enthusiasm for this trick, small dogs will quite naturally want to play helicopter, spinning in midair.

Teaching Shake

This old classic is still a crowd pleaser. Sit your dog facing you, kneel in front of him and reach for his pastern (which is the equivalent of our wrist). Especially if your dog is touch sensitive or easily spooked, do this calmly and gently. Tell him how good he is as you hold his paw in both hands and move it gently up and down. Release his paw and repeat the pattern several times. Do it prior to walks or feeding so he looks forward to the routine.

When teaching your dog to shake, the first thing you need to do is interest him in giving you his paw.

After a handful of experiences, add the simple command, "Shake," or get creative and say something like "howdy doody" or "what's up" as you look at his paw and reach for it. Become more animated in your praise and shaking his paw so he knows that's what you want.

The next step is to look distinctly at his front leg and give your command as you begin reaching toward it. Hesitate for a few seconds before touching his paw. Ideally, he'll surprise you by lifting his leg and offering his paw. If not, continue practicing, and when he finally does offer his paw let's hope you have a sirloin steak waiting in his bowl to acknowledge his greatness on that day!

CHAPTER 13

Other Things to Do with Your Dog

Fortunately for today's dogs and dog owners, there are countless activities that involve both canine and human. Some are training intensive, while others are somewhat less demanding. It depends what you and your dog are into. Dogs who love what they're doing—and see that you love doing it, too— are incredibly adept at learning new things that help them get better at what they love. By working together on whatever goals you develop for your chosen sport(s), your bond will grow deeper, you'll become more accomplished as a team, and your life will be fuller for the experiences.

The Canine Good Citizen® Test

Realizing that it wasn't enough for a dog's owner to speak for him, the American Kennel Club developed a ten-point test for dogs which, when completed successfully, earns a dog the right to be called a Canine Good Citizen. A CGC-certified dog demonstrates appropriate behavior in a variety of everyday situations as opposed to performing specialized requests in a competition (formal obedience). The idea was a hit, and since its introduction in 1989, hundreds of thousands of dogs have been certified.

FACT

Just as friendships deepen through shared experiences like running together or belonging to a crafting club or being in a play, so your bond with your dog will deepen through shared experiences. There are lots of things to do together, so enjoy!

The ten parts of the Canine Good Citizen® Test are:

Test 1: Accepting a friendly stranger. This shows that your dog will willingly accept the friendly advances of a stranger.

Test 2: Sitting politely for petting. In a controlled sit, your dog should allow a friendly stranger to pet him.

Test 3: Appearance and grooming. Your dog needs to be well groomed and should welcome being gently groomed and examined by a friendly stranger.

Test 4: Out for a walk (walking on a loose lead). This shows that you can walk your dog under control without him pulling at or lunging on the leash, and that he is attentive to your presence as his handler.

Test 5: Walking through a crowd. Your dog should be able to pass by several strangers without displaying any inappropriate behavior.

Test 6: Sit and down on command and stay in place. With this test your dog will demonstrate that he understands these basic commands.

Test 7: Coming when called from about ten feet away.

Test 8:   Reaction to another dog. This shows your dog can behave politely around other dogs as a handler approaches with his dog and engages in casual conversation with you.

Test 9:   Reaction to distraction. When presented with a couple of common distractions—such as a dropped chair or cane or a person jogging by—your dog should show interest but not panic or aggression.

Test 10:   Supervised separation. The objective of this test is to see if your dog can be left on his own with a trusted person. With you out of his sight, your dog should remain calm until your return.

If you intend on making your dog a significant part of your life (especially if you live in an urban or suburban area), then taking advantage of Canine Good Citizen® testing is a very good idea. It's not only fun to learn and do, but it's valuable to be able to trust your dog and how he interacts with others. The Canine Good Citizen® Test is open to all dogs, so your friend doesn't need to be registered with the AKC to participate, even though the program is under the auspices of the American Kennel Club. Many local obedience trainers include the CGC test as part of their courses, or you can find out more about the Canine Good Citizen® Test by calling the AKC at (919) 233-9767 or visiting their Web site at *www.akc.org/events/cgc.*

Agility

Agility is the fastest-growing activity for dogs and their owners. Dogs are timed as they travel over a course that includes jumps, weave poles, ramps, A-frames, and other colorful obstacles. Their handlers guide them through the course, ordinarily running beside them to indicate which obstacle is next. Combining precision with speed, agility is just plain exciting—and dogs love it.

FACT

Agility is an all-inclusive sport, and dogs of all shapes and sizes and pedigrees can compete. Smaller dogs go over smaller obstacles, larger dogs over larger obstacles. It's great fun to watch.

Several organizations conduct agility trials across the country and around the world, including the American Kennel Club and the United States Dog Agility Association. Agility offers the opportunity to hone your training skills and compete in a sport that requires less discipline than that of formal obedience. You might compare it to the difference between learning to sing opera vs. blues, or playing with the symphony vs. a rock-and-roll band. Since Agility tends to get more exciting as you move into higher and higher levels, Agility trainers aren't as likely as Obedience competitors to have to devise clever ways to keep practice sessions fresh.

Agility is the fastest-growing canine sport, and when you see it in action—or better yet, do it with your dog—you'll understand why. All dogs can do it, it's high-energy, and it's great fun!

The American Kennel Club offers three types of classes: Standard, Jumpers with Weaves, and Fast Class. The first includes contact obstacles which are marked with yellow contact zones. To properly negotiate the obstacle the dog is required to step on or "hit" the certain zones. Jumpers with Weaves has no contact obstacles, just jumps, tunnels, and weave poles. Fast Class requires handlers to work farther away from their dogs, demonstrating an ability to take direction at a distance. All divisions award four titles: Novice, Open, Excellent, and Master. Dog/owner teams that have earned Excellent Standard and Excellent Jumper titles can compete for the Master Agility Championship title.

Obedience Competitions

In a nutshell, obedience training will make life easier for most owners. The idea is to be able to train your dog so that she can eventually be trained to comprehend and respond instantly and reliably to commands off-leash. In Obedience, there are three levels of increasing difficulty: Novice, Open, and Utility. In any trial, the dog must score 170 or more of the possible 200 points to earn her title.

1. Novice is the first level, and the title your dog earns is called a CD, which stands for Companion Dog. There are six simple exercises your dog needs to complete before she can have this title conferred upon her: stand for examination, heel on and off lead, recall, and group sit- and down-stay.
2. The Open level is a little more difficult. The exercises required are heeling off lead, drop on recall, retrieving on the flat and over a jump, broad jump, long sit, and long down. After earning three qualifying scores, your dog will have a CDX, which stands for Companion Dog Excellent.
3. Utility-level work is ranked as the hardest for good reason. These are some of the most advanced trials there are. There are five complex tasks: hand signals, scent discrimination, moving stand, directed retrieve, and directed jumping. If your dog earns three passing scores, she receives a UD, or Utility Dog, certificate. Of course, there are those overachievers who have earned a UDX (yes, Utility Dog Excellent!) and even the

OTCh (Obedience Trial Champion). Find out what your dog needs to do to earn these prestigious titles by visiting the Web site at *www.akc.org* and looking up obedience trials.

Conformation (Dog Shows)

So, you're a consummate stage mother? Maybe you bought Fido because he came from champion bloodlines, and you wanted to try your hand at showing? Maybe you've been to a dog show and it looked like fun—or maybe it's just something you want to try once. You're not alone. The AKC alone sanctioned more than 600 all-breed dog shows in 2006, in which nearly 1.5 million people competed with their dogs. Be forewarned: Dog showing is very competitive. Dog-show people are very dedicated to their sport, and don't take dabblers very seriously; however, if you are eager to try and willing to listen and learn, you will be welcomed.

FACT

Breed clubs are authorized by the AKC to set and define a breed's standard of perfection, otherwise known as the "breed standard." Clubs may choose to modify the standard to clarify ideals or to recognize new markings or colors. Sometimes they even change the name, such as when the Japanese Spaniel Club of America changed the breed's name to the Japanese Chin in 1977.

How a Dog Show Works

Dog shows are not run by the AKC; rather, they are sponsored by a licensed organization—typically a dog or breed club—that must conform to the AKC's rules and regulations regarding the conduct of dog shows, equivalent to "Robert's Rules of Order" for business meetings. There is a certain way that the dogs must be entered in the classes and presented to the judges, just as the judges are honor-bound to evaluate the dogs based on the breed's standard.

In this typical scene inside the ring at a dog show, a judge examines a Scottish Deerhound while the handler keeps the dog focused, awaiting the judge's next request.

It seems complicated, but in essence it's fairly simple. There are seven groups of breeds—Hound, Herding, Sporting, Working, Terrier, Toy, and Non-Sporting—each composed of a certain number of individual breeds. By the end of the dog show, there will be one dog representing each of the seven groups. These seven dogs compete for Best in Show.

To get to these coveted spots, the dogs go through classes within their own breed until one of them is awarded Best of Breed. Every Best of Breed (BOB) winner from a particular Group competes with the other BOB winners for the awards of Group I, II, III, and IV. Group I winners are those who go on to compete for Best in Show.

But wait—there's more! The classes that dogs in an individual breed compete in on their way to Best of Breed include:

- Puppies (6 to 9 months and 9 to 12 months)
- Novice
- Bred by Exhibitor
- American-Bred
- Open (Champions only)

Each class is also broken down by sex, with the female dogs (bitches) competing against each other and the dogs doing the same. The first-place bitches in the regular classes compete for "Winners Bitch," and the first-place dogs for "Winners Dog." These two compete in the Open class against dogs and bitches who have already earned their championship for the possible Best of Breed honor. If BOB is a dog, a bitch is also chosen as Best of Opposite Sex (BOS). If BOB is a bitch, a dog is chosen as BOS.

FACT

The dogs are judged on general appearance according to their standard, which includes things such as head, neck, forequarters, hindquarters, coat, color, gait, and temperament.

Getting Started in Showing

If you want to enjoy and be successful at showing, you need to start from the very beginning. Go to a show as a spectator only. Choose a local show where the competition might not be as intense as, say, Westminster. Talk to people. Watch the handlers. Get a program and see what it says about the dogs and the event. See if anyone showing the dog(s) you're interested in lives near you. Perhaps that person could be your mentor. Also, see if conformation handling classes are offered by a local kennel club.

There's more to showing a dog than you think! The people you see in big shows like the Westminster Kennel Club have been showing for years, so they make it look easy. Having your dog do what the judge asks at just the right time, and turning him out so he looks his best, are essential parts of showing that take time and training to master.

Before you step into a ring with your dog, you will need to learn how to properly present her. This means learning to show off the defining features of the breed. Your dog will need to be groomed to perfection. Dogs who are spayed or neutered cannot be shown. You will need to know about gaiting patterns and what the judges of your breed expect. It's a lot, but it's part of becoming a professional in this sport. Preparation on the front end will prevent unnecessary heartbreak, disappointment, and wasted money on the back end.

Professional Handlers

There are people in the dog-show sport called handlers. They make a living showing other people's dogs in competitions. Many breeders use handlers because they cannot travel all around the country, showing their many dogs. Some breeders will have more than one dog on the road. In situations like these, some breeders don't see their dogs for months and months at a time. They will sometimes fly into a city just to visit their dog and handler and watch the show, and then leave the dog with the handler and fly back home. This is the life of a champion dog for people who are serious about dog shows.

In the end, people show dogs because they love them. Don't forget about your dog(s) in the often fast-paced and seemingly political arena of the dog show.

Specialized Sports

The AKC sanctions and different clubs sponsor a variety of events that allow dogs to demonstrate what they were originally bred to do. For Labrador and

Golden Retrievers, for example, this is hunting; for Sheepdogs, it's herding; for Terriers, it's going to ground in the pursuit of vermin; and for sighthounds like Basenjis or Rhodesian Ridgebacks, it's lure coursing.

Great strides have been made in the past several decades to keep the working abilities of breeds alive and well, and these sports are where they are safely—and competitively—played out. There is nothing like seeing your Beagle work a scent trail or your Shetland Sheepdog corral a flock of geese.

FACT

A dog who is doing what he was bred to do is truly alive. You will immediately see the difference in your dog when he is engaged in something that is in his blood to do. It's an experience that's worth every effort on your part and that will fill you with love and pride.

The specialty sporting events offered by the American Kennel Club are:

- Coonhunting (Coonhounds)
- Earthdog Tests (Terriers and some Hounds)
- Field Trials and Hunting Tests (Sporting breeds and Hounds)
- Herding Trials and Tests (Herding breeds)
- Lure Coursing (Sighthounds)

Very brief descriptions of each are included here, but if any of these sound intriguing to you, be sure to find an event near you and go take a look. It may lead you to do things with your dog(s) that you never thought possible. Find out more about the individual events through the AKC's Web site, *www.akc.org,* or by doing an Internet search of the activity.

Coonhunting

If you live in the southern United States, chances are you are familiar with this sport. It tests the ability of Coonhounds to find and tree raccoons. Raccoons are nocturnal animals, so the hunts are conducted at night, with dogs and handlers going out onto a course with only a headlamp to guide them. The "music" Coonhounds make as they pick up and follow the scent of their quarry is truly magical. Coonhounds are also shown. The titles that can be earned at Nite Hunts are: CNC (Nite Champion); CGN (Grand Nite Champion); and CSGN (Supreme Grand Nite Champion). Coonhounds also compete in Bench Shows (dog shows), Field Trials, and Water Races, each specific to a particular set of abilities.

Earthdog Tests

In an entry-level earthdog test, two large mice or rats are placed safely and securely in a cage at the end of a long underground tunnel. A Terrier or Dachshund is let loose at the entrance of the tunnel. The dog is judged on his desire to do everything necessary to get to the cage. The challenge is increased as the length and direction of the tunnels change. There are three Earthdog titles: Junior Earthdog (JE), Senior Earthdog (SE), and Master Earthdog (ME).

Field Trials and Hunting Tests

These are two distinct types of competitions. Field Trials are for retrievers, spaniels, and pointing dogs. The idea is that these dogs go into a field and spot game, marking it for their companion hunters and the other dogs. These are very competitive events. The dogs are tested and judged against one another. There are two titles awarded in Field Trials—Amateur Field Champion (AFC) and Field Champion (FC).

Hunting tests tend to be more open and involve many of the sporting breeds as well as Beagles, Basset Hounds, and Dachshunds. Here, the dog is judged against a level of performance. Although hunting tests are a little less competitive, they are still an excellent means of judging dog and hunter alike. There are three titles for hunting: Junior Hunter (JH), Senior Hunter (SH), and Master Hunter (MH).

Herding Trials and Tests

The relationship with herding dogs is one of the oldest relationships humans have. Herding trial exercises are used to gauge the development of what is still a very important job for many herding dogs. The AKC separates herding dogs into four distinct groups: Shepherd (usually used with sheep and usually lead a flock); Drover (works livestock from behind, usually sheep or cattle); Livestock Guarding (they do not move livestock, but guard it from other predators); and All-Round Farm Dogs (these usually can respond quickly to different situations and can perform a number of different jobs).

The first few exercises are called tests. They measure the general innate instincts of your animal and his ability to be trained. There are six higher levels of achievement. The first two tests are Herding Tested (HT) and Pre-Trail Tested (PT). In these, your dog's abilities are judged, again, based on inborn reaction as well as certain trained functions. The next levels are progressively harder. The idea is that a dog must keep ducks, sheep, or cattle together, sometimes under very difficult circumstances. The other four are Herding Started (HS); Herding Intermediate (HI); Herding Excellent (HX); and Herding Champion (HCh).

Lure Coursing

In this competition among and between the sighthounds, dogs are released to chase a flag across an open, but rigged, course. The flag is typically a piece of brightly colored plastic, called a lure, and it is propelled over a zig-zagging course that tests the dogs' ability to keep the lure in sight while running full-speed. Sighthounds include Afghan Hounds, Basenjis, Borzoi, Greyhounds, Ibizan Hounds, Rhodesian Ridgebacks, Salukis, Scottish Deerhounds, and Whippets. The dogs are judged on overall ability, quickness, endurance, follow, and agility. There are three titles to be earned: Junior Courser (JC), Senior Courser (SC), and Field Champion (FC).

Other AKC Activities

The American Kennel Club also oversees a couple of sports that are open to all AKC-registered breeds. These include Tracking and Rally.

Tracking

Tracking tests a dog's ability to find and follow a scent over an extended distance. Courses are created in expansive rural areas where a dog may need to maneuver over fields as well as across roads and through woods.

Tracks are laid as long as five hours in advance, and the handler is not told where the track leads. The judges plot the courses the day before and on the day of the event the track is laid according to those specifications by tracklayers. The plot will indicate the length of the legs, angle and direction of the turns, and where to drop the articles that the dog will subsequently need to indicate. The plot may also include a cross-track which challenges the dog's ability to continue following the original and more aged scent.

It is a fascinating sport to watch and participate in, especially if you are interested in a vigorous, noncompetitive sport and love spending long stretches of time with your dog outside.

There are four titles, including Tracking Dog (TD); Tracking Dog Excellent (TDX); Variable Surface Tracking Test (VST); and Champion Tracker (CT). Occasionally, tracking dogs go on to do search and rescue work.

Rally

For those whose training has evolved past the Canine Good Citizen but not quite to Obedience competitions, Rally is their sport. Designed to promote a more casual learning environment—with the added challenge of being judged—rally tests a dog's responsiveness to his owner through a course stationed with certain tasks. There are typically ten to twelve stations, and some of the tasks include sit, about turn, pivot turns, face forward, moving at various paces, and so on. There are three levels—novice, advanced, and excellent—and four titles: Rally Novice (RN); Rally Advanced (RA); Rally Excellent (RE); and Rally Advanced Excellent (RAE).

Therapy and Other Neat Stuff

These dogs aren't in need of therapy—they help give it. They are the therapy. It's well known in the medical community that animal visits to long-term care facilities often bring about tremendous reactions from the patients. The dogs that make the grade for these types of assignments must be well-behaved and love affection. Therapy dogs seem to have a sense for who needs them most, though they give their all to everyone. If this is something that sounds interesting to you because you think your dog could make a difference—and you have the time to work with him and go to the place that needs you—learn more about what's involved from an organization like the Delta Society (*www.deltasociety.org*) or Therapy Dogs International (*www .tdi-dogs.org*).

Dogs who work as therapy dogs are certified to do so after receiving specialized training. They are then able to work with different kinds of people in need in different kinds of environments. You can see how this dog is responding to this boy.

Other Neat Stuff

There are other options to compete with your dog, including Flyball, Flying Disc (Frisbee), and Canine Freestyle.

Flyball is fast-paced and exciting. Dogs are run against each other in lanes. They are released onto a course that has several hurdles they must jump on their way to a flyball box. At the box, they press a lever that shoots out a tennis ball. The dogs must catch the ball and return over the hurdles. It's finish first or go home. For big and small dogs alike (with different hurdle heights) Flyball is governed by the North American Flyball Association, and it confers three different titles: Flyball Dog (FD); Flyball Dog Excellent (FDX); and Flyball Dog Champion (FbDCh).

Flying Disc (or Frisbee) events don't seem difficult to figure out. Many folks do this all the time with their pets out in the parks, right? Wrong! This stuff is fast, furious, and wicked. To see some of the top Frisbee dogs do their stunts and tricks, and compete against others, is so spectacular that the best dog/handler teams are often chosen to entertain stadium crowds. Visit *www.iddha.com* or *www.ufoworldcup.org*.

Canine Freestyle is basically dancing with your dog. That's right! Handlers and dogs pair a piece of music with a choreographed series of movements to create a dance routine, just as other dancing pairs do. The routines need to satisfy certain requirements, but artistic expression counts for a lot of points, too. Performances can be truly mesmerizing. Take a look at the World Canine Freestyle Organization's Web site: *www.worldcaninefreestyle.org*. If you are curious and impatient and just have to see people dancing with their dogs right now, search for "canine freestyle" on *www.youtube.com*.

CHAPTER 14

Traveling with Your Dog

It's a great time to be a dog. There are loads of pet-friendly hotels, great equipment for making traveling safer and easier, and more people and places that seem to understand that having a dog along is just fine—in sum, traveling with your dog has never been as easy and enjoyable. But traveling with your dog isn't limited to vacations; it is also as matter-of-fact as driving to the veterinarian's office, the groomer, or any other place you need to take your dog regularly. The fact is, none of it will be easy or enjoyable if your dog is not a good traveler.

The Go-Everywhere Dog

For those of us whose dogs enjoy joining us in our vehicle of choice on the highways and byways of our country, we can go just about anywhere. Short rides, long rides, overnighters, visits to friends and family far away—for travel-happy dogs, it's not the length of the adventure, it's the adventure itself. Just as every time you come home is cause for celebration for your dog, so is seeing you give her the invitation to join you when you pick up the keys and head for the door. Dogs who are frequent travelers are as adept at settling themselves into their "seat" as we are—and often are settled before their owners, eager and ready to get going.

If yours is a dog who loves to come along with you, there are certain things you need to do to ensure her comfort and safety—as well as your own—on every trip, no matter how far you're going. So you don't forget anything, here's a handy list of what you'll need.

1. Some form of security

Allowing your dog to be loose in the car is like driving without your seat belt. Certainly there are plenty of times it's been done and nothing's happened—and in fact for years people drove without seat belts and dogs traveled in the open backs of pickup trucks—but those days are gone. The roads are more crowded, people tend to drive faster, there are more distractions, and it's simply not possible to think that traveling without a seat belt is wise for any passenger—including your dog.

Fortunately, there are many options, from specially made seat belts for dogs that work in conjunction with human seat belts, to booster seats with safety harnesses for small dogs, to tried-and-true crates, which keep your dog confined. You may even want to use different systems for different trips.

2. A couple of old blankets or towels

Use one to cover the car's cushion where your dog will be sitting. It is so much easier to move it or bring it in and wash it than it is to try getting every dog hair off the seat before someone else needs to sit in that spot. It's handy to have a second old towel in the vehicle if you go to the park with your dog and she gets wet or muddy. If your dog travels in a crate, you'll want to put a towel or blanket in it to keep it soft and cozy for her.

A specially designed seat belt keeps this Cairn puppy safe in the back seat of a vehicle.

3. Water and a bowl

You'll feel terrible if you take your dog to the park, go on a great hike, then get back to the car and see your dog panting and exhausted and realize you don't have any water for her. Even sharing your water bottle won't satisfy her need for fresh water, and it'll only waste the water you need for yourself (not that you shouldn't try this if it's your only option). Even if outdoor exercise isn't in your travel plans, dogs need a constant source of fresh water, and it's critical you have it with you so you can offer it to her at regular intervals.

Thoroughly rinse a used gallon container and fill it with cold tap water or buy one filled with spring water. It's best to be able to have a supply of the water your dog is used to drinking to prevent any gastric upset. Whenever you need to, fill your dog's bowl with water from this container. Keep it as cold as possible by keeping it in the shade while you're parked or near the air conditioning while you're traveling. The best kind of bowl to have on the road is a collapsible bowl. It pops up and holds plenty of water when you need it, then crushes down for easy packing when you don't.

4. Poop picker-uppers

Make it a habit to have a plastic bag or newspaper in your hand when you let your dog out of the vehicle to relieve herself. It is your responsibility and obligation to clean up after your dog wherever you travel with her. Having something handy to wrap it up and throw it away in makes quick work of this distasteful (but mandatory) chore.

5. Records

No, not the old vinyl LPs, copies of your dog's health records. You may need these in case of emergency, and it's so much easier to have them available than to try to get them should you need them. You'll want a copy of your dog's immunization records to show what shots she's had and when (rabies is especially important), as well as information about any medications she may be on, your veterinarian's phone number, and an emergency backup number of someone to call should something happen to you.

If you are going on vacation with your dog, you'll obviously need to pack his medication—and don't forget his flea and tick preventative and heartworm preventative. These need to be given on a regular basis, and you don't want to miss a dose.

6. A first-aid kit

Using a pencil-case-sized plastic container, fill it with gauze bandages, vet wrap (to secure a bandage), tweezers, antibiotic ointment, premoistened antiseptic wipes, a supply of your pet's regular medication, buffered aspirin, Mylanta, a pair of pantyhose for a make-shift muzzle, and anything else you think you might need. Label it as your dog's kit and stash it somewhere safe.

7. Extra collar, leash, and ID tag

Heaven forbid your dog's collar or leash should break or become lost while on the road. You will be thankful for the spare. Keep the information on the ID tag current (include your cell phone number), and stash these in a safe place as well.

8. Treats and toys

There's something about traveling that makes you hungry for snacks, so have something suitable on hand for your friend. She may love your extra French fries, but they may not agree with her. Healthy treats that won't make a mess are best. Some dogs love to chew while traveling, so an appropriate toy will keep her occupied.

9. Food

If your travel plans include staying overnight or longer, be sure to bring enough of your dog's regular food to last the trip. Changing foods—especially while traveling—can upset your dog's stomach or keep her from eating. Dogs tend to be excited while traveling and often won't eat normally, anyway. Don't resort to "spoiling" your dog with your restaurant leftovers; it's too risky. Mixing some healthy scraps, like lean cooked meats or plain rice, into her normal food is fine and may encourage her to eat if she's fussing, but don't overindulge.

Finding Dog-Friendly Lodgings

It's a great feeling to get into your vehicle packed and ready to go on vacation and know that you don't have to drop your dog at a kennel or other boarding situation. Rather than worrying about how he'll be treated while you're gone, you can look forward to enjoying your adventures with him by your side. Whether your accommodation of choice is a tent over a sleeping bag or a suite at a five-star hotel, it is not difficult to find a place at any range of the spectrum that will welcome you and your dog.

While there are lots of great places to stay with your dog, don't presume that any place you want to stay will be one that's pet-friendly. Some places that allow small dogs won't accept larger dogs or multiple pets. Always research where to stay ahead of time, call the lodging, and talk to them about their pet policy. Make a reservation. This gives you the security you need when traveling with your dog. You certainly don't want to arrive and find the place is booked solid even though it's their slow time of year. You can also request a certain type of room—you may want a first-floor room with immediate outside access, for example.

There are several pet-travel Web sites that you can visit, but one of the most trusted is Petswelcome at *www.petswelcome.com*. It has more than 25,000 listings for hotels, B&Bs, campgrounds, resorts, and beaches, many with user reviews. There is even an Info X-Change area where people can share information about all aspects of traveling with their pets.

There are guidebooks that list pet-friendly lodgings across the United States, and these can certainly help. Searching on the Internet is a great way to see what's out there, too. Double-check all listings; the pet policies at hotels and motels can change frequently.

At Your Destination

At last, you've arrived at your destination. Let the fun begin—right? Well, yes, but not quite. When you arrive at a hotel, motel, inn, or bed and breakfast with your dog, the first thing you want to do is let her out so she can relieve herself. Be discreet, and take her to a somewhat out-of-the-way location if possible. Other arriving guests may not appreciate watching your beloved urinate on the flowers lining the walkway to the front door.

It is absolutely necessary that you pick up after your dog when she defecates on public property. Nothing will cause an establishment to retract its "dogs allowed" policy faster than the neglect of owners who don't clean up after their dogs.

With her immediate needs taken care of and her waste properly disposed of, put your dog back in the car while you check in. Until you get the feel for the establishment, don't assume that everyone staying there will think your dog is the cutest and best-behaved they've ever met and will be thrilled to see her. In fact, assume the opposite. People checking into hotels have luggage, kids, agendas, and business meetings they need to get to, and often the last thing they want to deal with is your dog wanting to say hello. Give them the benefit of the doubt and keep things as calm as possible for everyone concerned.

At the front desk, remind the staff that when you made the reservation you asked about your dog and let them know that she is with you. They will probably have a note about it. Once you've found your room and are satisfied with it, *then* get your dog and bring her (and her stuff) to join you.

Settling In

Another thing hotels don't look too kindly on is damage to their rooms by unruly pets. Soiling, chewing, excessive shedding, towels that look like they've been used to bathe the dog—all of these are reasons hotels won't allow dogs. Be considerate and conscientious during your stay. Put one of the old towels or blankets you carry on the bed if your dog is going to sleep on it. Make sure he gets plenty of exercise to release some pentup energy. Feed him in the bathroom or on a noncarpeted part of the room so any spills will be easy to clean up. Consider ordering room service so you won't have to leave him in the room by himself while you get something to eat.

Going Out

The strange smells and sounds of new environments make dogs anxious. They need to explore to become more familiar with everything before settling down. Don't think you can check in, drop your dog with your luggage in the room, and take off again. For even well-mannered dogs this can be torturous.

At the same time, your dog should be well-adjusted enough that you can trust her to stay alone in the room for a few hours. Make sure she has been sufficiently exercised, that she's relieved herself, that she's had something to eat and drink, and that there is nothing in the room that could harm her while you're out. Close the door to the bathroom, put anything she might chew on in a closed drawer or closet, leave a light on, and leave the TV on for background noise (not too loud). Be sure to put the Do Not Disturb sign on your door so the staff won't come in.

FACT

The safest and most secure way of leaving your dog in your room while you go out is to put him in his crate (another great reason to crate-train your dog). His familiar crate will help him feel at ease. Knowing that he's secured in it means you won't have to worry about him getting into anything dangerous, making a mess of the room, or accidentally escaping should the staff enter your room.

When you return, tell her what a great doggy she is and take her out immediately to stretch her legs and do her thing. Be careful walking your dog after dark. Stay on lighted walkways and pay attention to landmarks so you don't get lost. Consider that you may come across local wildlife like skunks or deer—or other people's dogs or cats. If your dog can't be trusted to handle these encounters appropriately, only walk her where it seems safest.

Airline and Other Travel

Is it safe to fly with your dog? As safe as it is for you—though certainly not as comfortable. Unless you have a very small dog that can be brought into the cabin in an approved carrier, your dog will need to be crated and put in the baggage compartment. Before you even consider doing this, you need to do extensive research. Most U.S. domestic airlines and major intercontinental airlines have policies in place to make it as safe as possible to transport pets. You should read and compare them, and try to talk to people with experience. Owners of champion show dogs often travel by air to get to the biggest shows around the country and the world.

The airlines' policies also detail their strict requirements for the kind of carrier your dog can be transported in, what can be included inside it, how it should be labeled, and so on. A dog who isn't crate-trained is in for a very unpleasant experience. Even a dog who loves his crate at home may find the experience stressful.

ALERT!

You may think you can help your dog by sedating her for a flight, but it's not true! High altitudes and sedatives are a deadly mix and should not even be considered. Study the guidelines provided by the carrier and be sure your dog is healthy before taking to the skies with her.

If you have a large dog, chances are slim that you will be allowed to travel with him by train, bus, or boat—but it's worth checking! Large or small, if you plan to or need to take a train or a bus somewhere with your dog, try to find out well ahead of time if your dog is welcome.

At the time of this writing, cruise lines do not accept dogs onboard. Typically they cross over into international waters where quarantines and other regulations make accommodating dogs too restrictive. You can find charter outfits or sightseeing tours that allow dogs, but it takes some research.

Help for the Anxious Traveler

There are dogs for whom car travel is a miserable experience. They foam at the mouth, vomit, become extremely nervous, and can even become destructive to the car, other passengers, or themselves. Because there are times when it's necessary for a dog to travel in a vehicle to another destination (such as the veterinarian), if this describes your dog, you need to help her get over her fears.

Not traveling well is the result of either not being properly exposed to a car from puppyhood or having bad experience(s) in the vehicle. Either way, it's your job to reverse the negative associations so they become positive ones.

Slow and Steady

Before a dog can relax in the car, he needs to feel comfortable near the car. Using treats, reward him for not just approaching but being able to stay near the car. Leave the car door open so he can look into it, but don't in any way force him into the vehicle. Every day, for just a few minutes a day, make being near and getting into the car rewarding and safe for your dog.

Once he's in the car, secure him with a seat belt, close the door, and get in the driver's seat. Don't go anywhere; just pet him and give him a treat or two for just being in the car. Slowly work up to starting the car and making very short trips, always ending on a good note. You can judge how he does and work up to longer trips.

For dogs who become carsick, it's important not to feed them anything for several hours before a trip. This may mean missing a meal, but that's okay. The meal won't benefit your dog if she loses it on the ride anyway.

If your dog is fine getting into the car but gets carsick or upset as the trip goes on, you will need to adjust your strategy. You will need to make some trips that end at the first signs of upset. For example, get in the car with your dog as usual and begin to drive. As soon as you notice your dog looking "off," pull over, take him by the leash and collar, and get him out of the car. The fresh air and new smells should divert and calm him so he won't be sick. After a few minutes, and with your reassurance, put him back in the car and start driving again. Drive in the direction of home, and if he makes it all the way, praise him lavishly in the car before taking him out to relieve himself or go into the house. Working this way, your dog can learn that not all car rides end badly.

CHAPTER 15

Your Dog and the Law

You may not want to think about it this way, but your dog is your property as well as your responsibility. Considering that there are fewer and fewer places in the world today where dogs can simply be let outside to "do their thing," whether it be tending the livestock or simply exploring the neighborhood, it's more and more important to understand where your rights as a dog owner begin, and where they end.

Securing Insurance

It is a smart idea to have insurance for your pet. Take care to find homeowners or renters insurance that covers pet damage and dog bites. You may also want to consider purchasing a health insurance policy for your dog.

Homeowners Insurance

You feel like you're finally living the American Dream: you're in a secure relationship, you have a wonderful German Shepherd Dog (one of the most popular breeds in the country), and you're ready to move from a rental and buy your first home. After months of searching, you and your partner have found the perfect place, and you make an offer. Next thing you know, the insurance company is giving you a hard time. Not because you can't afford the insurance, but because of the fact that you have a German Shepherd.

In most parts of the country insurance companies are within their rights to deny people homeowners insurance or charge higher premiums because they have a certain breed of dog. Even if you have been with a carrier for a long time and it's time to renew, you may be refused a policy. Dog bites account for hundreds of millions of dollars in claims every year.

FACT

According to the Centers for Disease Control and Prevention, there are 4.7 million dog bites in the United States per year, 800,000 of which are serious enough to require medical care. About half of all medically treated dog bites involve children.

Be aware that owning a bully breed can increase your risk of being denied coverage. Ask fellow dog owners in your area for recommendations for companies and agents. Another place to start is with your state's insurance commissioner, who will have a list of all the companies that supply homeowners insurance wherever you live. Speak with multiple insurance agents at different companies and ask specific questions about their policies. Find out if there are any breeds they will not cover or for which they will charge you a premium. Some companies have a blanket ban on certain breeds, while others decide on a case-by-case basis. Ask if there are any ways to lower a premium by spaying or neutering your dog or showing proof of obedience training. You may be able to sign a liability waiver for dog bites. If there is no way a company will insure your dog, look into buying separate coverage for your dog.

Renting with a Dog

Many landlords do not allow lessees to keep dogs. If yours does, do your best to be courteous. Do not allow the dog to damage the property, and make sure your dog is spayed or neutered and properly trained. You should also get renters insurance, which is similar to homeowners insurance. This will cover you if your dog happens to bite anyone. Follow the suggestions outlined previously for finding homeowners insurance.

Pet Health Insurance

Veterinary medicine is one of the few areas of medical practice in the United States that is not financially based on insurance. That means that when you walk into a veterinarian's office for care, you're expected to pay for the care you receive that day in full. When your dog is a puppy and basically healthy and your veterinary visits are limited to routine checkups, vaccine protocols, and preventive care, your bills may not seem so bad.

But pet insurance isn't based on things going normally—or even particularly well. The reality is that your dog may be perfectly healthy one day and suffer a tear of her cruciate ligament the next; or she may get hit by a car and need surgery; or she may develop a congenital health problem that needs high-cost prescriptions and frequent veterinary visits. These are the unknowns that you want to try to insure against so that the bills they incur don't bankrupt you.

To find a policy that's right for you, consult your veterinarian, breeder, or rescue organization for recommendations on pet health insurance companies. Evaluate your needs and research the policies. Find out whether the plan includes the following:

- routine wellness
- vaccines

- spaying or neutering
- dental cleaning
- surgery and hospitalization
- prescription medication
- flea and heartworm preventives

Inquire about waiting periods, coverage for preexisting conditions, deductibles, and insurance caps. The most basic plans cost about $150 per year, while more extensive coverage can cost more than $500 per year. Either of these figures is less than what you would pay for a health emergency. Surgery, hospitalization, tests, and medication can easily cost you thousands of dollars without insurance.

Breed-Specific Laws and Legislation

Confess: Do you think Pit Bulls will maul to kill if incited to? Do you think a Doberman is an inherently dangerous breed? Would you worry if you owned a Yorkie and your neighbor owned a pair of German Shepherds? In all honesty, everyone harbors breed prejudices, born out of experience or media hype. Local legislators in some parts of the country have enacted laws regarding certain breeds. Most often, these include bully breeds that have received bad press for attacking people.

Some cities impose bans on certain breeds. Others require that owners of certain breeds get permits for their dogs and comply with regulations. Requirements may include spaying or neutering your dog, purchasing liability insurance, paying a higher licensing fee, and muzzling your dog in public. Find out what restrictions your city, county, or state has regarding dogs.

Breed-specific discrimination exists everywhere. The American Kennel Club actively assists clubs and individuals all around the country who face such problems. If you have any concerns about this issue, visit the AKC Web site at *www.akc.org/canine_legislation/index.cfm.*

If Your Dog's a Nuisance

If your neighbors are complaining about your dog because he's barking, roaming, fence-chasing, or fouling the sidewalks or peoples' yards, you have a problem. Your situation may soon escalate from slight misunderstanding to vendetta—with you and your family in the middle of the debate.

Barking

The truly frustrating thing about a barking problem is that it usually happens when you're away—in which case you may not have a real understanding of how serious the problem is. Then again, maybe you do. If you are always away when the barking occurs, you should put a tape recorder on so you can find out what's really going on. When does your dog start barking, and for how long does he bark?

Think about what's causing your dog to bark—loneliness, boredom, habit? Are you trying to make things as safe and comfortable for him as possible when you're gone? Is he confined to a room where there's not a lot of motion by the window(s)? Have you created some "white noise" to muffle the outside noises by leaving a fan on low or putting the radio on an easy listening or classical music station? Have you provided a desirable chew toy or something to occupy your dog in your absence?

FACT

If you want more information about the legal rights of dog owners, as well as perspectives on responsible dog ownership, check out the Web site of the American Dog Owner's Association (ADOA) at *www.adoa.org.*

If you're doing all this and there is still a problem, you need outside help. Contact a professional dog trainer and talk to her about how to solve the problem. The trainer will probably want to work with you and the dog, which may include visits to your home. It's important that your neighbors and possibly the police know that you are actively working to correct the problem.

Roaming and Fouling

It's nice to think about dogs living "freely"—able to meander at will, knowing which neighbors are friendly with treats and which aren't, having playmates they pal around with and certain spots in which they like to sleep, showing up for regular meals at their "real" house. Maybe it was like that for dogs once upon a time. But not anymore, and for a reason. Most parts of the country are too densely populated. Free-roaming dogs pose risks to traffic, other animals (including livestock), property, sanitation (by fouling wherever), and people (should they become aggressive or frightened).

Leash laws, licensing laws, dog-bite laws, and pooper-scooper laws are all ways to keep the peace in neighborhoods and other public places. You may walk your dog around the block off-leash because she listens so well and understands the rules of the road, but if one day you encounter a strange dog being walked on a leash and your dog runs up to say hello, frightens the dog, and inadvertently starts a fight, you're responsible.

To help people overcome their instinctual revulsion at having to pick up after their dogs, there are all kinds of products that make the job easier. These include pooper-scoopers, scented plastic baggies, even contraptions that can be buried in your yard where the waste will naturally decompose.

Similarly, some people find picking up their dog's feces so revolting they can't bring themselves to do it. When they walk their dog(s), they leave the feces. While they may justify to themselves that theirs is only one dog and can't make that much of a mess, it's easy to imagine how unsanitary and disgusting the sidewalks and areas around them would be if everyone made this same excuse. That's why towns make and enforce these laws and others—to protect everyone.

Aggression and Fence-Running

Dogs who charge at passers-by from behind a fence or who are quick to display aggressive behavior frighten others in the neighborhood. It's not okay that *you* don't mind your big, young dog's enthusiastic leaping at people or snapping and snarling as he runs along the fence. Both these situations are potentially dangerous: What if one day your dog gets out and actually attacks what's seemingly provoking him? What if your dog jumps on a child wanting to play and next thing you know he has the child pinned? Situations like these that appear to start off innocently enough have led to death. Before you have a neighborhood mutiny on your hands or people just stop visiting you, learn how to control your dog. Visit the Association of Pet Dog Trainers at *www.apdt.com*. You can learn how to choose a trainer in your area that will work for you.

In our relatively litigious society, there is never a shortage of reasons or excuses for lawsuits, many involving the care of animals who can't speak for themselves. For more detailed coverage of the common legal issues introduced in this chapter, check out *Every Dog's Legal Guide: A Must-Have Book for Your Owner* by Mary Randolph.

Working through a nuisance problem is one of the toughest challenges you'll face—with your dog, your family, your neighbors, and your community. You may feel all alone, frustrated beyond reason, even hopeless. Remember that your dog is sensitive to your moods and feelings toward him. If he senses that leaving him is stressful for you, he may feel stressed, which can contribute to the problems. Keep this in mind when the situation seems grim: If you work through this, you will have solved a problem (instead of ditching it), and you will have saved a life—that of your dog. It's worth it for both of you.

Your Dog and Your Will

Sure, you love your dog and have a special relationship with him. But if something happened to you, who would care for him in a way you could feel good about? The person you have in mind may not be a relative, and it may be someone you know only through your dog (like your dog's breeder, perhaps). If you have any concerns about how your dog will be kept and treated if for some reason you couldn't care for him, you need to take legal action to ensure that he will be entrusted to the person you select and not someone selected for you.

For many older people—and truthfully, for anyone—the reality is that their dog may outlive them. Dogs can be provided for in a will where the terms of the care are specified.

The other thing your dog will need is a certain amount of money entrusted for his care. You may think that Mrs. Clark will take excellent care of your dog, but making sure she has the money to do so can almost guarantee it.

It's best to name two caregivers in your will in case something happens to one of them. You can also specify that the executor of the will may place your dog with another responsible person should both your choices fall through, or that the majority of the beneficiaries can appoint a new animal caregiver. It's complicated but important, so be thorough and specific about your wishes.

Another option is to establish a legal trust fund for your dog. An appointed trustee would be responsible for monitoring the caretaker you chose for your dog over time. Few states currently allow a pet to be named as a beneficiary of a trust, though they will enforce a trust for the pet should the trustee be found negligent. The Humane Society of the United States lists the states that do allow and enforce pet trusts on its Web site at *www.hsus.org*.

The Partnership for Animal Welfare (*www.paw-rescue.org*) has some great advice for people who want to be well prepared in case of emergency. This is important to think about if you have dogs who are relatively easy to care for, but critical if any of your dogs are special needs—on various medications, for example.

FACT

Making provisions for your dog in case anything happens to you may not be the most comfortable for you, but it is necessary. It can certainly give you peace of mind. An excellent book on the subject is *When Your Pet Outlives You: Protecting Animal Companions After You Die,* by David Congalton and Charlotte Alexander.

The first step is to identify the person or people who will take care of your dog if anything happens to you. Ask them if they would be comfortable fulfilling such a role, and make sure they understand everything it would entail. If they live close to you, give them a key to your home and tell them where to find your veterinarian's contact information and your dog's medical history. If they live farther away, you will have to ask someone else to take care of your dog in case of an emergency. Make sure you list these people on your emergency contact information at work, and enter their phone numbers into your cell phone as "in case of emergency" listings. Alert your veterinarian to the people who will take care of your dog in your absence so your dog can continue to receive care.

You may come up against some resistance when you want to address the care of your pet in your will, but don't be intimidated or made to feel silly. People say things in nonemergency situations that they might not when catastrophe strikes. Dogs and other pets are often the first to be "cast off" when their owners pass away, even by well-meaning family members. Don't take a chance that yours could meet that fate.

Your Dog and Divorce

It is simply not fair that dogs become casualties in divorce situations, yet it happens so often! Why? Because there is so much else to take care of, and often someone is forced to move, frequently to places that may not take dogs. The truth, though, is that your dog can help you heal from divorce possibly better than any other person or animal in your life at the time. Dogs are forgiving, generous, honest, present, and comforting. A dog can give you a purpose when you may feel lost and all alone—she may be the only one you have to care for when the dust settles, and though you might find it an imposition at first, you'll be thankful for it in time.

FACT

It is often difficult for children to understand and accept their parents' divorce. If there is a lot of arguing in the household, a dog can quickly become a child's source of solace and safety. The dog may be the only family member the child truly trusts, and separation from the dog can be another major blow to a child of divorce. Parents are wise to do all they can to maintain the connection of the child to the dog even if it complicates matters.

Managing to keep your dog through a divorce may mean asking a relative or friend to care for her for a while. It may mean moving in with someone you don't want to move in with until you can find a place that accepts both you and your dog. It may mean hiring a dog walker because you have to work especially long hours. You may even feel you're not being fair to your dog, but what are your options? If you think surrendering her to a shelter or rescue will be better for her in the long run, visit a shelter or call a rescue organization and talk to them to see if it is a feasible option.

CHAPTER 16

Your Dog's Health

There is nothing better than seeing your dog in great health, living life to the fullest. Her eyes are bright, her skin and coat are soft and lustrous, her energy is right, she is ready for any adventure that comes her way—in sum, she is a healthy, happy dog. When you love your dog, there is nothing worse than watching her suffer with itchy skin, chronic ear infections, gastrointestinal upset, or any number of things that can take your dog off her game. This chapter will help you better understand the common health problems dogs face and how to cope and deal with them.

Basic Preventive Care

Most of the early chapters in this book tie in to the basic preventive care your dog needs to be and stay healthy. What does preventive care mean? It means taking care of your dog the way you take care of yourself. It means:

- Brushing him regularly
- Checking his eyes, ears, and mouth regularly
- Keeping his toenails short
- Feeding him a high-quality diet
- Making sure he always has access to cool, clean water
- Keeping his environment clean
- Giving him the attention and exercise he needs
- Spaying or neutering your dog
- Keeping him current on all his vaccines
- Taking him for a regular veterinary checkup at least once a year

Preventive care means being aware of and in touch with your dog's physical and mental condition. It means doing all you can to prevent your dog from becoming ill. Even with sound preventive care, though, things happen. Through your attention to detail and to slight changes in your dog's demeanor, you can hopefully catch a health issue before it gets too serious. This chapter examines common problems particular to a dog's bodily systems so you can help determine what may be ailing him.

Common Problems of the Skin

The dog's skin is a dynamic and vital organ. No matter if your dog is short- or longhaired, her skin is always shedding dead cells and replacing them with new ones. The skin is made of two layers: the epidermis, or outer layer of skin cells, and the dermis, or second layer. A dog's skin is prone to many problems that can affect either or both layers of skin—most notably, itching, hair loss, swelling and inflammation, and flaking. Because skin problems are often the most visible and pronounced of ailments afflicting dogs, it's not surprising that they represent a large percentage of the overall cases referred to veterinarians.

Scratching and Itching

While all animals occasionally scratch themselves (including we humans!), excessive or constant scratching or itching is the sign of a problem. The most common causes are fleas, hypersensitivity (an immunologic or allergic reaction), and pyoderma (a bacterial infection). If the underlying cause isn't determined, the condition can grow increasingly worse.

At the first signs of itching, check your dog for fleas. You can do this by moving the fur backwards and looking for fleas themselves or for "flea dirt"— the digested blood fleas excrete that indicates their presence. If your dog has fleas, you will need to remove them from her body and from the environment.

Some dogs are so sensitive to flea bites that they develop flea allergy dermatitis. The dog develops an immunologic hypersensitive reaction to the saliva injected by the flea when it feeds on the dog. By constantly licking, scratching, and chewing at her skin, the dog develops areas of hair loss, which can further progress to open sores that lead to infection. The area most affected seems to be the base of the tail and lower back.

Flea allergy dermatitis typically develops when a dog is three to five years old, and it can be extremely tough to reverse, even if your dog is flea-free! The sooner your veterinarian can diagnose the condition, the sooner you can begin treatment and hope to alleviate the symptoms. Treatment will involve being vigilant about keeping your dog and home flea-free, the use of special shampoos, dips, or ointments to prevent itching, and possibly a prescription for anti-inflammatory drugs.

Your dog's itching may be caused by an infestation of mange, another external parasite that aggravates the skin. If there is no sign of fleas on your dog or in your home, you can suspect mange. A skin scraping and examination by your veterinarian will confirm the condition if it exists, and you can begin treatment.

Allergies

Dogs can also develop immunologic hypersensitivities to foods—anything from beef to wheat to dairy. This is why so many premium diets feature ingredients such as lamb, rice, or turkey—protein sources to which dogs are less sensitive.

A hypersensitivity reaction to things in the environment, such as certain fabrics, detergents, molds, or fungi, usually means the dog is allergic to that thing. Symptoms usually develop when the dog is one to three years old and begin to show in the spring or fall. Areas of the body most affected include the face, stomach, paws, and, oddly enough, the creases of the elbows. If your dog is constantly rubbing his face, licking and scratching his paws, or itching his tummy or elbows, you should suspect an allergic hypersensitivity. Left untreated, the itching will lead to areas of broken, exposed skin that are ripe for infections. Often, paw licking will develop into a behavioral habit, perpetuating the condition.

Because of the enormous number of potential allergens in the dog's environment, your veterinarian will need to evaluate your dog's symptoms carefully and perform blood and skin tests to try to determine the allergen. Once this is pinpointed, elimination of the source is necessary, and you will probably need to use special shampoos and ointments to alleviate itching.

Infections

Bacterial infection is the result of skin that's under attack and losing the battle. The skin of a healthy dog has certain bacteria that live on its surface and within each hair's follicle. This "good" bacteria wards off infection by "bad" bacteria. But when something happens to disrupt the balance, harmful bacteria invade and proliferate, causing serious infection and some severe and very painful problems.

Hot Spots

These are quarter-sized areas of red, moist, swollen sores, typically found on longhaired dogs during warm, humid weather. They can be caused by the dog's licking itself in response to some other problem such as a parasitic infection or general hypersensitivity. Often the cause goes undiscovered. Treatment involves applying antibiotic ointment to the wound and using an Elizabethan collar on the dog so she cannot reach the spot to continue licking or chewing at it.

Skin-Fold Pyoderma

Dogs with areas of thick, folded skin on their bodies, such as Chinese Shar-Pei, Bloodhounds, Mastiffs, Pugs, and others, can develop infections in between the folds. That's because the fold creates a warm, moist spot—prime breeding grounds for bacteria. Regular inspection of the folds can help prevent infection, and antibiotic ointment can help treat it.

Another spot bacteria may breed rapidly is between the toes, and this is only exacerbated by the dog's licking. Scratches or cuts to the skin between the toes often go unnoticed, which can also lead to infection. Again, good grooming habits can go a long way toward preventing this condition.

Seborrhea

When there is an imbalance of new cell growth to replace dying cells, the result is a thickening of the skin with noticeable shedding of the dead cells. This is called seborrhea. Symptoms include extreme flakiness, an overall greasiness to the skin and coat, an unpleasant and persistent odor to the coat, itchiness, and bald patches of thick skin. The causes of seborrhea include hormonal imbalance, parasitic infection, excessive bathing or grooming, and nutritional disorders—all factors that contribute to the skin's not being able to properly regulate itself. Diagnosis is fairly simple, but treatment can be quite involved and may necessitate antibiotics, special shampoos, and anti-inflammatories.

Common Problems of the Eyes, Ears, and Mouth

These areas of the face are often the first line of defense for a dog. Think about it—if you were closer to the ground and spent most of your time sniffing and digging around to find out what was happening in your world, your eyes, ears, and mouth would be at greater risk of injury or infection, too.

Eyes

Eyes and their surrounding tissues are susceptible to a number of problems. Dogs have three eyelids: top and bottom, and a third eyelid called the nictitating membrane, an extra layer of protection against the elements. The eyelids and the nictitating membrane all produce tears to lubricate the eye.

If one or both of your dog's eyes is tearing excessively, suspect a problem. It could be that a speck of dust or dirt or a grass seed has lodged between the eyelid and the eyeball. If you can see the particle, you can try to remove it with blunt tweezers or a moistened paper towel or cotton ball. To help the eye heal, apply some antibiotic ophthalmic ointment just inside the lower lid. Likewise, if an eye appears red or swollen, the dog may have an infection caused by a foreign body. It is best to consult your veterinarian if such a condition exists.

Entropion and Ectropion

Sometimes eye irritation is caused by a congenital defect of the eyelid. If the eyelid rolls inward, causing the eyelashes to aggravate the eye, the condition is called entropion. When the eyelid rolls outward, the condition is known as ectropion. Dogs with ectropion have exposed eyelid tissue that's particularly prone to damage and infection. Entropion and ectropion are both common congenital defects that require surgical repair.

Conjunctivitis

The membrane that lines the inner sides of the eyeball up to the cornea is called the conjunctiva. If it becomes infected, you'll notice a discharge from the corner of the dog's eye. The discharge may be clear and watery or opaque and thick. Typically this is the result of a bacterial infection. Your veterinarian can give you the best diagnosis.

Eye Problems of Older Dogs

As your dog ages, she becomes prone to dry eye and cataracts. As the name implies, dry eye is a condition in which the surface of the eye appears dull instead of shiny and bright. Dry eye is a condition of the tear glands, indicating that something is at fault with them. Consequently, they cannot supply the moisture necessary to lubricate the eye properly, which in turn leads to infection. Your veterinarian may be able to stimulate the tearing mechanism, or artificial tears will be prescribed.

Cataracts are clouding of the cornea that lead to blindness. They usually appear as milky colored or bluish-gray spots in the dog's eye. All older dogs are prone to developing cataracts. Other dogs at risk are diabetic dogs and dogs with a congenital problem that causes cataracts to form early.

The Ears

Dogs' ears come in all shapes and sizes, from small and erect to long and pendulous. The most common problems they're susceptible to are cuts, hematomas, and infections. Many breeds' ears are cropped both to enhance appearance and to reduce the incidence of ear infection.

The Inner Ear

The skin of a healthy inner ear should be pink with some waxy light-brown secretion in the ear canal. If you notice your dog scratching at his ears, excessively rubbing the side of his face against the floor or other surfaces, or whining with discomfort when you stroke around his ears, suspect an infection or other problem. The skin that lines the ear canal is the perfect host for bacteria, which thrive in warm, moist environments. Dogs who swim regularly, who live in humid environments, who have long, hairy ears, or whose ears are not regularly inspected for excessive dirty wax buildup can easily develop an infection. Your veterinarian will diagnose it and give you instructions for treatment.

ALERT!

Ear mites can be another source of itchy, inflamed inner ears. These microscopic parasites also like warm, moist environments, where they feed on skin flakes. A scraping at the vet's office will confirm this diagnosis.

The Outer Ear

Ear flaps are most prone to cuts, bites, and hematomas. As long as a cut is not deep, it is simple to treat by cleaning it thoroughly and applying antibiotic ointment. Often dogs involved in a fight will get their ears bitten. If the bite is deep, take the dog to the veterinarian; otherwise, wash it thoroughly, apply antibiotic ointment, and monitor it for infection.

Hematomas are the result of a pooling of blood in the ear flap. This can happen after a dog shakes her ears violently, scratches them excessively, or knocks them against a sharp object. Consult your veterinarian about the best way to deal with a hematoma.

Deafness

Some breeds of dogs have genetic defects that cause them to either be born deaf or develop deafness at an early age. Conscientious breeders will test their dogs if they suspect a problem and remove affected dogs from their breeding programs. This is most common in Dalmatians and some Terrier breeds. Older dogs lose some or all of their hearing. They still manage to get around in familiar, safe environments, but special care should be given to them.

The Nose

First of all, forget the folk remedy that says a dog with a warm, dry nose is sick. Yes, a dog's nose should typically be cool and moist, and if it's not, the dog may have a fever. But some sick dogs will have cool, runny noses. Regardless, the nose is an all-important organ to the dog. Smell is her most acute sense; through it she learns the most about her environment and the other creatures in it.

Runny Nose

Because the nose itself doesn't have any sweat glands, when a dog is excited or sick, the nasal mucous membrane will secrete water. Only secretions that persist for several hours indicate a problem.

Sneezing

This indicates an irritation to the front of the nasal cavity (coughing or gagging means the irritation is further back). It could be the inhalation of dust or dirt, which would cause the dog to sneeze several times and then stop, or it could indicate a fever or infection if it persists. If the sneezing is accompanied by discharge from the nose and/or eyes, see your veterinarian.

The Mouth

The dog's mouth is made up of the lips, teeth, gums, and tongue. It is the passageway to the esophagus. While the lips and tongue can be injured by cuts or burns, injury and disease most commonly affect the teeth and gums, and it is on these that you must concentrate.

Teeth

The average adult dog has forty-two teeth in her mouth (this can vary by breed, with shorter-faced breeds having fewer teeth). With improper oral hygiene, the teeth can become encrusted with plaque and tartar, leading to smelly dog breath, inflamed or infected gums, tooth loss, and general deterioration of the mouth.

Because of the high incidence of dogs suffering from periodontal disease, veterinarians and others in the pet industry have gone out of their way to educate owners and provide them with materials that make taking care of their dogs' teeth easy.

During your annual checkups at the veterinarian's office, the doctor can advise you whether your dog's teeth need to be surgically scraped to have any lingering or stubborn tartar removed. Since this procedure requires anesthesia, discuss it with your vet at length before subjecting your dog to it.

When they're young, dogs have stain-free, shiny teeth. To keep them looking that way (for beauty and health reasons), you should brush them several times a week with a toothpaste made especially for dogs.

Gums

Healthy gums are pink and should be firm. Red, swollen, painful gums are a sign of gingivitis and require immediate attention. Your veterinarian will probably need to scrape your dog's teeth to remove offending tartar, after which you'll need to aggressively brush and inspect your dog's teeth. Severe gingivitis can lead to infection and tooth decay.

Choking and Gagging

If your dog starts to choke or gag, there may be something caught in the back of his mouth. If possible, try to remove the object yourself. If it's lodged too firmly and your dog is struggling and choking, take him to the veterinarian immediately. Try to calm and reassure the dog.

Common Problems of the Digestive System

This system is made up of the esophagus, stomach, small intestine, liver, gall bladder, spleen, colon, rectum, and anus. The problems most typically associated with this system include vomiting, bloat, diarrhea, constipation, flatulence, and anal sac disorders. Every dog will experience upsets of the digestive system in the course of her life; most problems are easily treated and symptoms resolve within hours or days.

FACT

Older dogs experience a certain amount of incontinence. It is a natural part of aging. Older dogs tend to experience bladder control problems first. Owners need to be understanding in these instances. Lack of bowel control also follows with some dogs. Veterinarians can often prescribe medicines to help dogs control these functions and return them to some normality.

Vomiting

Dogs sometimes gag and throw up as a matter of course. The most common cause of vomiting is simply overeating, or eating so quickly the food is gulped down and then comes back up again. Dogs will also commonly vomit after eating grass, and some dogs get carsick. If your dog infrequently vomits what's obviously partly digested food or chewed grass or is distressed by the car, don't worry about it.

This doesn't mean that if your dog is vomiting it shouldn't concern you. If it relates to anything unusual, or if you notice blood in the vomit, or if the vomiting is severe and frequent, make an appointment to see the veterinarian immediately. These are signs that your dog is truly not well.

Bloat

This condition is also called gastric dilatation, which is exactly what it is: a swelling up of the stomach due to gas, fluid, or both. When the stomach fills up this way, it is prone to twisting, which quickly leads to shock and death. The exact cause of bloat is unknown, but it's suspected that dogs can develop bloat by eating too much dry kibble, exercising vigorously after eating, or gulping their food or their water. Some breeds seem prone to it, and it appears to run in some breed lines. Dogs experiencing bloat become restless, drool heavily, try to vomit or defecate unsuccessfully, and cry in pain when their stomachs are palpated. It is imperative to get your dog to the veterinarian as soon as possible if you suspect bloat.

As your dog enters his older years, he'll need some help so that accidents don't happen in places where you don't want them. Baby gates might be a good idea to keep your long-time friend out of rooms where incontinence might create a real problem for you. Remember, older dogs often lose bladder or bowel control without even knowing it.

Diarrhea

Like vomiting, the type and consistency of diarrhea vary depending on what's really wrong with the dog. When all is normal, the dog eats and drinks and her digestive system absorbs nutrients from the food and water and passes along undigested materials in the stool, which should be firm and consistent in color. Any irritation to the intestines or the bowel will trigger diarrhea. These irritations can vary from a change in food or water to overexcitement to eating something that can't be digested or is toxic or that produces an allergic response. The color, consistency, odor, and frequency of the diarrhea can help you and your veterinarian determine the underlying cause and set about providing the proper treatment.

ALERT!

Certain medications can cause loose stools, so be sure you ask your veterinarian and read about the potential side effects whenever your dog is on a prescription medication. Better to know ahead of time that this may happen than be surprised or unduly worried.

Constipation

If you notice your dog straining to defecate, or even whimpering or whining while doing so, with the result being no passing of stool, your dog is constipated. Most cases of constipation are caused by inappropriate diet, which causes stools to form improperly and either block the colon or be painful to pass. Try giving your dog one-half to two tablespoons of a gentle laxative such as milk of magnesia. This can be tricky, as dogs don't like the taste. The best way to give it is to measure the amount into a syringe or turkey baster so you can direct the medicine to the back of the dog's throat without getting your fingers in the way. Once squirted in, close the dog's mouth so he is forced to swallow. Then take the dog out often so you don't risk an accident in the house. If you don't get results in about twelve hours, consult your veterinarian.

Flatulence

Having an overly flatulent dog is no fun! Through no fault of his own, a dog who passes gas can clear an entire room in no time. Peeyew! While it is normal and natural for all creatures to pass some gas, excessive flatulence is a problem. You can most likely chalk your dog's flatulence up to inappropriate diet. A diet high in meats, fermentable foods such as onions, beans, or even some grains or dairy products can lead to excess gas. Review your dog's diet carefully, including the ingredient list of his dog food, and slowly integrate a diet change. If this doesn't yield results, your veterinarian can help.

Anal Sac Disorders

Dogs have two anal sacs, one on each side of the rectum at about 5 and 7 o'clock, commonly called "scent sacs." They secrete a distinctive odor that leaves the dog's scent when she defecates. If the sacs become blocked, they can become sore and infected and will need to be expressed. If your dog frequently scoots across the floor dragging her bottom or wants to lick the area often, suspect an anal sac problem and ask the vet to show you how to handle expressing them to relieve the buildup—or have the procedure done by your veterinarian or professional groomer. They have experience with it and can probably handle this messy, smelly task better than you can.

Common Problems of the Respiratory System

Dogs breathe through their respiratory system, a series of airways that comprise the nasal passages, throat, windpipe, and bronchial tubes that lead to the lungs. Any of the following symptoms indicate a problem in the system: rapid breathing, noisy breathing, and coughing.

Rapid Breathing

Dogs will breath heavily and rapidly in a number of circumstances, such as after strenuous exercise, in excessive heat, or if they're excited or stressed. If your dog is breathing rapidly while at rest and you can't attribute her condition to any of these other factors, consult your veterinarian.

Noisy Breathing

This includes wheezing, sneezing, labored breathing, hoarseness, and any odd sound the dog makes while trying to breathe. Owners of some short-faced breeds live with this problem. Their dogs have shorter airways and will regularly snort, snore, or breathe heavily. For other dogs, noisy breathing is generally due to an obstruction, though it can also indicate a lung disease or heart failure. It's best to have your veterinarian listen and look.

Coughing

Coughing results from the effort to extricate an obstruction in the airways, whether it's a bone chip, a collapsed windpipe, or fluid buildup in the lungs caused by a respiratory disease such as kennel cough. Kennel cough is highly contagious between dogs and can spread rapidly at a dog show or in a kennel. There is a vaccine to help prevent kennel cough, and if it's caught early, treatment is successful.

Common Problems of the Circulatory and Nervous Systems

At the center of the circulatory system is the all-important heart, a muscle that pumps blood to the rest of the body. Diseases that affect the canine heart include birth defects, aging, infectious disease, and heartworms. Heartworm is a condition that can be deadly, but is easily avoided by giving regular preventive heartworm medication.

All activity in the nervous system generates from the brain, the spinal cord, and the peripheral nerves. Spinal cord diseases, seizures, head injuries, and paralysis are some of the problems that can result from injury or disease of this system.

Seizures and Epilepsy

A seizure is caused by a sudden burst of electrical activity in the brain, affecting the entire body by causing uncontrolled convulsions: foaming at the mouth, jerking of the limbs, snapping of the jaws, rolling of the eyes. Depending on the seizure's severity, the dog may collapse and slip into unconsciousness. Seizures can be caused by trauma to the brain or the healing associated with it, or by a hereditary condition.

Epilepsy is a state of recurrent and similar seizures that typically happen in three phases: sudden restlessness accompanied by chomping or foaming at the mouth; falling to the ground with head thrown back, pupils dilated, and slobbering and drooling; and a recovery phase in which the dog is disoriented. The more violent phases, one and two, happen in just a few minutes; the recovery phase may last hours. You must consult with your veterinarian and your dog's breeder if your dog has epilepsy.

Paralysis

Complete paralysis is the result of permanent damage to the spinal cord, but a dog can experience partial paralysis due to a spinal cord disease or infection. Advances in canine care have led to the development of support systems for dogs with partial paralysis. These include specially designed carts and lift mechanisms so your dog can continue to get around.

Lyme disease, which is caused by a tick bite, can cause a form of paralysis in which the effects come on slowly, impairing movement to the point of paralysis. A speedy diagnosis is key to recovery. Normally the paralysis resolves with treatment by antibiotics.

Common Problems of the Musculoskeletal System

Bones and muscles support the body and protect the internal organs. All dogs, regardless of size, have an average of 319 different bones in their bodies. The bones are connected by ligaments and surrounded by muscles.

If your dog is limping or is favoring a particular leg, chances are he's got a bone or joint disease, a strained muscle or tendon, or possibly a broken bone. The causes range from something as severe as a congenital disorder, such as hip or elbow dysplasia, to something as ordinary as a strained muscle or age-related arthritis. Your veterinarian should give you a professional diagnosis.

Hip Dysplasia

Canine hip dysplasia (often referred to as CHD or just HD) is a disorder of the hip socket. In a healthy hip, the head of the thigh bone (femur) should fit snugly in the hip socket (acetabulum). If the ligaments around the socket are loose, the head of the femur will start to slip from the socket. This causes gradual hind-end lameness and pain. Treatment varies depending on the age of the dog, the severity of the condition, and the options available to dog and owner. Rapid advances are being made in the treatment of hip dysplasia.

While a specific cause of CHD has not been identified, it is suspected to be an inherited disorder, and breeders are encouraged to X-ray their dogs before breeding and to only breed dogs that have been certified free of the disease. It has happened, however, that CHD-free parents have produced pups that develop hip dysplasia. Weight, nutrition, and environment have all been implicated in the possible exaggeration or development of CHD, which normally manifests at an age of rapid growth.

FACT

The Orthopedic Foundation for Animals was established in 1966 to study and improve the condition of canine hip dysplasia. Now in its forty-first year, the Foundation's expanded mission is ". . . to improve the health and well-being of companion animals through a reduction in the incidence of genetic disease." Learn more about them at *www.offa.org*.

Arthritis

Millions of dogs in the United States are living with this painful degenerative joint disease. The vast majority of these dogs are seven years or older. Dogs with arthritis usually show the following signs:

- Stiffness when getting up or lying down
- Lowered activity level
- Reluctance to walk very far or to climb stairs
- Flinching or snapping when touched
- Swollen joints that seem hot or painful

Arthritis doesn't have a cure, but a number of medications are available to relieve the pain of those achy-breaky joints. Your veterinarian can prescribe a nonsteroidal anti-inflammatory drug (NSAID) to relieve pain and inflammation. These drugs are similar to the ibuprofen or acetaminophen you might take for yourself, but they're formulated specifically for dogs. In fact, your ibuprofen or other NSAID can be toxic to your dog, so never give her anything like that without your veterinarian's okay. Canine NSAIDs are generally safe, but they can have side effects—vomiting, diarrhea, and liver or kidney damage—and some dogs (Labs in particular) are highly sensitive to them. Your veterinarian may need to adjust the dose or try a different drug if your dog develops these problems, and she will probably require periodic blood work to check liver and kidney values before renewing a prescription.

If you have a small dog, lift her on and off furniture throughout her life, but especially as she gets older. This helps prevent cumulative damage to her joints. Keep your dog's weight at a healthy level to reduce stress on the joints, and consider providing your dog with a heated bed. Warmth is one of the best ways to relieve joint pain.

Common Problems of the Urinary and Reproductive Systems

The components of the urinary system are the bladder, prostate, and urethra, as well as the kidneys and ureters. The system works together. The two kidneys' jobs are to siphon excess waste created by ordinary metabolism, and regulate water and minerals. Wastes are deposited into the ureter, which empties into the bladder. Urine passes from the bladder to outside the body via the urethra (in the male, the urethra also transports semen).

Potential Problems

If all is functioning well, your dog will urinate regularly (not frequently), and his urine will be clear and yellow in color. A problem of the kidneys, bladder, urethra, or prostate will be evident as straining to urinate, blood-tinged or cloudy urine, excessive drinking accompanied by excessive urination, or pain upon urination. The problem could be something as minor as dehydration or as complicated as renal failure. You must consult your veterinarian for a diagnosis.

FACT

Blood in the urine is a sure sign of a urinary tract infection—if not a more serious condition—and you should consult your veterinarian immediately. Often, feeding your dog a simple bowl of beef or chicken broth is a solid start toward getting your dog back on track, because he'll want to drink it, thereby replenishing the fluids in his body. Discuss this option with your vet before moving forward.

Spaying or Neutering Your Dog

Consider spaying your female or neutering your dog as preventive care for a number of reasons. Healthwise, a spayed female is far less prone to diseases of the reproductive system, because her reproductive organs have been removed. A neutered male is immune to testicular and prostate cancers. As for behavior, you'll be spared the mess of the female's biannual season, and your male will be less likely to lift his leg in your home, roam in search of females in heat, or engage in aggressive behavior.

The female's reproductive organs include two ovaries, a uterus, and fallopian tubes. A spayed female will have all of these removed. Intact females will experience regular heats and are prone to false pregnancies and infection of the uterus, called pyometra. Some believe that a spayed bitch is prone to obesity. While it is true that she will not be under the same hormonal influence that keeps an intact bitch in form, with regular exercise and the proper diet a spayed bitch can be kept in top shape.

The male dog's reproductive system includes the testicles, penis, and prostate gland. Intact males are prone to damage or injury of the penis or scrotum, cancer of the testes, and inflammation, enlargement, or cancer of the prostate. Once again, you and your dog will live happier, healthier lives if the dog is neutered. Neutering is the surgical removal of the testicles. The empty scrotum eventually shrinks and leaves no scar. Neutering not only guarantees the male won't develop testicular cancer or prostate problems, it also lessens a male's territoriality, making him (with proper care and training) a friendlier pet. Neutering does not significantly change a dog's temperament, however; if you have an aggressive male, neutering will not solve the problem, but combined with training, it can certainly help.

CHAPTER 17

Vaccines and First Aid

Vaccines are given so that pets and people can be protected from potentially fatal diseases. This is a wonderful thing. Unfortunately, some pets (and people) are sensitive to a particular vaccine or a combination vaccine, and their sensitivity can lead to becoming sick from the vaccine itself. Because of this, and because the formulations and types of vaccines are always evolving, it's important to understand what the vaccines your dog should receive are actually for, whether your dog should receive them, and whether they should be given individually or in combination.

Puppy Shots

Though there is a lot of debate concerning which vaccines to give and how often, no one will argue that vaccinating puppies is absolutely necessary. It wasn't that long ago that puppies and dogs routinely died from diseases like distemper and rabies. Now only unvaccinated dogs are at risk of developing a life-threatening case of either, and these numbers are low since a rabies vaccine is required by law in most states.

FACT

The American Animal Hospital Association (AAHA) issued Canine Vaccination Guidelines for the General Veterinary Practice in 2006. You can access them through the Web site at *www.aahanet.org*.

In sum, vaccines have been categorized as "core" and "noncore" to assist veterinarians and owners in determining which are absolutely necessary and which are recommended and why. The AAHA guidelines also give specifics about what age puppies and dogs should be when they receive the vaccinations.

Core and Non-Core Vaccines

The core vaccines are those that are absolutely necessary. They are given to protect against the highly infectious diseases of parvovirus, distemper, adenovirus (hepatitis), and rabies.

The non-core vaccines are those that have been determined to be advantageous in certain situations (for example, in kennels where many dogs live together) or that provide temporary relief in some cases. The vaccines listed as non-core in the AAHA guidelines are the distemper-measles vaccine, parainfluenza virus, bordetella, leptospirosis, and Lyme (Borrelia burgdorferi). It's important to note that the connotation of non-core doesn't necessarily mean your dog shouldn't receive it; rather, its use should be considered as relevant to the individual circumstances of the dog (for example, dogs living in areas of high Lyme disease exposure will benefit from the vaccine).

A puppy vaccination schedule should begin around the age of six weeks and continue through the age of sixteen weeks. Your veterinarian will provide you with the complete schedule for when your pup needs to come in to receive all his shots at the right times.

How the Vaccine Works

A vaccine is intended to work with the immune system to fight against invasive infections of bacteria and viruses. The injection contains a harmless amount of the organism the body may someday need to fight off. This "jump-starts" the immune system to respond to that organism again if it enters the body. Without vaccines, dogs are far more susceptible to contracting infectious diseases from other dogs and other animals.

The Diseases Vaccines Protect Against

It's important to know the diseases for which vaccines exist so that you can fully understand why protection against them is so vital for your dog.

Especially for those who spend a lot of time at the local dog park letting their dogs socialize with others, kennel cough is almost a certainty. It is akin to sending your child off to kindergarten: a guarantee she'll pick up almost everything. Make sure your puppy and mature dog are always up to date on their vaccinations. Socialization is very important, so make sure you do it. But know that some sickness will come from all the interaction, just like young kids in school for the first time.

Adenovirus (Canine Hepatitis)

Hepatitis, a viral disease, attacks body tissue, particularly the kidneys and liver, and most often strikes dogs under one year of age. Symptoms include increased thirst, loss of appetite, abdominal discomfort, high fever, and lack of energy. Eyes may appear to have a blue tint. The disease is spread through contact with an infected dog or his urine or feces. It is a core disease against which to be vaccinated.

Distemper

This is a viral disease that attacks a dog's nervous system and progresses to affect every tissue in the body. It is an airborne disease that can strike at any age but is most deadly if acquired young, which is why it's one of the first shots a pup receives. A dog with distemper will secrete a thick, yellowish discharge from his nose and eyes. He'll run a fever and he will not want to eat. The pneumonia, encephalitis, and dehydration that can result can be deadly. This is a core disease against which to be vaccinated.

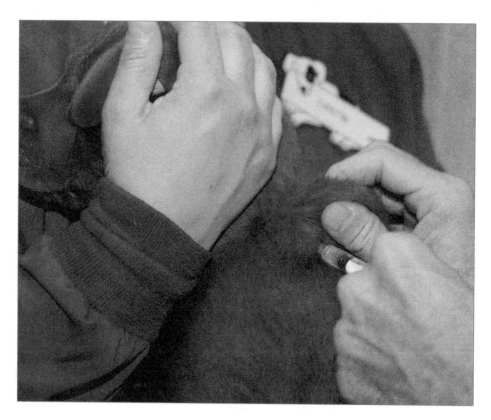

Knowing which vaccines are necessary for the long-term health and safety of your dog will ensure that she stays free from potentially fatal infectious diseases. Her schedule for receiving the shots starts in puppyhood.

Parvovirus

This viral infection manifests itself as an inflammation of the intestinal lining, causing sudden vomiting, bloody diarrhea, a high fever, and rapid weight loss. It is transmitted through the feces and can survive outside a dog's body for three to six months. The disease is extremely debilitating and rapidly lethal; treatment is intensive and often unsuccessful. It is a core disease against which to be vaccinated.

Rabies

The rabies virus attacks the central nervous system, causing unpredictable and often aggressive behavior. This erratic behavior is what, in turn, can cause the virus to spread, because it is through the bite of an infected animal that another animal is infected. Rabies can be transmitted from species to species, too, making it a health hazard to domesticated animals and people. This is why it is a core disease, and all states require that dogs and cats be vaccinated against rabies. Rabies is common in the northeastern United States, where there are large populations of skunks, raccoons, foxes, bats, and groundhogs. If you observe erratic behavior in any of these animals, call your local animal warden immediately.

FACT

The CDC is working with partners around the world to eliminate canine rabies globally. September 8, 2007, was the inaugural World Rabies Day, and a symposium brought together professionals from all over the world to discuss and examine how to eliminate rabies around the world. The United States is already considered rabies-free. For more information, go to *www.worldrabiesday.org*.

If your dog is bitten or scratched by any wild animal, you should alert your veterinarian and your local animal warden immediately.

Bordetella (Kennel Cough)

Kennel cough is the common name given to the respiratory condition that results in a harsh, dry cough in a dog that sounds like a case of bronchitis in a person. It is caused by the bacteria *Bordetella bronchiseptica*, though the bacteria doesn't always act alone. Dogs who live in kennels, who will be boarded with other dogs, or who visit strange dogs frequently should be vaccinated against the disease. It's highly contagious, though it can be treated with antibiotics, rest, and the proper environment. Affected dogs must be isolated from other dogs, and especially from puppies, who are more severely stricken than older dogs.

FACT

Kennel cough is the most common sickness passed on from dog to dog at dog runs and dog parks. It is the equivalent of a cold passed from one first grader to another. It is annoying, but if properly treated, it disappears in less than two weeks. The constant coughing sometimes becomes difficult to bear, but it will end. And then it's like chicken pox—luckily, dogs tend to only get it once.

Leptospirosis

Lepto strikes the liver and also the kidneys, but this disease is caused by bacteria. Severe infections cause shock and death, but if it's caught early, aggressive treatment with antibiotics can fight it off. Symptoms include vomiting, excessive thirst with decreased urination and dehydration, and abdominal pain. Lepto is highly contagious, and an infected dog can also pass the bacteria through his urine for some time, even after treatment. Dogs who spend a great deal of time outdoors seem most affected. The disease is also contagious to people. It is a non-core disease against which a vaccine should be given if the dog or his environment is susceptible.

Lyme Disease

Lyme disease is a tick-borne viral disease that often causes debilitating joint pain. While once a disease predominantly of the eastern United

States, it is now documented in the northern Midwest and Pacific Coast areas of the United States. It is a non-core disease, but dogs living in areas of high possible infestation should be vaccinated.

Lyme disease is caused by the bacterium *Borrelia burgdorferi*, and is transmitted by tick bites. To infect a dog, a tick must remain attached to its host for several hours, so finding and removing ticks is essential to protecting your dog. Typical symptoms include fever, fatigue, swollen lymph nodes, limpness, loss of appetite, and inflamed joints. Your veterinarian can diagnose a dog with Lyme disease, and treatment is usually effective if the disease is caught early enough.

Other Vaccines

Some potentially life-threatening conditions for which vaccines currently exist are periodontal disease and rattlesnake venom. Both are fairly new to the market and are still being clinically evaluated for their overall benefits. Neither are considered core vaccines. Certainly if you are concerned about the potential for your dog to be bitten by a rattlesnake, or if you are especially concerned about how poor dental health can affect your dog's teeth, gums, and other body systems, discuss these with your veterinarian.

Vaccinating as Your Dog Gets Older

It was once standard practice that the veterinarian needed to see your dog once a year after she was given her full range of vaccines. This was to administer booster shots as well as to give an overall evaluation so your dog's condition could be monitored as she aged. Now, it is understood that vaccines can continue to protect a dog for longer than one year, and that to over-vaccinate is potentially harmful. Does this mean that if your dog is looking and acting healthy she may not need his annual veterinary visit? No!

Is a combination vaccine safe for my puppy or dog?
Now that leptospirosis is considered a non-core disease that not all dogs may need to be vaccinated against, fewer puppies and dogs are given what was once a standard combination vaccine: DHLPP (distemper, hepatitis, leptospirosis, parainfluenza virus—a contributor to kennel cough—and parvovirus). Ask your veterinarian if any of the shots your puppy or dog is scheduled to receive is a combination vaccine and what the advantages or disadvantages might be.

At her yearly checkup, the vet will examine your dog from head to tail, including her eyes, ears, mouth, feet, limbs, chest, back, and anus. He will ask you about any lumps or bumps he might detect, or any swellings or tender spots. He'll let you know if your dog's teeth need a scraping (as ours do occasionally), and he'll advise you about your dog's weight and overall condition.

If you live in an area with a high susceptibility to a particular kind of disease, or if you plan to board or travel extensively with your dog, your veterinarian may recommend a vaccine to protect your dog.

There is a lot of controversy about how frequently dogs (and people!) should be vaccinated, and how much of a vaccine to use. While you certainly want to protect your dog against potentially fatal diseases, you don't want to introduce an ailment by over-vaccinating. In trying to decide what is best for your dog, it's important to work with a veterinarian whom you trust. There is much conflicting information on the Internet, even though it's a handy source for investigating issues.

One thing that many veterinarians do before giving a vaccine is to perform a blood test to assess the level of antibody concentration in the blood. This test, known as a titer, can let the veterinarian know whether your dog is adequately protected or whether she needs a booster shot of any kind. This is especially helpful if you're concerned about something like Lyme disease or kennel cough in your area.

If you've been following the preventive measures described here, you will be proud to hear your veterinarian tell you how healthy your dog looks and acts. Way to go! That's a compliment to the kind of care you're giving your best friend. Keep it up.

First Aid and Handling an Emergency

Emergencies elicit two states that don't help matters any—shock and/or fear in the dog and panic in the owner. When dealing with an emergency, keep reminding yourself to stay calm and stay focused on what you can do for your dog. The first thing to do is call your veterinarian or the emergency clinic and let them know that you are on your way and why. Ideally, you should have someone drive you to the clinic while you manage your dog. After you've called the veterinary clinic and gotten someone to help if you're alone with the dog, follow these steps:

1. Evaluate the dog's condition and deliver any first-aid procedures, such as reducing bleeding, putting on a muzzle so the dog doesn't bite you or someone else, applying any ointment, or wrapping a wound.
2. Keep your dog still and warm by reassuring him and keeping a blanket on him.
3. Make preparations to transport him so he experiences as little turbulence and commotion as possible. Be very careful when lifting him. Use a large sheet as a kind of hammock in which to contain him or lift him onto a board that will keep his body flat and somewhat immobilized.

Once your dog reaches the veterinarian's office, all you can do is await the doctors' assessment of your dog's condition. Try to stay calm until you have the facts. Since coping with emergencies usually involves having to transport the one who needs care, it's a good idea to have something in the car to help you stay calm and focused. That could be something as simple as chewing gum, or some hard candies to suck on. You might also consider keeping a small bottle of Rescue Remedy® in your glove compartment. This homeopathic formula was created for just such purposes, and since it is not a barbituate, you can use it safely even while driving. In fact, your dog could benefit from it, too. The bottle includes dosage recommendations that are applicable for dogs. It is a homeopathic remedy, so you can't overdose—though certainly you shouldn't give more than a few drops at a time.

Common First Aid

The scouts have it right when they say Be Prepared. When you are scared or upset about something that's just happened to your dog, you won't think as clearly. You might end up scrambling for supplies that could, instead, be ready and waiting for you. Where? In your handy first aid kit.

A first aid kit is simple to put together yourself, and if you do you'll know it has what you need in it when you need it. Use a container that can be securely closed and stored so that it's also easy to use. A large, plastic pencil holder can do the job, as can a shoebox. Once you have the container picked out, be sure it is clearly marked with something like FIRST AID FOR DOG. The supplies you'll need include:

- Gauze pads
- Antibiotic ointment
- Nonstick first-aid tape
- Cotton balls and swabs
- A roll of stretch bandage
- Tweezers or hemostats
- Styptic pencil
- Rectal thermometer
- Long strip of fabric or old pair of nylon hose for use as a temporary muzzle
- Thin plastic gloves for treating wounds and heavier gloves for possible bite protection

Other supplies you should have on hand for your dog's (or your family's) general care include hydrogen peroxide 3 percent for cleaning and disinfecting; Pepto-Bismol or Maalox for minor gastrointestinal upset; syrup of ipecac to induce vomiting; a topical anti-inflammatory; and plain aspirin for pain.

CHAPTER 18

Keeping Your Dog Pest-Free

A parasite is an organism that feeds off of another organism. Internal parasites are those that grow by feeding inside the body (worms, for example); external parasites are those that grow by feeding outside the body (fleas, for example). Finding ticks or fleas on your dog is not pleasant—but it's certainly better than not finding them and then realizing you have a flea infestation or a dog who has contracted a tick-borne illness! There are other pests that can wreak havoc on your dog, too—microscopic mange and mites and internal parasites in the form of worms. Because these critters are all over the dog's environment, they present some of the greatest ongoing challenges to dog owners. Because of that, there are many products and programs on the market to help control and combat them.

Dealing with Fleas

Fleas have been annoying humankind and animals for centuries, and they're almost as tough to control today as they were in the days of ancient Rome. The flea's exoskeleton is amazingly resilient, and fleas can jump several hundred feet to land on an unsuspecting host.

Despite what many dog owners believe, fleas do not spend most of their lives on their pets. In fact, fleas only stay on dogs to feed and breed. They feed by biting the dog and sucking its blood. Because fleas often harbor tapeworm larvae in their systems, fleas can transmit tapeworm disease to the animal through the bloodstream or by being eaten when a dog tries to chew the fleas off himself. When fleas mate, the females lay hundreds of eggs. These drop off the dog and into the environment. Larvae hatch from the eggs in two to three weeks, and these feed on environmental debris such as human or animal dandruff, mold, and other protein and vegetable matter.

Fighting fleas can start from the inside out with your dog. There are foods and supplements you can give that boost your dog's immune system—and a healthy dog is both less susceptible to these pests and better able to fight them off. These ingredients include brewer's yeast, garlic, B vitamins, and—for the skin—calcium, phosphorous, and zinc. For more information, check out *The Goldsteins' Wellness & Longevity Program for Dogs and Cats.*

From the larval stage, the flea develops a cocoon shell in which it matures. In the cocoon stage, the flea can live with no nutrients for almost a year. Then all it takes is the slight vibration of an animal's passing for the cocoon to release the adult, which jumps onto its host and begins the life cycle all over again.

Your dog can pick up fleas almost anywhere—outdoors, in a neighbor's house, even from another dog. Chances are, by the time you spot adult fleas on your dog, you have an infestation in your home and/or yard.

You'll know you and your dog are in trouble when you see him itching or licking himself suddenly and with real purpose. To confirm your suspicions, part your dog's hair to the skin or brush it backward and see if you notice any black specks. The specks can be dense around the dog's groin area, in the hair at the base of the tail, and around the ears and neck. With a moist paper towel, wipe the specks. If they turn red, they're flea dirt—particles of digested blood the flea has excreted.

Facing the Problem

Now that you know your dog has fleas, you will have to be diligent about removing them from the dog *and* the environment. If you only remove the fleas from your dog without eliminating the flea eggs, larvae, and cocoons from the environment, you are guaranteed a continuing problem.

One flea and tick preventive measure is to apply a topical product onto your dog's skin between her shoulder blades. From there it will spread to the rest of her skin, but she can't lick it directly.

Dog owners are fortunate to have a wide range of flea-fighting products to choose from, ones that are safer than ever for dogs and the environment. You should consult with your veterinarian before waging a war on the fleas that have infiltrated your happy home; you'll want to be sure that the products you select for use on your dog and your home are appropriate for your dog's age, weight, and skin type, and that the ingredients don't clash with a product you choose for your home and yard.

FACT

The active ingredient in many of the topical flea products on the market these days is pyrethrin, a natural compound that's toxic to fleas but won't harm pets or people. There are also formulations that stop flea eggs from developing, interrupt the reproductive cycle, and break down the flea's tough exoskeleton.

Once you've selected the flea-fighters you'll need, plan a systematic approach to ridding your dog, home, and yard of all stages of the flea life cycle. Take every step seriously if you want to completely eliminate the problem. You'll need to vacuum thoroughly, using several vacuum-cleaner bags and disposing of them all in air-tight plastic bags. You'll need to wash all the dog's bedding in very hot water. This may include your family's bedding, too, if the dog shares anyone's bed. Any place that your dog passes through or sleeps in can be considered a flea "hot spot" and potentially infested. Concentrate your efforts there.

To remove fleas on your dog, first wash her with a flea-killing shampoo to kill and rid your pet of some of the pests, then comb through the dog's wet fur with a fine-toothed flea comb. Dip the comb in a large glass of soapy water or rubbing alcohol to drown and kill any fleas that survived the bath. After a nose-to-tail combing, rinse your dog with a conditioning rinse to remove any excess soap or alcohol, and to help soothe the skin.

Dry your dog thoroughly, and don't let her roll in her favorite hole in the yard or lie down in her usual spot on the porch—these are possible hot spots, too, and they need to be treated with an outdoor insecticide. Once you've treated the dog, house, and yard, you'll never want to repeat the process, so you'll need to step up your preventive measures.

Preventing a Flea Problem

Figuring your dog can get fleas any time he steps out of your home and into a well-populated area, you should check him regularly before coming inside. Run a flea comb through his fur. This will snag any free-loaders before they start breeding. Kill them on the comb by crushing them with your fingernail or immersing the comb in a glass of soapy water or rubbing alcohol.

During the warm months, when fleas are at their worst, bathe your dog regularly with a flea-preventive shampoo, and ask your veterinarian about other products designed to keep fleas from settling on your pet. Vacuum your home frequently, and make sure to keep your pet's bedding fresh and clean.

ALERT!

There are several over-the-counter flea control products available for the war against these insidious pests. While keeping your dog flea-free is most desirable, remember that these products are pesticides. Some are not recommended for puppies. It's critical that you read their instructions completely and use them according to the directions. Discuss any concerns with your veterinarian.

Flea Bite Sensitivity

Many dogs are allergic to the saliva that fleas inject into their skin when they bite them or are particularly sensitive to fleas living on them. These dogs can develop serious skin ailments from their allergies and sensitivities, which often linger even after the flea problem has been eradicated. The excessive scratching, licking, and fur-biting they indulge in to get at the fleas leaves their skin damaged, causing further itching and, often, infection. The infection can leave the skin swollen or patchy and can lead to permanent hair loss. Besides being unsightly, a flea allergy or sensitivity is extremely irritating to your dog. Your veterinarian will advise you on how best to treat this many-symptomed problem.

Dealing with Ticks

There are many types of ticks throughout the United States, the most common being the brown tick, the wood tick, and the deer tick. All adult ticks seek out dogs and other animals as hosts for feeding and breeding. The brown tick is typically the size of a match head or small pea when engorged. The wood tick is a larger tick that, when full, swells to the size of a kernel of corn. The deer tick is a tiny tick that even when engorged is no larger than a speck. The brown tick is known to transmit Rocky Mountain spotted fever, while the deer tick is the carrier of Lyme disease, both of which can be deadly.

Unfortunately, it's almost impossible to keep ticks off your dog if you spend any time outdoors with him. Your best bet, yet again, is preventive care: bathing your dog with a flea and tick shampoo formulated for his needs, taking your veterinarian's advice about what products work best to keep ticks off your dog, and always checking your dog thoroughly when you return from an outdoor adventure.

Ridding Your Dog of Ticks

The sooner you spot a tick on your dog, the better. You need to remove the tick immediately, then monitor the spot from which you removed it. To take a tick off your dog, first wet a cotton ball with alcohol. Apply this to the tick to suffocate or numb it. Then, with tweezers or with gloves on your hands, pull the tick gently off the dog. Deposit the tick in a jar filled with alcohol or nail polish remover. If your dog comes out of a trip to the woods loaded with ticks, you may want to get a tick dip from your veterinarian to help remove them all at once.

ALERT!

It used to be that Lyme disease was only a serious threat to dogs in certain parts of the United States, most notably the East Coast. Today it is a concern of dog owners in nearly all parts of the country and is so common that there is a vaccine for it. Talk to your veterinarian about whether the vaccine can help your dog.

Tick bites rarely become infected, but you'll want to keep an eye on your dog's skin in the area from which the tick was pulled off, especially if it was a deer tick. A red, circular rash that develops around the bite is an early indicator of Lyme disease. With a dog's fur, though, this is often difficult to detect. The best thing to do is let your vet know that you pulled a deer tick off your dog. If she's not vaccinated against the disease, you may want to start her on a low-grade antibiotic to be sure the disease does not infect her. It is much simpler and safer to fight off a low-grade infection up front than to have to eradicate a full-blown infection. In fact, the disease has been known to linger for years, causing severe pain.

Dealing with Mange Mites

Mites are tiny creatures that resemble spiders and that can only be detected under a microscope. The most common kind of mange mite that affects dogs is sarcoptic mange. Another name for it is scabies.

The adult females who find their way onto dogs burrow into their skin and lay eggs. These hatch in a few days, and the young feed off the top layer of skin until they mature and perpetuate the life cycle. Dogs affected by scabies become very itchy, and infected areas tend to become red and sore. A veterinarian can quickly confirm a scabies infection with a skin scraping and will then prescribe the dip and/or ointment to treat the infection. Your dog may need to wear an Elizabethan collar to keep her from licking at the spots until they are healed.

FACT

The medications your veterinarian may prescribe to rid your dog of mange can further compromise her immune system as well as her skin. Support the treatment with safe, all-natural remedies such as a naturally medicated shampoo (it should contain neem oil or tea tree oil) and immune-system stimulators such as vitamins C, E, A, and the addition of whole foods to the diet.

Fortunately, this type of scabies cannot live on a human host. They also can't survive off a host for longer than about thirty-six hours, so while it certainly helps to disinfect your dog's sleeping areas by vacuuming or washing in hot water several times during treatment, scabies is eradicated from the environment fairly quickly.

Dealing with Worms

Like the infectious diseases that are easily avoided by proper vaccinations, worms are another potentially deadly enemy of your dog's health that are easily avoided and treated with proper care, hygiene, and attention. There are several types of worms that infect dogs. Tapeworms, whipworms, roundworms, and heartworms are the most common.

Dogs become infected by worms through contact with contaminated soil; raw, contaminated meat (such as a dead animal in the woods); or ingestion of an infected host (such as a flea). That's why it's so important to clean up after your dog in the yard and around the house, and to have fecal exams performed by the veterinarian regularly (microscopic examination is often the only way to detect the presence of internal parasites).

You might suspect your puppy or dog has worms if his appetite decreases, he has an upset stomach, he loses weight, and you see blood or mucus in his stools. These symptoms are characteristic of an advanced state of parasitic infection; dogs can have a slight infection and appear normal until your veterinarian detects worms in his feces. For common infestations, safe, effective, and fast-acting worming medications are available.

Besides avoiding places where your dog or puppy may become infested with worms and being alert to the signs of a potential infestation, you can further help your friend by feeding him a high-quality diet so that his system can naturally fight off any of these pests as effectively as possible. This doesn't mean that a diagnosed infection shouldn't be treated with traditional medications as prescribed by your veterinarian; rather, it means that there are foods that will naturally help your dog stay worm-free.

Heartworm

The heartworm is a particularly deadly parasite because it infests and grows in the canine heart. Left untreated, heartworms literally strangle the heart, causing it to fail and the dog to die.

Heartworm is transmitted by infected mosquitoes. When they land on a dog to bite, heartworm larvae are deposited on the skin. The larvae burrow their way through the dog's skin, growing into small worms as they go. When they finally reach a blood vein, the worms travel to the heart, where they mature. Heartworms can grow four to twelve inches long, and a dog can be infected for years before symptoms are noticeable. A dog diagnosed with heartworm is in trouble either way. Treatment is intense and can even cause the death it seeks to avoid.

Today's dog owners are extremely fortunate to have heartworm preventive medication readily available. In some parts of the country veterinarians suggest giving dogs the preventive daily or monthly (depending on the type) only in seasons in which the mosquito is most active; in other parts of the country, veterinarians keep dogs on the preventive all year round as a safety precaution. Ask your veterinarian what's best for your dog and stick with the program. If you take your dog off of the preventive for more than several months, she must be tested for the presence of heartworm before being allowed to go back on it.

Tapeworm

Tapeworms can actually be seen upon close examination of an infected dog's feces; sometimes they are visible around the dog's anus, as well. That's because tapeworms are long, segmented worms. They can grow to twenty inches, and the segments reproduce at the front of the worm and are cast off at the back. Castoff segments are the ones that are released by a dog when he defecates. Tapeworms attach and feed in the small intestine. They are transmitted by fleas, so when a dog licks or bites off a flea, it might contain the tapeworm larvae.

Fortunately, a tapeworm infestation is easily treated, though if the problem may have started because of the presence of fleas, it can easily recur if the flea problem isn't handled as well.

Roundworm

Roundworms can be found in the soil and in other infected animals. Dogs can get them by simply walking in infected dirt, or even nursing from an infected mother. Once in a dog's system, the roundworm can remain encysted for years, which is why even healthy mother dogs can end up passing the worms on to their pups. When the worms get active again, they move to the lungs where they develop into a larval stage. They get coughed up, and upon being swallowed, find their way to the intestines where they mature and reproduce. They can grow up to seven inches, and an infestation can clog the intestines. Affected dogs vomit and have diarrhea. It can take several rounds of medication to rid an infected dog of the worms.

Whipworm

This worm also thrives in the dog's intestine. It gets its name from its whip-like appearance, and these long worms can quickly form a mass that will easily obstruct the large intestine, causing bloody diarrhea and a very sick dog. Repeated treatments are usually necessary before a dog is free of these pests.

In sum, be forewarned that internal and external pests can make your dog seriously ill and potentially lead to death. Use common sense when you're out with your dog. Avoid areas that appear to be heavily trafficked by other animals or in which many strange dogs urinate and defecate. Keep your home and yard as clean as possible. Wash your dog's bedding. Groom him regularly and be on the lookout for fleas and ticks. These critters can be largely avoided if you're clean and conscientious.

CHAPTER 19

Alternative Health Care

When someone you love becomes ill, it is instinctual to do everything you can to try to help. If that someone is your dog, you will want to learn everything you can about how best to treat her to help her heal. These days, it's not enough to simply take the advice of your veterinarian—though you should certainly start with it and consult with your veterinarian as you explore other healing modalities. The fact is, nontraditional healing methods are gaining in credibility and becoming more mainstream because in many cases they're proven effective.

Is It Right for Your Dog?

Making full use of any possible healing modality when treating an illness makes perfect sense and is therefore "right" for any dog or other living creature. Still, it can be scary to venture into areas where you don't have some familiarity, or where you may not be assisted by someone you've come to know and trust with the care of your dog. There's still a stigma associated with alternative health care because it's not mainstream. It can be hard enough to find a traditional veterinarian with whom you have a trusting relationship—how can you find someone else practicing in a field with which you may have little familiarity?

FACT

Alternative care is also referred to as holistic, integrative, or complementary, as well as nontraditional. It includes everything from using herbal supplements to administering acupuncture to ease your dog's aches and pains.

There are a number of resources at your disposal, made handier by the Internet. The best place to start is with the American Holistic Veterinary Medical Association (AHVMA) at *www.ahvma.org*. Founded in 1982, the AHVMA helps veterinarians and pet owners expand their understanding of treatment options. When a veterinarian takes a holistic approach, she not only works from a complete physical examination, but also examines the influences of nutrition, behavior, past medical history, stress, and any other factors that could be contributing to the disease. Holistic medicine takes all of these factors into account together and uses them to come up with an effective treatment plan.

The AHVMA Web site allows you to search for an holistic veterinarian by name, state, zip code, area code, and modality of treatment. Let's take a look at some of the treatments.

Nutrition and Behavior

We don't stop to think about it too often, but it is so true and so obvious that we are what we eat—and it's no different for our dogs. Many of the commercially manufactured foods we feed our dogs have had the nutrients cooked right out of them. When you consider that most dogs do not eat a varied diet—and what they do eat may be lacking in elemental nutrients—is it any wonder that so many have skin conditions, gastrointestinal conditions, and behavior issues, or that they develop illnesses at younger and younger ages?

A change in diet may not be the complete answer to a particular health issue, but it's a good place to start if you want to make a difference. Look at the ingredients in your dog's primary food source and learn about how to evaluate them. Think about how you can improve the overall quality of the nutrients your dog receives on a daily basis.

By affecting how the body functions, nutrition also plays a part in how we behave. For humans, we can think about the effects of fatty foods, too much caffeine, too much sugar, chemical preservatives and additives, and so on. For dogs, we can think about the effects of malnutrition—where the body isn't getting enough sustaining nutrients. A chemical imbalance caused by poor nutrition will certainly affect behavior.

Again, just as our doctors do for us, veterinarians can run blood tests to get a sense of what may be high or low that's contributing to the imbalance. If your dog hasn't had one in a while, your veterinarian should perform a comprehensive blood test.

Massage and TTouch (Tellington Touch)

Renowned inspirational speaker and author Leo Buscaglia, Ph.D, had this to say about touch: "Too often we underestimate the power of a touch, a smile, a kind word, a listening ear, an honest compliment, or the smallest act of caring, all of which have the potential to turn a life around." Dogs are enablers for all of these simple, compassionate acts that make such a difference in our lives. For some, the unconditional love received from a dog is what can get us through the day. The connection we establish and maintain with our dogs through touch is magical and miraculous.

The impulsive act of petting a dog can be easily converted to a therapeutic massage by becoming more focused on where and how you are touching your dog.

Channeled into therapeutic massage and Tellington Touch (TTouch), touch is something we can give back to our dogs that helps them (and us) live with less pain and more joy.

Massage

The difference between simply petting your dog and giving him a therapeutic massage is almost as slight as the focus you bring to the act. The way you pet your dog conveys many things to him, from a friendly tap to let him know he's done something you like to a caressing of his head or face to let him know how much you love him. Dogs are super-sensitive to our body language, and they sense what emotions we may be bringing to them before we even make contact with them.

The intention of massage is to knead, rub, or pat the body in order to stimulate circulation. Increased circulation means better blood flow, which leads to the release of stress, improved breathing, and a general feeling of well-being.

Massage therapy has been known to reduce anxiety levels of students taking exams, assist cancer patients with the effects of their treatments, lessen depression in those who are grief-stricken, promote weight gain in malnourished infants, and much more. For athletes, the benefits of increased circulation translate to better-functioning joints and muscles and improved performance.

Massage can benefit dogs in as many ways. It can reduce fear and anxiety, help the body fight off disease, improve physical performance, and enhance bonding. Consider massage as a treatment for a dog who is especially athletic if you notice that he's sore, for a senior dog whose circulation could be boosted by it, or for a sensitive dog who needs to relax. There are many books and even some DVDs that can teach you about massage techniques that benefit dogs.

TTouch

Not long ago, a competitive rider and horse trainer named Linda Tellington-Jones wanted to explore the mind-body connection through touch as a way to work with her horses' behaviors. Basing her work on techniques developed by Moshe Feldenkrais for humans, Tellington-Jones started using circular touching motions to actually interrupt unacceptable behaviors so that the desired behavior patterns could emerge. Her system has become known around the world as TTouch, and it has revolutionized how people relate to their pets. TTouch improves relationships between dog and human, resolves behavior problems, and even assists in healing physical problems.

ALERT!

Tellington-Jones's TTouch method is beneficial for dogs with problems ranging from barking and chewing to pulling on the leash, jumping up, resistance to grooming, car sickness, and the effects of aging. Learn more at *www.ttouch.com*.

Chiropractic and Acupuncture

Taking the work of touch to the next level, the use of chiropractic techniques and acupuncture on dogs (and other animals) are also becoming more widely used as more and more dogs are benefiting from them.

Chiropractic

The term chiropractic comes from two Greek words—*cheira* and *praktikos*—and means "done by hand." It is the practice of assessing mechanical abnormalities of the spine and musculoskeletal system to affect relief through the nervous system. The premise is that pain is the result of an impaired nervous system as influenced by the position of the spine. Once adjustments are made to the spine and the surrounding musculature, the pain is relieved. Treatment depends on the condition being addressed.

The best way to find a cure is by actively seeking one based on your dog's health issues. All searches should begin with a trusted veterinarian who can give you the best conventional perspective. From there, the search can and should continue with the simplest and purest of intentions: to make the quality of life of your dog the best possible.

Chiropractic is more and more commonly practiced on horses and companion animals—particularly those involved in competitive sports such as show jumping, dressage and eventing for horses, and agility and other physically demanding sports for dogs. It's not always easy to find a canine chiropractor near you, but as success stories emerge and demand grows, their numbers are increasing. Animal practitioners need to be trained just as human chiropractors do. The American Veterinary Chiropractic Association (AVCA) provides credentials, and on its Web site (*www.animalchiropractic.org*) you can find referrals as well as other information.

Acupuncture

The ancient practice of acupuncture takes stimulation to yet another level: through needles applied directly to "meridians" in the body that correspond to the area that needs relief. This is an outrageously oversimplified summary of a healing procedure that dates back nearly 10,000 years and whose use in western veterinary medicine is still in its infancy. In fact, it was only in 1998 that the American Veterinary Medical Association (AVMA) finally gave the nod to acupuncture, stating in its Guidelines for

Complementary and Alternative Medicine that acupuncture and acutherapy were integral parts of veterinary medicine.

Aromatherapy

The nose is one of the dog's strongest sensory organs. Dogs have approximately four times as many scent receptors as we do! So it stands to reason that they are affected by what they smell around them, whether it's the kitty litter, the garbage can, pizza crusts, or an hours-old scent trail through difficult terrain. A dog's world is guided by what she smells around her far more than we realize.

Aromatherapy Defined

Using the scents of flowers, roots, and trees to promote healing and wellness—which is what aromatherapy is all about—can be highly effective with dogs. Their sensitivity to smells, though, makes using aromatherapy with them both easier and more difficult—easier because the scents are absorbed much more quickly through their noses, more difficult because they can be overpowering.

Aromatherapy is done with essential oils. These are produced by steaming or otherwise extracting the scents from their sources—whether those are flowers, herbs, or trees. The oils are bottled and sold in pharmacies, health food stores, and even some grocery stores. They can be used in many ways, including being diffused through a heat source; combined with other ingredients to make things such as soaps, insect repellents, and so on; or diluted in a base solution (typically an oil, such as sunflower or grapeseed oil) to be applied directly to the skin.

QUESTION?

Which essential oil should I try with my dog?
Understanding which oils do what is critical to getting started. There are lots of books you can learn from, and of course many Web sites, as well. To get started, check out *www.aromaweb.com*.

Getting Started

Once you've targeted some oils that are suggested for the ailment you're working with, it is extremely important that the proper dilution is made with the essential oil before exposing it to a dog (or any animal) because of potential sensitivity. As you learn more about how to use the oils, you'll find advice on dilution concentrations, too. Aromatherapy practitioners who work with animals say that this is the beginning of an amazing journey of discovery for you and your dog. Besides their great sense of smell, dogs and other animals have an innate sense about what's good for them (well, except when they raid the trash). They should be offered a few of the smells to see which they naturally select.

Aromatherapy isn't a substitute for conventional medicine—especially for a potentially life-threatening problem. But like other complementary therapies, it has the potential to make a difference, and in a way that may make lots of other changes possible as well.

Flower Essences

Wait a second, wasn't there just a discussion about essences—essential oils? Yes, there was, and in fact essential oils (which are plant derivatives) and flower essences do share the fact that they are extracts that promote healing. The difference is that the essences used for aromatherapy have strong smells and they are held in an oil-based solution. Flower essences have no smell, are typically taken through the mouth, and are prepared only in one place using specific directions as established by their founder.

Flower Essences Defined

The "father" of healing flower essences is Dr. Edward Bach. An English physician, Dr. Bach came to see disease as the result of physiological and psychological imbalances at work in the body. Healing, therefore, would come not in using something that would mask or annihilate the disease, but in something that would restore balance of the mind, the emotions, and the body. He believed the balancing elements were to be found in nature, and he went on to identify thirty-eight healing flowers and plants that now form his comprehensive Bach Flower Remedies.

FACT

The most popular Bach formulation is Rescue Remedy®, a combination of five essences. It is intended to calm and reduce stress and is suggested for anyone facing a situation from which they need to feel "rescued," such as an important examination, speaking in public, handling a trip to the emergency room, and so on. It is as helpful for dogs as it is for humans.

Getting Started

Like essential oils, flower essences won't be of maximum benefit unless it is determined with some accuracy before taking them which ailment they should be addressing. In other words, looking for something to calm a dog is not as specific as looking for something to relieve the stress associated with loud noises (such as vacuum cleaners or thunderstorms). Similarly, flower essences can be used to reduce a dog's desire to lick himself all the time—but it helps to understand the source of the licking (is it nervousness, insecurity, boredom?).

ALERT!

A leading creator and supplier of flower essences in the U.S. is Anaflora, which offers thirty-two essences primarily for animal healing and deepening of bonding and communication. Learn more about them at *www .anaflora.com.*

To assist in targeting the correct remedy, Bach provided detailed descriptions of what each is for. There are many books that also help explain which remedy (or combination of remedies) is best for which problem(s). You can start your search on the Web site *www.bachflower. com.* A reassuring thing to know is that the essences are harmless; you can't overdose on them—of course, to get the desired results you need to choose the correct essence and take it according to the directions, which is in small doses over time.

Animal Communicators

This chapter has introduced you to alternative, complementary, nontraditional ways to address and treat health and behavior issues of dogs. It has progressed from discussing treatments that are performed on the body to those that work on the emotions and even the spirit of the animal being treated. It is fitting to end with a discussion of animal communication.

Even those who have owned and loved dogs for decades, who have wondered how they could have helped an ailing or misbehaving or obviously stressed animal have a better life, who feel they tried everything—even these folks react with skepticism when the subject of animal communication and communicators comes up. At least the first time.

The objective of this chapter isn't to sell you on animal communicators any more than it is to get you to use flower essences, aromatherapy, or acupuncture. One of its goals, though, is to present it as something that could be helpful—especially if your dog is suffering, you or your family is suffering as a result of your dog, or you're simply at your wits' end. It may come down to asking yourself, "Why not?"

Marta Williams, author of the books *Learning Their Language* and *Beyond Words,* describes animal communication as an intuitive exchange of thoughts, images, and emotions. This is something animals do between themselves and other animals (including humans) all the time. Intuitive communication can happen in four ways: through feelings (clairsentience); through mental telepathy (clairaudience); through visual images (clairvoyance); and through a feeling/knowledge that something is absolutely true even if you didn't know it before. Humans describe intuition as having a hunch—for example, getting a phone call from someone soon after you've thought about them. While it's easy to disregard these feelings as simply superstitious or coincidental, others believe otherwise.

If you're intrigued and you do a Google search for "animal communicator," your search will yield close to a million results. That can be overwhelming enough to end it for you right there. Animal communicators, all claiming to be effective, have proliferated since Dr. Sonya's show "Pet Psychic" debuted on Animal Planet TV. The best way to find and work with an animal communicator you can trust is to get referrals from an holistic veterinarian or a friend with similar interests.

CHAPTER 20

Your Senior Citizen

You think it's never going to happen: The rambunc-
tious puppy who chewed through three armchairs
and took three years to train to heel is starting to
slow down! You begin to notice changes in your dog
at around age five or six (depending on your dog),
and next thing you know, you have a canine senior
citizen.

The Aging Process

As scary as it is to know that time is catching up with your dog, there are a lot of wonderful things about this time in your dog's life. You and she have a strong bond, and you know what to expect from each other. Your dog probably listens more. She sleeps more, even though she still loves to go to the beach or for walks, and is generally more mellow, predictable, and even-tempered.

In fact, these may be some of the most enjoyable years you'll spend with your dog. She'll love going for car rides with you and will wait patiently while you do your quick errands. She'll be the first out the door if you let her know you want to play ball, but she'll be ready to stop when you tire of the game. Take the time to appreciate and savor these moments.

FACT

A dog's body ages in some of the same ways as a human's: metabolism slows; the immune system slows; arthritis may set in; vision, hearing, and smell can be impaired; there may be loss of bladder and bowel control; and there is usually an overall slowing down.

It's tough to see your dog go through these changes, and sometimes it's tough for you and your family, too. Your older dog may not be able to hold it through the night, and you may wake up to find accidents in the house. Older dogs know these are mistakes and may look at you with real apology in their eyes. Take pity on your older dog and let her know you understand. You may want to set your alarm an hour or so earlier in the morning so that your dog won't have to wait as long at night.

When your dog reaches six to eight years or so, you should take her to the veterinarian for a senior examination. Even if she seems as healthy as ever, your veterinarian can take whatever tests she may think are necessary to evaluate your dog's condition. These can include blood tests, urine tests, and vision and hearing tests. Your veterinarian should know your dog already and can provide objective commentary on her overall state.

Feeding Your Older Dog

One of the major influences on overall geriatric health is nutrition. If your senior citizen is eating too much fat and not enough fiber, not only does he risk becoming obese, but he may become constipated or have other gastro-intestinal upsets. Also, just as humans become allergic to things that didn't affect us before as we age, the same happens with dogs. The tried-and-true food you gave him for most of his life may now be causing him to itch or sneeze, or it may bother him in other ways.

The levels of proteins, fats, carbohydrates, vitamins, and minerals that a dog needs vary according to age. A growing puppy or an active dog in his prime is going to need a lot more to keep his body going than will a semi-retired, couch-loving senior dog. Discuss your dog's activity level with your veterinarian to determine the best diet. There are now specific dog foods for growth, maintenance, and senior years, including diets for particular health issues, "lite" foods, and foods supplemented with beneficial vitamins and minerals like glucosamine and chondroitin. Do some research about what supplements might benefit your senior dog, and discuss them with your veterinarian.

Another temptation is to spoil your older pal by giving him special treats. Spoiling the ones we love is natural; just remember, the more weight your dog carries around, the poorer his overall health is going to be. You may be indulging him in the short run, but those indulgences could mean less time with your dog in the long run. If you give a special treat, just cut back on his regular diet for a day or so. Ideally, you'll have kept your dog fit and trim throughout his lifetime, in which case it'll be easier to maintain this same condition into his senior years.

You should also provide your older large dog with raised food and water bowls from which to eat and drink. This makes eating and drinking easier on his back, neck, and shoulders.

Grooming Your Older Dog

Throughout her life, your dog will benefit from regular grooming (as explained in detail in Chapter 8). As she ages and her skin becomes less supple, her fur less lustrous, her ears and breath a bit stinkier, you may feel less inclined to keep her looking her best. However, this is when dogs seem to appreciate being groomed most. Older dogs seem to particularly love the attention they receive from grooming, and seem to understand that they look better with your help.

Skin and Coat

Regular brushing will keep shedding under control and continue to stimulate the natural oils in your dog's skin that keep his skin and coat looking and feeling their best. For dogs with longer hair who spend more time lying down, regular brushing will also keep mats from forming in the coat. These can be painful to detangle for older, more sensitive dogs.

Seniors should still be bathed—in fact they may need more frequent bathing if they accidentally soil themselves. Pay particular attention to the water temperature you use, take care in getting your dog in and out of the tub, and avoid drafts. Keep a "waterless" shampoo on hand for quick cleanups.

Teeth and Gums

If you haven't been keeping your dog's teeth and gums clean and healthy until now, you're in trouble. The accumulated plaque and tartar of a lifetime can have serious effects on the teeth and gums. Your dog may start to lose her teeth, which exposes the mouth to infection. She will probably have bad breath, which will make her a less lovable companion in close quarters (through no fault of her own!). Her gums may become so sore that she isn't able to eat the kibble that is her best source of nutrition.

ALERT!

Don't forget to keep your older dog's eyes and ears clean of dirt or waxy buildup. Both tend to increase with age, so make a point to go over your dog's face with a soft cloth every day and wipe her ears gently with a cotton ball or gauze pad. Report anything unusual to your veterinarian. This could include excessive discharge, redness or swelling in or around the eyes, cloudiness in the pupil (a sign of cataracts), or other signs.

Being able to continue to exercise means a lot to any dog, but it's especially helpful and important for senior dogs, as it keeps them physically and mentally connected to their world, providing inspiration for life. This lucky senior has a cart outfitted to support his hind end so he can still make his rounds in the yard.

If you've been keeping up with regular veterinary visits, you should know whether your dog's teeth and mouth are in good shape. Your dog may even have needed to have her teeth cleaned under anesthesia. The thing is, you don't want to subject an older dog to this procedure if you don't have to, because older dogs are more prone to the ill effects of anesthesia. Keep brushing!

Exercising Your Older Dog

Your dog may be slowing down, but that doesn't mean he shouldn't get out. In fact, he'll be happier and healthier if you keep him exercising. Th' doesn't mean going on the same five-mile runs you did when he was s' seven. Take into consideration the fact that his joints are stiffer, his energy level is lower, and his systems are working harder to keep up. All dogs are individuals, and the amount of exercise they can handle varies with the dog's breed, age, regular activity level, and so on. The point is, you know your dog and you know what he's capable of. Don't push him, but don't sell him short, either.

One thing you should continue to do as long and as often as possible is get your senior out for his regular walks. Not only are these good for his body (to keep those joints and muscles moving a bit and not stiffening up from lack of use), they're good for his soul. Without his walk, your dog is cut off from a great deal of the world—the one he knows by the smells he finds as you take your walk, wherever it may be.

The other activity you should continue with your dog as often as possible is to take him for car rides as you did throughout his life. For dogs who love their car rides, these can be the highlights of their day or week. They will reinvigorate your senior. While this may not seem like exercise per se, getting to the car, into and out of the car, and being wherever it may be that you go in the car are all opportunities to use his body and mind.

Common Problems of Older Dogs

Just as preventive care was stressed in the health chapter, it will be stressed again here. You can fend off so many major problems by being alert and attentive to your dog's overall health every day.

Aching and Stiffness

If your dog is having trouble getting up and down stairs, or takes some lame steps every once in a while, you can suspect an arthritis problem. Your veterinarian can suggest something to alleviate the pain. Options abound these days, and you should do all you can to keep your older dog comfortable. Your veterinarian can go over recommended treatments with you.

Your veteraniarian can supply a number of well-known prescription drugs to help your long-time friend over some of the affects of this most common of aging ailments. However, light exercise—such as short, slow walks—is also helpful to ward off the effects of the onset of arthritis. Talk to your veterinarian about how much exercise your dog should get.

Suspicious Lumps and Bumps

Many dogs develop lumps and bumps over their bodies as they age. If you notice any on your dog, you should have them examined by the veterinarian as soon as possible. Most are simply fatty growths, but some can be tumors, and it's important in those cases to have them biopsied to determine if they're cancerous.

Vision and Hearing

Other functions you'll want to monitor are your dog's vision and hearing. Most dogs develop cataracts (clouding of the eye lens) as their vision deteriorates, but not all do. Your dog may be losing her sight and you may not notice. Dogs with impaired vision are still able to get around almost normally, especially in familiar territory, because they are so familiar with their homes and immediate vicinity and because their other senses are so developed. The same can be true of hearing loss. Your dog may not respond to you as quickly, but if she sees you calling to her or knows that when you come home she gets her dinner shortly thereafter, she'll still respond. The veterinarian can perform more conclusive tests if you suspect your dog is losing her sight or hearing.

Special Considerations for Older Dogs

There are a number of things you can do around the house to make your older dog more comfortable.

If you know his sight and/or vision are deteriorating, put off any major redecorating or remodeling plans. Your old dog can navigate around familiar sofas, chairs, or tables and will know the smells of familiar carpets or other floor surfaces. Making major changes to the layout of familiar rooms will thoroughly confuse a blind dog, which will further stress him and make his condition worse.

Don't yell at a dog who can't hear well. Communicate more through sight and touch. Pet your dog to get his attention, then beckon him to where you want him to be. Use the hand signals you taught him over the years to help him understand what you want.

If your dog is having trouble getting up and down the stairs, can't jump up on the sofa to watch TV with you, or has trouble getting in and out of the car, you should lift or carry him if you can. If your dog weighs too much for you to be able to do this, consider building some simple ramps to help him. The ramps will need to be covered with some kind of nonslip material. Your dog will be so much happier if he is not banned from his favorite spots because of his failing health.

FACT

Your dog may not be able to get up and down stairs as easily as she used to. Some pet suppliers offer hand-held slings, which can be used to help your friend up and down the stairs with relative ease. These can also be a helpful tool when getting in and out of automobiles. Ramps are also a popular alternative when your dog has problems negotiating inclines such as steep steps or access to your automobile.

Speaking of favorite spots, these are usually the softest, coziest places in the house. Older dogs especially appreciate them. A flip through any dog supply catalog will show that there are all sorts of beds made to make geriatric dogs more comfortable, from egg-carton foam beds to specially heated pads. These are designed to relieve arthritic joints and to keep calluses from forming on the joints.

"Other Dogs" and Old Dogs

Is it a good idea to get a younger dog or a puppy when your dog starts getting old? Will this new addition reinvigorate your canine senior citizen, or will it send her into an irreversible funk and bring on a quicker death? Will you find yourself so involved in caring for the new dog that you somehow neglect your old friend when she may need you most?

These are all things to think about before you add another dog to your household while your own dog is in her golden years. She may, in fact, find a new friend invigorating and revert to a kind of second puppyhood. Or she might withdraw altogether. Puppies are truly irresistible, while older dogs have their share of problems that are not always pleasant to deal with. Even unconsciously, you may find yourself giving all your attention to the newcomer, which will not make your older dog feel good.

Before you get another dog, sit down and really think about how your dog may react. Don't get a puppy so there will be another dog in the house when your old dog's time comes. Don't get another dog if your dog is used to being Number One and is not particularly well socialized.

When—and How—to Say Goodbye

No matter how well you take care of your dog throughout his life, old age will eventually catch up to him. It may be a slow decline or a rapid decline. There may be good days—those during which your dog wakes with his renowned zest for life, eats well, and wags his tail enthusiastically when you talk to or pet him—and bad days—those during which your dog won't even want to get out of bed for his favorite toy or treat. The good days will renew your hopes, and the bad days will break your heart.

As your dog's caretaker and friend, it's up to you to determine when the bad days can't go on and decide if it's time to put your dog to sleep. When your old friend suffers at the end of his life, euthanasia is the gift you can give him to bring his life to a peaceful close with you by his side. It is a terribly painful decision to have to make, but it is a wise and humane one.

Discuss putting your dog down with your family so everyone can be prepared for it. Call your veterinarian and talk to him about your decision. When you agree the time is right, your veterinarian should make the time to take you right away so that you can be in a quiet room alone with your pet. If it is going to stress out your dog to take him to the vet's, ask for a mild sedative you can give him before you come over, then go pick it up so you can give it to your dog at the right time.

Dogs are extremely sensitive to our moods, and the pain you experience watching him suffer and considering euthanasia will bring additional stress to your dog. It is your job as her friend and caretaker to keep your emotions in check and focus on her. Talk to her, sing to her, tell her about your favorite times together, let her know how much you love her, recall the joy you shared. Hold her with love and tenderness in her last moments.

Think about what you want to do with your dog's body when he is no longer. If he's small enough, do you want to bury him near your home? Do you want to bury him in a pet cemetery so you can visit his gravesite for many years to come? Do you want the veterinarian to have him cremated? Make a decision that's right for you and that you won't regret later.

Euthanasia is a painless procedure in which a lethal dose of anesthesia is injected into a vein. As the drug enters the bloodstream, the dog loses consciousness and his systems cease functioning, bringing on a peaceful, pain-free death. You can be assured that all he feels is the slight prick of the needle.

You should be with your dog until the very end. Talk to him and tell him what a good friend he's been and how much you'll miss him. It's normal to cry, so don't be embarrassed. Your veterinarian will certainly understand if you want to be with your dog for a few minutes after he passes away.

When Your Friend Is Gone

You may be surprised at how deeply you are affected by the loss of your dog. When you think about it, even though you may have known deep down that this time was coming, you were still trying to be strong and optimistic, if only to give your dog hope. Now that your friend is truly gone, you will grieve for her loss, but you will find a release for all the days, possibly years, of hanging on that you did for her sake.

Your home will not be the same without your dog there, and everything will remind you of her—her old bed, her old bowls, her old collar, her favorite toys, and her favorite spots. We are lucky to live in a time when it's acknowledged how deeply people love their dogs; in fact, some people feel stronger love for their dogs than for other people in their lives, so naturally they are going to feel their loss more deeply. Your family will also be grieving, and it's important to allow everyone to grieve in their own way and time, and to talk about those feelings.

FACT

There are a number of Web sites for grief counseling upon the loss of a pet. There are memoriam spaces and online support groups. This is a tough time for many people, and you should consider taking advantage of these services, as the loss of such a friend is always difficult to accept.

If you or anyone in your family is having a particularly difficult time, or if you just want to know that there are others who have gone through similar pain, you can find books on coping with the loss of a pet in your bookstore or library or online. Speaking with other dog owners can help, too, since chances are they've had a similar experience and understand what you're going through. There are also pet-loss hotlines you can call to speak with people who can lend a kind ear. It's important to honor the memory of your friend. Your heart will heal with time, and you know she will always be with you.

APPENDIX A:

Canine Organizations and Associations

Owning a dog brings you instant membership into the worldwide community of fellow dog owners— a passionate group, for sure! There are numerous organizations associated with the care and keeping of your canine companion. This appendix lists some of the largest and most established, and can serve as a base and a springboard for discovering others.

Registries

The American Kennel Club

The most famous organization that represents purebred dogs in the United States is the American Kennel Club. Established in 1884 to advance the interests of purebred dogs, today the American Kennel Club recognizes more than 150 breeds in seven groups (Sporting, Non-Sporting, Working, Herding, Terrier, Hound, and Toy) as well as a host of breeds in the Miscellaneous Class as well as its Foundation Stock Service (FSS).

The AKC is a nonprofit organization whose members are not individual dog owners but breed clubs. Each member club (and there are currently more than 500 of them) elects a delegate to represent the club at AKC meetings. The delegates vote on the rules of the sport of dogs—they are the legislative body of the American Kennel Club. The delegates elect the AKC's twelve-member Board of Directors, who are responsible for the overall and daily management of the organization.

Most people are familiar with the prestigious Westminster Kennel Club show that's televised from Madison Square Garden every February. Westminster is one of the member clubs of the AKC—one of the oldest, too. Besides the hundreds of member clubs, there are nearly 5,000 affiliated clubs that conduct AKC events (dog shows and other events) following AKC rules of conduct.

The AKC oversees the establishment of recognized breeds in the United States, and also enforces the standards by which breeds are judged. To carry out its many functions, the AKC maintains offices in New York City (where it was founded) and Raleigh, North Carolina. It has several divisions: Registration, of course, but also Judges' Education, Performance Events, Publications, and more. The AKC maintains a reference library of more than 20,000 books, including editions of some of the earliest books ever published on dogs.

What does all this mean to you? It means that when you buy a purebred puppy and register him, you are joining a very large and time-honored family of people who are crazy about dogs. If you want, you can look up fifty generations of your Golden Retriever's ancestors. That's what being purebred means—not that your puppy is some kind of elite dog, but rather, that all the caretakers of his family before you wanted to breed the same kind of dog over and over. The AKC's purpose is to preserve the integrity of its registry of purebred dogs, to sanction events that promote the purpose and function of purebred dogs, and to ultimately protect and ensure the continuation of the sport.

The AKC works very hard to make sure that the dogs it registers and awards show points, championships, and performance titles to are the best examples of their breed. However, the AKC is quick to point out that having an AKC-registered dog does not necessarily mean your dog will be free of health problems, or that it is of championship quality. All it means is that your dog's parents are registered purebreds, and that those dogs' parents are registered purebreds, and so on. Never forget the family and the network you are joining by registering your puppy with the AKC. Don't abuse registering or owning a purebred dog. Be proud of your dog's heritage and your dog's health.

American Kennel Club
51 Madison Avenue
New York, NY 10010
or
5580 Centerview Drive
Raleigh, NC 27606-3390
www.akc.org

The United Kennel Club (UKC)

The United Kennel Club was founded in 1898 by Chauncey Z. Bennett. The UKC registers more than a quarter-million dogs each year. Their largest number of registrations are for American Pit Bull Terriers. Those two important facts make the UKC the second oldest and second largest all-breed dog registry in the United States. They are located in Kalamazoo, Michigan.

The UKC, like the AKC, sponsors events of many kinds, from dog shows to a host of performance events. The UKC is made up of over 1,000 different clubs that oversee several thousand licensed annual dog events. Many of their events are very easy to enter and compete in, promoting owners to show and compete with their dogs, as opposed to hiring professional trainers or handlers.

United Kennel Club
100 East Kilgore Road
Kalamazoo, MI 49001-5598
www.ukcdogs.com

The American Rare Breed Association (ARBA)

The mission of the American Rare Breed Association is to serve and protect what are considered rare breeds of dogs in the United States. This includes promoting and educating the public dog fancier about 130 or more breeds from around the world that are not now recognized by the American Kennel Club.

American Rare Breed Association
100 Nicholas Street NW
Washington, DC 20011
www.arba.org

The Canadian Kennel Club (CKC)

Much like the AKC, the CKC is the primary registering body and overseer of the sport of purebred dogs in Canada. Many Canadians who want to compete in the United States register their dogs in both clubs. Much like the AKC, the Canadian Kennel Club is devoted to encouraging, guiding, and advancing the interests of purebred dogs and their responsible owners and breeders in Canada.

Canadian Kennel Club
Commerce Park
88 Skyway Avenue, Suite 100
Etobicoke, ON M9W 6R4
Canada
www.ckc.ca

The Kennel Club (UK)

Founded in 1873, the primary objective of the Kennel Club is to promote in every way the general improvement of dogs. The Kennel Club is able to offer dog owners an unparalleled source of information, experience, and advice on dog welfare, dog health, dog training, and dog breeding.

The Kennel Club
1-5 Clarges Street
Piccadilly
London W1J 8AB
✐*www.thekennelclub.org.uk*

The Fédération Cynologique Internationale (FCI)

Currently based in Belgium, the Fédération Cynologique Internationale was created in 1911 with the aim to promote and protect cynology and purebred dogs by any means it considers necessary. The founding nations were Germany (Kartell für das Deutsche Hundewesen en und Die Delegierten Kommission); Austria (Osterreichischer Kynologenverband); Belgium (Société Royale Saint-Hubert); France (Société Centrale Canine de France); and the Netherlands (Raad van Beheer op Kynologisch Gebied in Nederland). The Federation disappeared due to the first World War and in 1921, the Société Centrale Canine de France and the Société Royale Saint-Hubert re-created it. Today the organization sponsors two of the world's largest dog shows: The European Dog Show and the World Dog Show.

Fédération Cynologique Internationale
Secrétariat Général de la FCI
Place Albert 1er, 13
B-6530 Thuin
Belgium
✐*www.fci.be*

Pet Advocacy and Therapy Groups

The American Society for the Prevention of Cruelty to Animals (ASPCA)

The ASPCA is one of the most active pro-pet groups in the world. A nonprofit company, the ASPCA sponsors countless numbers of groups and events to protect animals' and pet owners' rights. The ASPCA has attempted to reduce pain, fear, and suffering in animals through humane law enforcement, legislative advocacy, education, and hands-on animal care.

The ASPCA was founded in 1866 by a diplomat named Henry Bergh, who served in the U.S. delegation to Russia. Bergh modeled the ASPCA on England's Royal SPCA. The ASPCA managed to get the nation's first anti-cruelty laws passed in the state of New York in its first year. The ASPCA provided ambulance service to horses in New York City two years before the first hospital provided them for humans. In seven short years, twenty-five states, a number of territories, and Canada had used the ASPCA as a model for their own humane organizations.

Today, the ASPCA supplies a number of different services to pet and animal lovers all across the country. They are perhaps best known for helping shelter strays and foster adoptions. Their foster care program encourages sympathetic people to help animals who are "too young, sick, or aggressive to be offered for adoption right away a chance to have a long and healthy life by placing them in temporary homes."

People often confuse the New York-based ASPCA with other SPCAs around the country. There are Societies for the Prevention of Cruelty to Animals (SPCAs) in many states. The Massachusetts and San Francisco SPCAs are particularly active in promoting animal welfare through adoption and public education.

ASPCA
424 East 92nd Street
New York, NY 10128-6804
(212) 876-7700
www.aspca.org

The Humane Society of the United States (HSUS)

The Humane Society of the United States (HSUS) is another of the nation's largest animal-protection organizations. While the ASPCA is more focused on pets, especially dogs and cats, the Humane Society has a much wider scope. HSUS promotes the "humane treatment of animals and to foster respect, understanding, and compassion for all creatures." The HSUS uses such venues as the legal system, education, and legislation to ensure the protection of animals of all kinds.

The HSUS was founded in 1954 and currently has nine major offices in the United States. Unlike the ASPCA, the HSUS does not have any affiliate shelters. The HSUS mainly concerns itself with wildlife protection, companion animals, and animal research violations. However, they do sponsor many events for pet owners and do encourage pet rescue (adoption). Some of the events they sponsor include free spaying clinics for pet owners of insufficient means.

Humane Society of the United States
2100 L Street NW
Washington, DC 20037
www.hsus.org

The American Humane Association (AHA)

Based in Englewood, Colorado, and founded in 1877, the American Humane Association (AHA) is a welfare organization involved in assisting both animals and children. These days the AHA oversees the treatment of animals on movie and television sets and is working to establish standards for dog trainers, among many other things.

American Humane Association
63 Inverness Dr. East
Englewood, CO 80112
www.americanhumane.org

Delta Society

The Delta Society was established in 1977 in Portland, Oregon, under the leadership of Michael McCulloch, MD. The organization's first president was Leo K. Bustad, DVM, PhD, dean of a veterinary college and a pioneer in human-animal bond theory and application. From the beginning, Delta has sought to better understand why animals are important to the general population and specifically how they affect health and well-being. Delta provided the first comprehensive training in animal-assisted activities and therapy to volunteers and health care professionals, and it continues to develop standards-based training materials. It is committed to its mission to improve human health through service and therapy animals.

Delta Society
P.O. Box 1080
Renton, WA 98057
www.deltasociety.org

Therapy Dogs International (TDI)

Elaine Smith founded TDI in 1976 to create an organization dedicated to regulating, testing, and registering therapy dogs as well as their handlers. Through this process, they are better prepared and able to assist in visits to nursing homes, hospitals, and other institutions where therapy dogs are needed.

Therapy Dogs International
88 Bartley Road
Flanders, NJ 07836
www.tdi-dog.org

Training and Behavior

The Association of Pet Dog Trainers (APDT)

Founded in 1993 by Dr. Ian Dunbar, the APDT has grown to become one of the largest dog training organizations in the world. It is committed to developing better trainers through education, and offers individual pet dog trainers a respected and concerted voice in the dog world, promoting dog-friendly dog training to the veterinary profession and the public.

Association of Pet Dog Trainers
150 Executive Center Drive Box 35
Greenville, SC 29615
www.apdt.com

National Association of Dog Obedience Instructors (NADOI)

Founded in 1965 to promote modern, humane training methods and at the same time elevate the standards of the dog-training profession, NADOI members need to demonstrate that they have attained certain skills and knowledge through testing measured by their peers. The NADOI's mission is to endorse dog obedience instructors of the highest caliber; to provide continuing education and learning resources to those instructors; and to continue to promote humane, effective training methods and competent instructors.

National Association of Dog Obedience
Instructors
PO Box 369
729 Grapevine Hwy
Hurst, TX 76054
www.nadoi.org

Health

American Veterinary Medical Association (AVMA)

A convention of veterinary surgeons in New York in 1863 led to the foundation of the United States Veterinary Medical Association. There were forty delegates from seven states in attendance. It was created to serve as a resource for veterinarians across the country, and began publishing a review. In 1889, the name was changed to the American Veterinary Medical Association, and in 1900 its review's name was changed to the Journal of the American Veterinary Medical

Association. By 1913, the AVMA had 1,650 members; today there are over 75,000 members. The AVMA serves the veterinarians who care for the nation's millions of pets of all kinds, as well as those who serve in medical research, prevention of bio and agro terrorism, food safety, and those who contribute to scientific breakthroughs throughout the world.

American Veterinary Medical Association
1931 North Meacham Road, Suite 100
Schaumburg, IL 60173-4360
www.avma.org

Animal Poison Control Center

(888) 426-4435

Since 1978, the ASPCA Animal Poison Control Center (APCC) has been the premier animal poison control center in North America. The center, an allied agency of the University of Illinois, is the only facility of its kind, staffed by twenty-five veterinarians—including nine board-certified toxicologists (seven have both American Board of Toxicology and American Board of Veterinary Toxicology certification) and thirteen certified veterinary technicians. Located in Urbana, Illinois, the specially trained staff provides assistance to pet owners and specific analysis and treatment recommendations to veterinarians pertaining to toxic chemicals and dangerous plants, products, and substances twenty-four hours a day, seven days a week.

www.aspca.org

The American Kennel Club Canine Health Foundation (AKC CHF)

Founded in 1995, The AKC Canine Health Foundation is currently the largest nonprofit funder of exclusively canine research in the world. The foundation works to develop significant resources for basic and applied health programs with emphasis on canine genetics to improve the quality of life for dogs and their owners. The foundation funds research and supports canine health scientists and professionals in their efforts to study the causes and origins of canine disease and afflictions in order to formulate effective treatments.

www.akcchf.org

PennHip for Diagnosis of Hip Dysplasia

PennHip stands for University of **Penn**sylvania **H**ip **I**mprovement **P**rogram, and is a not-for-profit program. It involves a special technique that assesses the condition of a dog's hips to determine the severity of current or developing hip dysplasia. The information is saved in a database which continues to grow and serve veterinarians trying to understand and treat this condition.

www.pennhip.org

APPENDIX B

Furthering Your Knowledge and Understanding of Dogs

Believe it or not, while this book gives you an excellent overview on the fundamentals of having a dog in your life, there are lots of other ways to learn about dogs, whether it's your particular breed, training needs, activities you may want to become involved in, health concerns, and so on. This list includes the names of magazines and books that, in the opinion of the authors, are some of the very best among the many that are available. Enjoy!

Magazines

AKC Gazette and *AKC Family Dog*
Publications of the American Kennel Club
✎*www.akc.org*

Bloodlines Journal, Coonhound Bloodlines, and
Hunting Retriever
Publications of the United Kennel Club
✎*www.ukcdogs.com*

Canine Review and *Dogs in Canada*
Publications of the Canadian Kennel Club
✎*www.ckc.ca*

Dog Fancy, Dogs for Kids, Dogs in Review, and
Dog World
All from Fancy Publications
✎*www.animalnetwork.com*

Bark Magazine
The Modern Dog Culture Magazine
✎*http://thebark.com*

Dog and Kennel Magazine
From Pet Publishing
✎*www.dogandkennel.com*

Dogs Today
Britain's Biggest and Best Dog Magazine
✎*www.dogstodaymagazine.co.uk*

Kennel Gazette
A Publication of The Kennel Club
✎*www.thekennelclub.org.uk*

Books

General

The Complete Dog Book, by The American Kennel Club (Howell Book House)

The Complete Dog Book for Kids, by The American Kennel Club (Howell Book House)

Dogs Never Lie About Love: Reflections on the Emotional World of Dogs, by Jeffrey Moussaief Masson (Three Rivers Press)

The Intelligence of Dogs, by Stanley Coren (Free Press)

Pack of Two, by Caroline Knapp (The Dial Press)

Pet Sitting for Profit, by Patti J. Moran (Howell Book House)

The Quotable Dog, by Greg Snider (Contemporary Books)

Spotted in France, by Gregory Edmont (Rodale)

Adoption and Rescue

Save That Dog! by Liz Palika (Howell Book House)

Second-Hand Dog, by Carol Lea Benjamin (Howell Book House)

Health

Dog Owner's Home Veterinary Handbook, by Delbert G. Carlson, D.V.M., and James M. Giffin, M.D. (Howell Book House)

The Everything Dog Health Book, by Kim Campbell Thornton (Adams Media)

Feeding Your Dog for Life: The Real Facts About Proper Nutrition, by Diane Morgan (Doral)

The Goldsteins' Wellness & Longevity Program: Natural Care for Dogs & Cats, by Robert S. and Susan Goldstein (TFH)

Training and Behavior

Bones Would Rain from the Sky, by Suzanne Clothier (Grand Central Publishing)

The Culture Clash, by Jean Donaldson (James & Kenneth Publishers)

Dr. Dunbar's Good Little Dog Book, by Ian Dunbar, Ph.D. (James & Kenneth Publishers)

Dog Behavior, by Ian Dunbar, Ph.D. (TFH)

Don't Shoot the Dog, by Karen Pryor (Bantam)

Dual Ring Dogs, by Amy Ammen and Jacqueline Frasier (Howell Book House)

For the Love of a Dog, by Patricia McConnell, Ph.D. (Ballantine)

Hip Ideas for Hyper Dogs, by Amy Ammen (Howell Book House)

People, Pooches & Problems, by Job Michael Evans (Howell Book House)

Surviving Your Dog's Adolescence, by Carol Lea Benjamin (Howell Book House)

Training in No Time, by Amy Ammen (Howell Book House)

Pet Loss

The Loss of a Pet, by Dr. Wallace Sife (Howell Book House)

When Your Pet Dies, by Jamie Quakenbush (Simon & Schuster)

Videos

Training DVDs by Amy Ammen
Amiable Basic Dog Training
Amiable Novice Dog Training
Amiable Open Dog Training
✍*www.dogclass.com*

APPENDIX C

A Dog's Life Online

There are millions of Web sites devoted to dogs, and more are launched every day. They have to do with everything from breeders showcasing their dogs, to hard-to-find supplies, to important health research, to poems for and about dogs. This is but a brief selection of sites to get you started.

THE EVERYTHING DOG BOOK

General

If you want to start surfing somewhere, just any-where, try

www.dogpatch.com

For general info on all things dog-related

www.canismajor.com

For all kinds of fun stuff, check out

www.i-love-dogs.com

An organization that provides lots of information on dogs and all animals is

www.animalplanet.com

Another site that has solid information about dogs and other pets is

www.petplace.com

Health

American Academy of Veterinary Acupuncture

www.aava.org

American Animal Hospital Association

www.aahanet.org

American College of Veterinary Internal Medicine

www.acvim.org

American College of Veterinary Ophthalmologists

www.acvo.com

American Holistic Veterinary Medical Association

www.ahvma.org

American Veterinary Chiropractic Association

www.animalchiropractic.com

Complementary and Alternative Veterinary Medicine

www.altvetmed.org

International Veterinary Acupuncture Society

www.ivas.org

Veterinary Cancer Society

www.vetcancersociety.com

Training and Behavior

Learn more about Amy Ammen and Amiable Dog Training.

www.dogclass.com

The Association of Pet Dog Trainers can help you find a trainer in your area.

www.apdt.com

Grooming

If you want to know more about this industry, take a look.

www.petgroomer.com

Supplies and Accessories

Cherrybrook—All kinds of supplies

www.cherrybrook.com

DogWise—The world's largest online dog book store

www.dogwise.com

Drs. Foster and Smith—All kinds of supplies

www.fostersmith.com

Earth Animal—Natural care and nutrition for dogs

www.earthanimal.com

In the Company of Dogs—Gifts and gear for dogs and the people who share their lives

www.inthecompanyofdogs.com

J-B Wholesale—All kinds of supplies

www.jbpet.com

Planet Dog—Premium products made for the dog by dog lovers

www.planetdog.com

Specialized Sports and Activities

Agility
✍*www.akc.org* or ✍*www.usdaa.com*
Flyball
✍*www.flyball.org* or ✍*www.flyballdogs.com*
Freestyle
✍*www.worldcaninefreestyle.com* or
✍*www.canine-freestyle.com*
Herding
✍*www.akc.org* or ✍*www.ahba-herding.org*
Carting
✍*www.cartingwithyourdog.com* or
✍*www.workingdogweb.com*
Hiking
✍*www.hikewithyourdog.com* or
✍*www.dogplay.com*
Frisbee®
✍*www.skyhoundz.com*
Hunting
✍*www.akc.org* or ✍*www.ukcdogs.com*

Travel

To find pet-friendly lodgings of all kinds, visit
✍*www.petswelcome.com*
To find dog parks in your area or places you may
be traveling, see
✍*www.dogpark.com*

INDEX